REVOLUTIONARY SOLDIERS

IN

KENTUCKY.

CONTAINING

A Roll of the Officers of Virginia Line who received Land Bounties ;
A Roll of the Revolutionary Pensioners in Kentucky; A List
of the Illinois Regiment who Served under George
Rogers Clark in the Northwest Campaign

ALSO A ROSTER OF THE VIRGINIA NAVY

COMPILED BY
ANDERSON CHENAULT QUISENBERRY,
FROM VARIOUS SOURCES.

Baltimore
GENEALOGICAL PUBLISHING CO., INC.
1982

R 973.344

11·83   tube

Originally published in the *Year Book of the*
Kentucky Society, Sons of the American Revolution
Louisville, Kentucky, 1896
Reprinted: Southern Book Company
Baltimore, 1959
Reissued: Genealogical Publishing Co., Inc.
Baltimore, 1968, 1974, 1982
Library of Congress Catalogue Card Number 68-22328
International Standard Book Number 0-8063-0283-6
Made in the United States of America

Introduction.

IN no State in the Union, perhaps, are there so many descendants of Revolutionary soldiers, in proportion to population, as in Kentucky, where, more than in any other State whatever, the blood of the fathers has been kept pure and free from intermixture with that of the post-revolutionary immigrants to our shores. Professor Shaler, in his charming work on his native State, says: "In Kentucky . . . we shall find nearly pure English blood, mainly derived through the Old Dominion, and altogether from districts that shared the Virginia conditions. It is, moreover, the largest body of pure English folk that has, speaking generally, been separated from the mother country for two hundred years." In other words, the Kentuckians of to-day are mainly descended from people who, on an average, had already been established in Virginia, or some other American colony, for a hundred years when the Revolution began. Less than one per cent of the people of the State are descended from those people who came to this country subsequently to the war for independence. While Virginia furnished most of the original settlers of the State, Maryland, the Carolinas, and Pennsylvania each contributed not a few, and the other colonies, without exception, supplied some.

Nearly all the original adult male settlers of the State had seen service in the Revolutionary War, and especially was this the case with those from Virginia, very many of whom had been granted lands in Kentucky by that State on account of their services in the war. Kentucky was then "the great West" of the Union — the land of abundance and of promise —

> "The Unknown Land, that on the sunset rim
> Stretched over distance limitless and dim —
> Lay with its spread of plain and vale and hill,
> Beyond the eye, mysterious and still."

So when the veteran patriots laid down their arms at the advent of the peace they had conquered, and returned to their homes broken in fortune, but rich in hope and courage, their eager eyes saw the brilliant bow of promise toward the land of the setting sun, and thither many thousands of them wended their way with wives and children and lares and penates, to build new homes and carve out new fortunes in the forests primeval.

Such men, says Shaler, were, by their native strength and their deeds, the natural leaders in the new settlements, both in peace and in war. Thus the Kentucky spirit was the offspring of the Revolution. The combative spirit left by the war for independence was elsewhere overwhelmed by the tide of commercial life; here it lived on, fed by tradition, and by a nearly continuous combat, down to the time of the Civil War.

These men of the Revolution practically controlled affairs in Kentucky, and so long as they lived they were called upon to fill not only the highest but essentially all the public offices of the State, and their descendants have done so after them. The spirit of those old heroes is nowhere better exemplified than in the names given to the counties of the State as they were organized from time to time. Almost invariably some brilliant hero of the Revolution was honored at the creation of each new county, until later wars began to put forward new heroes to be honored. And even in the later wars many of the veterans of the Revolution, though beginning to bend beneath the weight of years, performed a full and noble share, often side by side in the ranks with their sons and grandsons, and under the command of their old leaders, who had learned war with Washington at Monmouth and at Trenton, and had suffered with him the hardships and privations of the historic camp at Valley Forge. In 1815, at New Orleans, "the hunters of Kentucky," who so signally defeated the British troops who later in the same year assisted in vanquishing the great Napoleon and his unparalleled "Old Guard" at Waterloo, reasserted that invincible courage by which they, or their fathers, had destroyed the haughty hosts of Patrick Ferguson at King's Mountain.

> "When Pakenham, with England's proudest means,
> Swept boldly down on salient New Orleans,
> Who held the sacred bonds of union then
> Like young Kentucky's stalwart riflemen?"

Lyman Draper, one of the most accurate of historians, says that nearly all the men who served under Campbell and Shelby and Cleveland and Sevier at King's Mountain, settled in Kentucky either before or after the close of the Revolution. Isaac Shelby, one of the leaders in that great fray, became the first Governor of the State. What an honor it was for old Kentucky to become the home of such heroes!

Than King's Mountain there has scarcely been a more glorious battle in history; certainly no more glorious one in the history of America. When the darkest hour had arrived for the American cause, when even the most sanguine had begun to despair, and when the Southern colonies were almost totally subjugated and overrun by the victorious and arrogant hosts of the foe, suddenly a glorious light of hope and promise broke resplendently forth from a new and wholly unexpected quarter. A few hundred settlers on the Holston, the Nolichucky, and the Watauga, being threatened with invasion by Ferguson, who in derision called them "backwater men," quietly unhooked their horses from the plows, carried meal for bread in sacks across their saddles, and driving their beef on foot before them, swiftly crossed the Apalachian range, and, almost before the haughty Ferguson knew that danger was impending, they fell upon him at King's Mountain, and in about an hour annihilated his band of rough riders (equal in numbers to themselves), who with fire and brand and bloody hand had gloried in harrying the patriots of the Carolinas so unmercifully and cruelly. Then these "embattled farmers" quietly recrossed the mountains to their humble homes on "the back waters," and resumed their plowing. Their service had been entirely voluntary. They received no pay, were furnished no rations, transportation, arms, or equipments. They went at their own expense, and merely from a sense of duty, and having abated a nuisance that annoyed them, they resumed their daily avocations. To the credit of the Government be it said, many of these men were afterward pensioned; though, as they were not regularly in the service, they could not, under a strict construction of the law, be considered as entitled to pensions.

Major Patrick Ferguson was one of the crack officers of the

British regulars, and had trained and drilled his troops until they were the best disciplined soldiers on the continent. The utter destruction of his force was the turning-point of the war, and from that time forth new courage animated the hearts of our ancestors, and they pressed steadily onward to the final victory at Yorktown, which gave us independence, and made it the highest honor in this land to-day to be a Son of the American Revolution.

And let it never be forgotten that nearly all the victorious heroes of King's Mountain settled in Kentucky, and have there to-day thousands upon thousands of descendants!

The one event of the Revolution the most far-reaching and important in its results, was the conquest of the Illinois by that gallant Kentucky pioneer, George Rogers Clark, with a handful of Kentuckians and Virginians. The Virginians almost to a man afterward became Kentuckians. A more thrilling and romantic enterprise than the conquest of the Northwestern Territory has seldom, if ever, been recorded.

By her charter Virginia possessed the great extent of country north of the Ohio and south of the lakes, but it was occupied by the British, who had posts at Kaskaskia and Vincennes. In the winter of 1777, General George Rogers Clark, then a citizen of the District of Kentucky, recognizing the importance to the American cause of Virginia holding her own, proposed to the Governor, Patrick Henry, to permit him lead an expedition for the reduction of those posts. Clark was thereupon supplied with means and with several companies of troops, partly from Virginia and partly from Kentucky, for this purpose; and in the summer of 1778 he marched swiftly through the intervening wilderness with his small but stout-hearted band, and surprised and captured Kaskaskia, after which he proceeded to Vincennes and took that post also. Father Gibault, a priest, assembled the terrified French citizens in a church, assured them (as he was authorized by Clark to do) that the Americans were their friends, and they then "took the oath of allegiance to the Commonwealth of Virginia." The rolls of Clark's regiments, published herewith, show that he received many of these Franco-Virginians as recruits in the ranks of his little army.

During the winter Colonel Hamilton, the Governor of Canada, advanced from Detroit and surprised and retook Vincennes, and, it was said, purposed during the coming spring to retake Kaskaskia also, and then march southward and invade Kentucky.

When this intelligence reached him, the intrepid Clark determined to literally " steal a march " on Hamilton, and by a vigorous and decisive winter campaign to frustrate his plans. The Kentuckians responded with encouraging alacrity to the summons to march against Hamilton, whom they greatly execrated because of his having inhumanly offered the Indians a premium for every Kentucky scalp they would bring him. The Kentuckians dubbed him "the Hair-buyer General." In February, 1779, General Clark set out from Kaskaskia with one hundred and fifty men and two small cannon ; and a march unparalleled in history began. A detachment was sent with the cannon to ascend the Wabash by boat ; and Clark followed with his remaining troops by land. The weather was very cold, and the country through which they had to win their way was a dense, unbroken wilderness ; but the dauntless Kentuckians pushed bravely onward until they reached the point, some fifteen or twenty miles from Vincennes, where the White River flows into the Wabash. For many miles around, the low grounds of the Wabash valley were covered with water to the depth of several feet, upon which thin ice had formed, and it seemed impossible to traverse them, but Clark determined to make the attempt. He and all his men blackened their faces with moistened gunpowder to give themselves an air of ferocity. A little drummer boy was placed upon the shoulders of a very tall man, " and was bade to beat for his life ; " and then, to the music of the " spirit-stirring drum," Clark stepped gayly into the water, followed eagerly by his troops, and a terrible and unprecedented feat of war began.

The water was often breast-deep to the tallest men, and was frozen, but the leaders broke the ice before them, and the others, holding their rifles and powder above their heads, struggled bravely on. As far as the eye could reach was an almost unbroken expanse of water. Small islands appeared here and there, but often they were four or five miles apart. The men in front sometimes reanimated those behind them by the false cry of "land, ho!" which quickly passed back along the line and gave new courage to those whose spirits were beginning to sink. But at last their courage and fortitude were rewarded, and they reached "a hill of dry land which was almost in sight of Vincennes, and here they heard the boom of its evening gun as they rested, while Clark dispatched a messenger who was directed to tell the people of the place that his friends might remain in their homes, but the friends of the King were to "repair to the fort and join the 'Hair-buyer General.'" The wading was then resumed, and shortly they sat down before the fort, upon which fire was opened without delay, after some slight defenses had been hastily thrown up.

Hamilton was taken completely by surprise, for it was considered wholly impossible that any troops could have passed the widely-extended "drowned lands;" but there they were, "and looking like devils," with their powder-blackened faces. Hamilton made a stubborn resistance with both artillery and small arms, and for fourteen hours the darkness of the wilderness and of the night was lit up by the lurid flashes and the red glare of battle. At dawn Clark commanded him to surrender at once, saying that if he was compelled to storm the place the Governor "might depend upon such treatment as is justly due to a murderer." Hamilton declined to surrender, saying that he "was not disposed to be awed." But at length he proposed a truce which Clark refused to grant. He must "surrender at discretion," and so he did, on February 25, 1779, and the Kentuckians marched in with loud cheers, and raised again the American flag which has never since been lowered in all the Northwest Territory by the hand of a foeman.

Says the historian Cooke: "Fourteen hours of fighting between two inconsiderable bodies of troops decided who was to possess the entire region north of the Ohio. At the conclusion of peace, in 1783, the principle of the *uti possidetis* was adopted by the Commissioners, empowering Great Britain and the United States to remain in possession of all the territory which they held at the termination of the war. Upon this provision the Northwest Territory was claimed by the American Commissioners on the ground of its capture by Clark and 'the possession of it by the Americans at the time of the conference.' The claim was acquiesced in, and the country accordingly fell to the United States."

By this conquest the boundary line between the United States and Canada is the lakes instead of the Ohio River. Virginia, "Mother of Statesmen and of States," ceded to the general government that vast empire won by Kentucky valor under the leadership of the young "Hannibal of the West," which now comprises five great States.

Broadly speaking, every man, woman, and child who settled in Kentucky prior to the close of the war in 1783 was a soldier of the Revolution. The settlement of the State began in 1775, contemporaneously with the breaking out of the war. About the first of June, 1775, a party of hunters camped for the night in the Kentucky forest at what is now known as the Royal Spring, and so pleased were they with the surrounding country that they determined to take out patents for some of it and to found there a town. Professor Ranck says the name of the settlement that was to be was discussed with animation. One suggested "York," another "Lancaster," but both names were dropped with a shout for "Lexington" as the conversation turned to the strange news that had slowly crept through the wilderness, and which, after being weeks on the way, they had just heard, of how "King George's troops, on the 19th of April, had called Americans 'rebels,' and had shot them down like dogs in Massachusetts Colony." The story of the christening of Lexington, the historic fact of how she got her name, is as romantic as the legend of the beautiful Princess Pocahontas, and is far more interesting, because more true than the one told of the founding of ancient Rome. The date of this occurrence is undisputed, and the fact itself is established by the concurrence of the highest authorities upon Kentucky history. Bancroft relates the incident in his description of the opening of the Revolution when he says that the spirit of independence "breathed its inspiring words to the first settlers of Kentucky, so that hunters who made their halt in the matchless valley of the Elkhorn commemorated the 19th of April by naming their new encampment Lexington."

Professor Ranck adds, eloquently: "So the hunters called the new settlement 'Lexington' in memory of that bloody field hundreds of miles away. . . . How strange the story of that pioneer camp! Here, more than a hundred years ago, when Kentucky was a wilderness province of the royal colony of Virginia; here, far away from civilized life, in the heart of an unbroken forest, at the dead of night, a little band of adventurers erected the first monument ever raised on this continent in honor of the first dead of the Revolution!"

There has been erected in Massachusetts to commemorate the battles of Lexington and Concord one of the most beautiful monuments in this or any other country, and it is graced by an inscription of those stirring lines by Emerson :

"By the rude bridge that arched the flood,
  Their flag to April's breeze unfurled,
Here once the embattled farmers stood,
  And fired the shot heard 'round the world."

But that great event has a nobler monument still—the beautiful city of Lexington, founded almost contemporaneously with the event it commemorates by brave and patriotic men who were, at that very time, engaged in their way, and that by no means an unimportant one, in waging war for American independence. For Kentucky, in the manner of its settlement, was as a "flying wedge." There were no settlements to the north or south of it, though it made both possible in the after years. The wars waged upon the early Kentucky settlers by the Indians were incited by the British. Indeed, the savage foes of our fathers were often led by the British officers and under British colors. But the brave pioneers succeeded in holding these advanced outposts, and in so doing rendered their country a service that can not be too highly extolled. It was as signal a service as was rendered by the troops of the line at Saratoga, or Monmouth, or Yorktown, or elsewhere, for it held intact for the then future American Union all that vast territory, an empire in extent, which now comprises the great States of Kentucky, Ohio, Indiana, Illinois, Wisconsin, and Michigan. The story of the valor of those dauntless pioneers who subdued the savages with one hand and the wilderness with the other has never been sufficiently related — indeed, never can be, for it paragons description. Every man of them was indeed a soldier of the Revolution in some sense, for they were all enrolled in tne active militia of Virginia, and therefore their descendants should be eligible to membership in the Society of the Sons of the American Revolution; for the militiamen of the older parts of Virginia, and of all the other original colonies have, by common consent, been declared soldiers of that war equally with the troops of the line.

Colonel Thomas Marshall Green says, in " The Spanish Conspiracy" (pages 44, 45), "The impression has prevailed among many that nearly all the warfare in Kentucky and the West was the result of merely individual effort. But, so far from that being the case, the men engaged in all this fighting acted as a part of the regular militia system of Virginia, and while in active service were regularly paid by that State. Formal reports of the ammunition and commissary supplies furnished to Boonesboro, Harrod's, and St. Asaph's, were made by quartermasters to the Virginia executives, and the bills were settled by them. Some of those made by Joseph Lindsey (who fell at Blue Licks), the writer has examined. In every respect they would do credit to any quartermaster-general in the regular army."

Even such of the early Kentuckians as may not have been regularly enrolled in the militia served just as constantly and just as efficiently as if they had been. And, as has already been claimed, not only every man, but every woman and every child in Kentucky prior to the close of the Revolution was essentially a soldier of that war; for they all endured and suffered and strove equally for the common cause. Boys scarcely able to stagger under the weight of a rifle often did a man's duty at a loop-hole, or behind a tree, and on the foray as well. And the women were as brave and as true in times of danger as any helmeted warrior could have been. They ran the bullets and loaded the guns and bound up the wounds of the stricken in times of siege; and they bore themselves as bravely under equal exposure to danger as the men, and with zeal as unfaltering. Nor are instances wanting where they themselves used the trusty rifles of their husbands, with aim as unerring and with execution as deadly. There are even cases where the dauntless dames in the defense of their children, even with tomahawk or axe, laid the fell invader low.

In all history there is no instance of more lofty courage than that displayed by the women of Bryan's Station when they went out in a body, in the face of five hundred ambushed savages, and filled their buckets with water at the spring for the supply of the besieged garrison, marching bravely forth and back with songs upon their lips, knowing all the time that they were within a hair's breadth of instant and violent death!

> "The mothers of our forest-land!
>   On old Kentucky's soil,
> How shared they with each dauntless band
> War's tempest and life's toil!
> They shrank not from the foeman,
>   They quailed not in the fight,
> But cheered their husbands through the day,
> And soothed them through the night.
>
> "The mothers of our forest-land!
>   Their bosoms pillowed men;
> And proud were they by such to stand
> In hammock, fort, or glen;
> To load the sure old rifle,
>   To run the leaden ball,
> To watch a battling husband's place,
> And fill it should he fall!"

The ladies of Lexington have now in hand the laudable work of collecting funds to erect a monument to the memory of the heroines of Bryan's Station. This honor comes tardily, but none was ever more deserved.

The battle of the Blue Licks is officially recognized by the Government as one of the actions of the Revolutionary War. Then why not also "Estill's Defeat," and the thousand other "moving incidents by flood and field;" and also the siege of Bryan's, and the three sieges of Boonesboro, where largely superior forces of Indians under British officers, and flying the royal standard of King George, were held back and defeated before the sharp, defiant crack of the dauntless pioneers' unerring rifles?

To gather together the names of all those Revolutionary soldiers who are unquestionably recognized as such, and who settled in Kentucky, would now be an impossibility. The Society of the Sons of the American Revolution was organized mainly with a view to creating an interest which would impel people to search out from the records, many of which are still preserved, the proofs of their ancestors' services in the war for independence, so that they might be printed in the year books, and thus be put in shape to be preserved indefinitely. Similar societies have since been established, and already much has been accomplished in this direction, but hardly as yet a drop in the bucket as compared with what might be.

With a view to making a start in the proper direction, and of facilitating the researches of those who are disposed to discover the official evidence of their ancestors' services, I have arranged and edited a list of those citizens of Kentucky who were granted Revolutionary pensions up to the year 1835, as reported that year by the Secretary of War, to which I have appended a list of the names of many of those persons to whom the State of Virginia granted lands on account of their Revolutionary services; and also rolls of the soldiers of General George Rogers Clark's "Illinois Regiments," nearly all of whom settled in Kentucky; and of the Virginia Revolutionary Navy, many of whom also settled there, and others, descendants of whom are now living in the State.

The Revolutionary pensioners in Kentucky, first and last, aggregated about three thousand. Some names, but not many (except of widows), were added to the list subsequent to 1835, but these it is not now practicable to obtain, owing to the unaccommodating spirit shown by the officials of the Pension Office at Washington. Some of the additional names are preserved, however, in Collins' History of Kentucky, which contains a list of nearly nine hundred who were still living in the State in 1840, about sixty years after the close of the Revolution, many of them being of remarkable ages. I have appended to my lists, which are given by counties, only such of the names given by Collins as do not appear in the report of the Secretary of War in 1835. Mr. Collins states that some few of those in his list may have been soldiers in the Indian wars soon after the close of the Revolution, which is likely. Collins' list includes a few counties which were created after 1835, and in this way, probably, some duplications of names may have crept into my lists.

The Continental Congress, as early as 1776, began to provide for disabled soldiers of the Revolution by pension or half-pay enactments. From June 7, 1785, to September 29, 1789, the several States assumed the payment of pensions, on account of the inability of Congress to raise money by taxation, but after the adoption of the Constitution, Congress resumed their payment. However, payments under these early or " invalid " pension laws were only for disability or known wounds, and, comparatively speaking, the beneficiaries were not numerous.

The first service pensions granted were under the law of March 18, 1818, which gave twenty dollars per month to officers and eight dollars per month to privates who were in indigent circumstances, and who had served a term of not less than nine months in the Continental line at any period of the war, the pension to begin from the day the proof was completed. Under this act the applications for pensions soon amounted to about eight thousand. It appears that this " vast number " of applicants alarmed Congress, who seemed to fear that the treasury would be bankrupted by them. So the law of May 1, 1820, was passed, and in a measure restricted the benefits of the law of March 18, 1818, and took from the pension rolls many of the veterans who had been pensioned under the last-named act. The act of March 1, 1823, however, restored such of these as had not died in the mean time.

The act of May 15, 1828, provided for pensioning such officers and enlisted men as had enlisted in the Continental line for and during the war, and continued in service until its termination, but was restricted to officers who were entitled to half pay under the act of October 21, 1780, and to enlisted men who were entitled to a gratuity under the act of May 15, 1778. The beneficiaries of this law received the full pay of their rank when in active service in the Continental line. The act of May 31, 1830, was simply to construe or explain this act.

Under the law of June 7, 1832, a pension equivalent to the full pay of his grade was granted to each officer, enlisted man, and sailor (except privateers) who served in the Revolution for a term of two years, or for any term not less than six months, either in the Continental line, State troops, volunteers, or militia. Several Revolutionary pension laws were passed subsequently, but they were either to construe this one, or to admit the widows of Revolutionary soldiers or sailors to the benefits of pensions.

Naturally, a great many Revolutionary soldiers had passed away before the first general pension law of 1818, which benefited only troops of the Continental or regular line, and even barred a great many of them — all those who had served less than nine months continuously. Others who would have taken advantage of this law, and were preparing to do so, died in the interim between the Alarm Act of 1820 and the Rehabilitating Act of 1823. It was not until 1832, fifty years after the close of the war, that any of the State troops, volunteers, and militia were granted pensions; and even under this law those who had served less than six months — and there were many such who had seen hard service — were barred. Imagine how many thousands of those who would have been entitled to the benefits of the act of 1832 had joined the silent majority before that time arrived!

Many of the old heroes who were entitled to do so never applied for a pension. Collins, speaking of those in Kentucky, says: "Many refused a pension altogether, declaring that they could support themselves, and would not seem dependent, even for a portion of their bread, upon a country whose liberties they had fought to obtain, and were willing to fight again to preserve." In Collins' list the names of some widows appear, and they are generally new names — that is, names that had not appeared on the pension rolls of 1835, which goes to show that the husbands of those ladies had never applied for pensions.

There have been granted altogether to soldiers of the Revolution, and their widows, sixty-two thousand and sixty-nine pensions. Of these more than three thousand were Kentuckians. But, taking into consideration the great number of soldiers who had not served long enough to become entitled to a pension, or who refused ever to apply for one, or who died before one became available, it is apparent that there must have been in Kentucky, first and last, at a moderate estimation, at least three Revolutionary soldiers who never got a pension for every one who did. This would make an aggregate of twelve thousand of those old heroes who became citizens of the State. Fifteen thousand would probably come nearer the actual fact. They now have many thousands of descendants who are citizens of the State. In addition to these are thousands of others, descendants of Revolutionary soldiers, who have moved into the State during the last one hundred and twenty years, whose Revolutionary ancestors never were citizens of Kentucky. So, as has already been stated, there are probably more descendants of Revolutionary soldiers in Kentucky, in proportion to population, than in any other State in the Union.

The subjoined list of Kentucky Revolutionary pensioners gives the county they lived in; their rank or grade; the State they served from; and the character of their service — whether Continental, State, militia, etc.; the act under which they were beneficiaries; the date they were placed on the rolls; the date their pensions began; the amount of their annual pensions, and their ages.

The ages to which these men generally attained were very remarkable, as the lists will show. Of the two thousand eight hundred and ninety-six named, seven hundred and ninety-two were eighty years of age, or over, at the time the rolls were made, and many of them lived for years afterward. Eighteen were one hundred years old, or over; and of these several had attained the almost incredible ages of one hundred and six, one hundred and seven, one hundred and eight and one hundred and nine! The younger ones were probably drummer boys in the latter days of the Revolution, or young men who had served with St. Clair or Wayne in the Indian campaigns in the Northwest; but there were but few of these. The average age of the two thousand eight hundred and ninety-six pensioners was more than seventy-six years at the time the rolls were made, in 1835; and by the time they had all died, it had undoubtedly gone beyond eighty years! Considering the vicissitudes of their hard military service in the Revolution, and the still severer trials they endured in conquering their savage foes and in subduing the forests and brakes in Kentucky, the ripe age to which they almost universally attained must be considered the most wonderful showing ever yet made in vital statistics. Collins says: "And what is still more remarkable than the great age attained by them is that even at that great age, over two thirds (nearly three fourths) of them were still the heads of families, and themselves housekeepers — not content to live with, much less to be dependent upon, their children, or others; so strangely and strongly and sternly was the spirit of personal independence implanted in their natures by their very mode of life." This in 1840, sixty years after the close of the Revolution!

When the Revolution was ended, the British Government furnished homes in Upper Canada, on the Bay of Quinte, Lake Ontario, to large numbers of American Tories, or "United Empire Loyalists," as they called themselves, who had fought for the King. Dr. Canniff, a descendant of one of these Tories, has written an able and interesting history of those settlers; but it is filled with hatred and the bitterest prejudice against Americans. After vaunting the great age to which the Tory founders of Upper Canada attained, without stating how old they did get, he says (p. 638): "Upper Canada was planted by British heroes of the American Revolution. It arose out of that Revolution. The first settlers were United Empire Loyalists. The majority of the original settlers were natives of America, brought up in one or other of the provinces that rebelled. They were Americans in all respects, as much as those who took sides with the rebels; yet to-day the descendants of the United Empire Loyalists are as unlike the descendants of the rebels as each is unlike a full-blooded Englishman. The pure Yankee and the Canadian may trace their ancestors to a common parentage, and have the same name. . . . It is desired that we had statistics to show the difference as to longevity and general health."

The omission is now supplied. On behalf of the "rebels," Kentucky's veterans of the Revolution have furnished some

" statistics as to longevity and general health " that the United Empire Loyalists did not equal, much less surpass.

It is hoped that the appended lists may be of great benefit to those Kentuckians who wish to find the proof of their ancestors' services, with the view of becoming members of the Kentucky Society of the Sons of the American Revolution. So far as the pension lists are concerned, much fuller information may be had concerning any individual named in them by applying for it by letter to the Commissioner of Pensions, Washington, D. C. As a great many applications are now being made, the work of the office is behindhand, and answers to such letters should not be expected in less than a month or six weeks. No fee is charged.

Since the close of the Revolution a great many records of the war, especially numerous muster rolls of troops, have been preserved in the Treasury, State, Interior, and other departments of the Government, but in such a shape as to be practically inaccessible for reference. Recently these have all been turned over to Colonel F. C. Ainsworth, Chief of the Record and Pension Office, War Department, who has had them arranged, classified, and indexed, so that it is possible to ascertain in a very few minutes all that is to be learned about any one of the more than three hundred thousand names on the muster rolls. It was through the efforts of the Sons of the American Revolution that this great work was done, in order to meet the demand of the public for such information—which will be furnished promptly and free of charge on application to the Chief of the Records and Pension Bureau, War Department, Washington, D. C.

What should be particularly interesting to Kentuckians is the fact that the Virginia Magazine of History and Biography (Richmond, Virginia), is now publishing lists of the Virginia Revolutionary troops from the records preserved in the State Archives. This may supply a great many, if not all, of the deficiences in the records of the general Government, so far as Virginia troops are concerned. The Government has very few rolls of the State troops, volunteers, and militia furnished by the various States in our great struggle for independence.

Persons living in Kentucky counties that have been established since 1835, in looking for the names of their revolutionary ancestors among the pensioners, should consult the lists of the county or counties from which the newer counties were formed.

The rolls of the "Illinois" and Crockett's Regiments, as well as of the Virginia Navy, are published by permission of the Virginia Magazine of History and Biography, in which they first appeared.

This work does not pretend to give a full list of all the Revolutionary soldiers who lived in Kentucky, for that would be impossible to do at this late day; nor does it claim that all of those it names (the pensioners excepted), lived in the State, though most of them may have done so, and probably did. But it is hoped that very much of value may be found in the work by those Kentuckians who seek to know the deeds of their Revolutionary sires.

Anderson Chenault Quisenberry.

WAR DEPARTMENT, INSPECTOR GENERAL'S OFFICE,
WASHINGTON, D. C., May 14, 1895.

List of Bounty Recipients.

A Roll of the Officers of the Virginia Line in the Revolutionary Army who received Land Bounties from the State of Virginia; the lands being located principally in the States of Kentucky, Indiana, and Ohio. To which is added a List of Non-commissioned Officers and Privates to whom such bounties were also assigned. Compiled by A. C. Quisenberry, from the Virginia State Records, from a List prepared by Leonard S. Latham, of Chillicothe, Ohio, in 1822, and from other sources.

Major-Generals received . . . . 15,000 to 17,500 acres
Colonels received . . . . 8,888 acres (usually)
Lieutenant-Colonels received . . . . 6,666 acres (usually)
Majors received . . . . 5,333 acres (usually)
Surgeons and Surgeon's Mates received . . . . . . 2,666 to 8,000 acres.
Captains received . . . . 4,666 acres (usually)
Lieutenants, Ensigns, and Cornets received . . . . 2,666 acres (usually)

MAJOR-GENERALS.

Gates, Horatio   Steuben, Baron

BRIGADIER-GENERALS.

Barron, James	Mercer, Hugh	Stevens, Edward
Clark, Geo. Rogers	Morgan, Daniel	Weedon, George
Lawson, Robert	Muhlenberg, Peter	Woodford, William
	Scott, Charles	

COLONELS.

Baylor, George	Green, John	Parker, Thomas
Bland, Theodoric	Grayson, William	Reed, Isaac
Brent, William	Harrison, Charles	Russell, William
Buford, Abraham	Heth, William	Simms, Charles
Campbell, Richard	Lewis, Charles	Smith, Gregory
Crawford, William	Matthews, George	Stevens or Stephens,
Davies, William	McClanahan, Alex.	Edward
Finne, William	Marshall, Thomas	Stevenson, Hugh
Febiger, Christian	Muter, George	Spottswood, Alex.
Fleming, Thomas	Neville, John	Towles, Oliver
Gist, Nathaniel	Parker, Josiah	Wood, James
Gibson, John	Parker, Richard	

1

STAFF COLONELS.

Aylett, William, Dep't Com. Gen. of Stores
Balmain, Alexander, Chaplain
Hurt, John, Chaplain
Mumford, William G., Dep't Com. Gen. of Issues.

LIEUTENANT-COLONELS.

Allison, John
Anderson, Richard C.
Ball, Burgess
Ballard, Robert
Bird, Otway
Bowman, Abraham
Cabell, Samuel J.
Carrington, Edward
Clark, Jonathan
Cocke, Nathaniel
Crockett, Joseph
Cropper, John
Dabney, Charles
Darke, William
Edmunds, Elias
Elliott, Thomas

Eppes, Francis
Flemming, Charles
Gaskins, Thomas
Hawes, Samuel
Hopkins, Samuel
Hart, John
Harrison, Robert H.
Innis, James
Jameson, John
Joynes, Levin
Lee, Henry
Matthews, Thomas
Meade, Richard K.
Montgomery, John
Nelson, William
Neville, Presley

Porterfield, Charles
Posey, Thomas
Powell, Levin
Peyton, Francis (heir)
Richardson, Holt
Seayres, John
Taliaferro, William B.
Taylor, Richard
Temple, Benjamin
Trigle, Frederick
Thompson, John
Wallace, Gustavus B.
Warnock, Frederick
Washington, William
Webb, John
Yates, William

SURGEONS AND SURGEONS' MATES.

Baldwin, Cornelius
Brown, William
Carter, William
Christie, Thomas
Clements, Mace
Davis, Joseph
DeBenneville, Daniel
Dixon, Anthony F.
Draper, George
Duff, Edward
Evans, George
Fullerton, H.
Galt or Gault, P.
Gault, John M.
Griffith, David (also
  a Chaplain)

Greer, Charles
Holmes, David
Hoomes, Benjamin
Howell, Lewis
Irwine, Matthew
Johnson, Robert
Johnson, William
Julian, John
King, Miles
Knight, John
McAdams, John
McAdams, Joseph
Middleton, Bazil
Munroe, George
Overton, Thomas
Pelham, William

Pope, Matthew
Ramsey, John
Rickman, William
Roberts, John
Ross, Robert
Russell, Philip M.
Savage, Joseph
Skinner, Alexander
Slaughter, Augustine
Smith, Nathan
Smith, Samuel
Swope, John
Trezvant, John
Vaughn, Claiborne
Wallace, James
Yates, George

MAJORS.

Belfield, John
Boykin, Francis
Bruin, Peter B.
Call, Richard
Claiborne, Buller
Clough, Alexander
Crockett, Joseph
Croghan, William
Cunningham, Wm.
Dick, Alexander
Dickinson, E.
Eggleston, Joseph
Falkner, Ralph
Finley, Samuel
Fitzgerald, John
Flemming, John
Gilchrist, George
Graves, John
Hays, John
Helphenstine, Peter
Hendricks, James

Hill, Thomas
Holmer, Christian
Holmer, John
Hopkins, David
Johnson, James
Knox, James
Lee, John
Leitch, Andrew
Leitch, James F.
Lewis, William
Lucas, James
Magill, Charles
Massie, Thomas
Meade, Everard
Meriwether, Thomas
Monroe, James
Moseley, William
Moss, John
Parker, Alexander
Pelham, Charles
Porter, Benjamin

Poulson, John
Quirk, Thomas
Ridley, Thomas
Rudolph, John
Russell's, Maj., heirs
Scott, John
Scruggs, Gross
Snead, Smith
Snead, Thomas
Stephenson, David
Stephenson, John
Swan, John
Taylor, Francis
Taylor, John
Taylor, William
Tompkins, Robert
Waggoner, Andrew
West, Charles
Woodson, John W.
Woodson, Tarlton

CAPTAINS.

Anderson, John
Apperson, Richard
Arbuckle, Matthew
Armstead, Thomas
Armstrong, James
Ashby, Stephen
Atkinson, Thomas
Avery, William H.
Barbee, Thomas
Bailey, Henry
Baldwin, John
Barnett, James
Barrett, Chisholm
Barrett, William
Baylor, Walker
Baytop, James
Baytop, Thomas

Beall, Robert
Bedinger, Henry
Bell, Thomas
Bentley, William
Berry, Thomas
Biggs, Benjamin
Blackeny, William
Blackwell, John
Blackwell, Joseph
Blackwell, Samuel
Blackwell, Thomas
Blair, John
Bohannon, Ambrose
Booker, Lewis
Booker, Samuel
Boswell, Machen
Bowyer, Michael,

Bowyer, Thomas
Bradford, Samuel K.
Bradley, James
Brashear, Richard
Breckinridge, Alex.
Briscoe, Reuben
Brooks, Samuel
Brown, William
Brown, Windsor
Browne, Thomas
Brownlee, William
Buckner, Thomas
Burwell, Nathaniel
Butler, Lawrence
Calmes, Marquis
Calderwood, James
Carnes, Patrick

Carrington, Mayo
Carter, John C.
Casey, Benjamin
Chamberlayne, Geo.
Chaplin, Abraham
Chapman, John
Cherry, William
Chilton, John
Chilton, Thomas
Clark, John
Clay, Thomas
Cocke, Colin
Cocke, Pleasant T.
Cole, John
Coleman, Richard
Coleman, Whitehead
Conway, Henry
Cooper, Leonard
Cowherd, Francis
Craig, James
Crain, James
Crump, Abner
Culbertson, James
Cummins, Alexander
Currie, James
Dade, Francis
Dandridge, Alex. S.
Dandridge, John
Davenport, William
Davis, Jesse
Denholm, Archibald
Dillard, James
Dix, Thomas
Drew, Thomas H.
Dudley, Henry
Dun, Peter
Duvall, Daniel
Eddins, Samuel
Edmunds, Thomas
Edwards, Leroy
Emmet, James
Eppes, William

Ewell, Charles
Ewell, Thomas
Fauntleroy, Henry
Field, Reuben
Finn or Fenn, Thos.
Fitzgerald, John H.
Fitzhugh, Peregrine
Foster, James
Forsythe, Robert
Fox, Nathaniel
Fox, Thomas
Fowler, William
Frazier, William
Gaines, William F.
Gallapin, Charles
Gamble, Robert
Garland, Edward
Garland, Peter
George, Robert
George, William
Gerault, John
Gill, Erasmus
Gill, Samuel
Gillison, John
Gist, John
Goodrich, John
Gray, George
Gray, James
Green, Berryman
Gregory, William
Griffin, I.
Gum, James
Grymes, Benjamin
Grymes, William
Handy, George
Harrison, Benjamin
Harrison, John P.
Harrison, Valentine
Hawkins, John
Hawkins, Moses
Healey, Martin
Heard, James

Henderson, William
Heth, Henry
Higgins, Robert
Hite Abraham
Hite, Matthias
Hobson, Nicholas
Hockaday, John
Hogg, Samuel
Holt, John H.
Holt, Thomas
Holcombe, John
Hook, James
Hoomes, Benjamin
Hooper, Richard
Hopper, Thomas
Hord or Hoard, Thos.
Hudson, John
Hughes, John
Hull, Edwin
Israel, Isaac
Johnson, Gideon
Johnson, John B.
Johnson, William
Jones, Cadwallader
Jones, Churchill
Jones, Gabriel
Jones, Llewellyn
Jones, Peter
Jones, Samuel
Jones, Strother
Jouett, Matthew
Jouett, Robert
Jordan, John
Kelly, Thaddeus
Kelty, John
Kemp, Peter
Kendall, Custis
Kennon, Luke
Kennon, Richard
Kinley, Benjamin
Kirkpatrick, Abraham
Laird, David

Lamme, Nathan
Lee, Philip R. F.
Lee, R. T.
Lewis, Addison
Lewis, George
Lewis, William
Lind or Lynd, Arthur
Lindsay, William
Lipscomb, Bernard
Lipscomb, Reuben
Long, Gabriel
Long, William
Lovely, William
Lucas, Nathaniel
Lucas, Thomas
Mabon or Maborn, James
McCarty, Richard
McCraw, William
McCormick, George
McKee, William
McKinley, John
Madison, Rowland
Mallory, Philip
Marks, John
Marks, Josiah
Marshall, James M.
Marshall, John
Martin, Thomas
Mason, David
Maupin, Gabriel
Mercer, John F.
Meredith, William
Miller, William
Minnis, Callohill
Minnis, Francis
Minnis, Holman
M'nor, Peter
Moody, Edward
Moody, James
Moon, Alexander
Moon, Archibald

Moore, Andrew
Moore, Peter
Moore, Thomas
Morgan, Simon
Morris, Nathaniel G.
Morrow, Robert
Morton, Hezekiah
Mosby, William
Moss, Henry
Muir, Francis
Neal, James
Nelson, John
Nelson, John
Nicholas, John
Nixon, Andrew
Oldham, Conway
O'Neal, Ferdinand
Overton, John
Overton, Thomas
Page, Carter
Parker, Thomas
Parsons, William
Patterson, Thomas
Payne, Tarlton
Payne, Thomas
Pemberton, Thomas
Pendleton, James
Pendleton, Nathaniel
Penn, William
Peterson, Thomas
Pettus, John
Perault, Michael
Peyton, Henry
Peyton, John
Peyton, Timothy
Peyton, Valentine
Pierce, William
Porter, Thomas
Porterfield, Charles
Porterfield, Robert
Powell, Robert
Poythress, William

Price, James
Pryor, John
Purvis, James
Quarles, James
Quarles, Henry
Ragsdale, Drury
Randolph, Robert
Ransdell, Thomas
Ray, Thomas
Read, Edmund
Reddick, Jason
Reddick, Willis
Reid, Nathan
Rice, George
Roane, Christopher
Rogers, John
Rogers, William
Rose, Alexander
Roy, Beverly
Royall, William
Rucker, Angus
Rudolph, Michael
Ruffin, Thomas
Russell, Andrew
Sanford, William
Sansum, Philip
Sayres, Robert
Scott, David
Scott, sr., Joseph
Scott, jr., Joseph
Settle, Strother G.
Shepherd, Abraham
Shield, John
Shelton, Clough
Singleton, Anthony
Slaughter, George
Slaughter, Philip
Smith, Arthur
Smith, Ballard,
Smith, Granville
Smith, Gregory
Smith, Joseph

Smith, Larkin	Terrill, Henry	Waman, Thomas
Smith, Matthew	Terry, Nathaniel	Waters, Richard C.
Sommers or Sum-	Thomas, Lewis	Watts, John
mers, Simon	Thompson, William	Welch, Nathaniel
Spencer, Joseph	Thornton, Presley	West, Thomas
Spiller, Benjamin	Thweatt, Thomas	White, Robert
Spiller, William	Tinsley, Samuel	White, Tarpley
Spottswood, John	Todd, Robert	White, William
Springer, Uriah	Trent, Lawrence	Whiting, Henry
Steed, John	Triplett, Thomas	Williams, James
Steele, David	Triplett, William	Williams, John
Stith, John	Turberville, Geo. Lee	Wills, Edward
Stokes, John	Upshur, James	Wills, Thomas
Stribling, Sigismond	Upshur, Thomas	Winston, John
Stubblefield, Beverly	Valentine, Edward	Woodson, Frederick
Stubblefield, George	Valentine, Jacob	Woodson, Hugn
Swearingen, Joseph	Vance, Robert	Woodson, Joseph
Tabb, Augustine	Vause, William	Woodson, Robert
Taliaferro, Benjamin	Vowles, Walter	Wright, James
Taylor, Isaac	Walker, Jacob	Wright, Patrick
Taylor, Reuben	Walker, Thomas	Yancey, Robert
Teagle, Severn	Wallace, Andrew	Young, Henry
Tebbs, John	Wallace, David	Young, Stephen

CAPTAIN-LIEUTENANTS.

(These officers had the rank of Captain and pay of a Lieutenant, commanding a company or troop. The first or Colonel's company of infantry was commanded by a Captain-Lieutenant.)

Crittenden, John	Lipscomb, Yancey	Warman, Thomas
Eppes, William	Marshall, Humphrey	Warsham, John
Graham, Walter	Thomas, Lewis	Wyatt, Cary

LIEUTENANTS.

Allen, David	Archer, Richard	Barbee, James
Allen, Edward	Armstrong, Archib'ld	Barksdale, John
Allen, John	Arnold, Lemuel	Barnett, William
Alexander, George	Ashby, Benjamin	Baskerville, Samuel
Anderson, Nathaniel	Bacchus, Lieutenant	Baylis, Henry
Anderson, Robert	Baldwin, Wood	Baylis, William
Archer, John	Ball, Daniel	Baynham, John
Archer, Joseph	Ballard, William	Baytop, John
Archer, Peter Field	Banks, James	Beck, John

Bedinger, Daniel
Beeson, Edward
Bell, Henry
Bell, John
Bell, Samuel
Bernard, William
Blackmore, George
Bolling, Robert
Bowen, John
Bowyer, Henry
Boyce, William
Bradford, Charles
Breckinridge, Robert
Britton or Barton, Jos.
Broaddus, James
Brooke, Edmund
Brooke, Francis
Brooke, James
Brooke, John
Brookes, Walker
Brown, Jacob
Brown, Robert
Brownlee, John
Burfoot, Thomas
Bullock, Rice
Bunting, William B.
Burton, James
Burton, Hutchins
Butler, Samuel
Campbell, Archibald
Campbell, Samuel
Campbell, William
Cannon, Luke
Carney, Martin
Carroll, John
Carrington, Clement
Carrington, George
Carson, John
Claiborne, Richard
Clark, Edmund
Clarke, Richard
Clarke, William

Clay, Matthew
Clayton, Philip
Cobbs, Samuel
Collier, Thomas
Coleman, Jacob
Coleman, Samuel
Coleman, Wyatt
Cooper, Robert
Connor, William
Conway, Joseph
Courtney, Philip
Coverly, Thomas
Cowne, Robert
Crawford, John
Craddock, Robert
Crute, John
Currell, Nicholas
Custis, Thomas
Dandridge, Richard
Dandridge, Robert S.
Darby, Nathaniel
Darville or Daw-
  ville, W.
Davenport, Opie
Dawson, Henry
Delaplane, James
Dent, John
Digges, Dudley
Drake, Thomas
Drew, John
Drummond, John
Dudley, Robert
Due, John
Dye, Jonathan
Easton, Philip
Easton, Richard
Edmonson, Benj.
Eflin, Philip
Elliott, Robert
Emmerson, John
Erskine, Charles
Eskridge, William

Eustace, John
Evans, William
Ewing, Alexander
Fauntleroy, Griffin
Field, Henry
Fiely, Michael
Fitzhugh, Peregrine
Fitzhugh, William
Fleet, John
Foster, John
Foster, Richard
Foster, Robert
Foster, Simpson
Fowke, John
Frazier, Falvey
Galloway, John
Garnett, Benjamin
Gibbs, Churchill
Gibbs, Harrod
Gibson, John
Giles, John
Gillaham, H.
Gilmore, James
Glasscock, Thomas
Goodwin, Stephen
Gordon, Ambrose
Gordon, Arthur
Gratton, John
Graves, William
Gray, Francis
Gray, William
Green, Francis
Greene, Robert
Gregory, William
Guthrie, George
Hackley, John
Hamilton, James
Haney, Holland
Hardiman, John
Hargis, John
Harris, John
Harris, John

Harrison, James
Harrison, John
Harrison, Richard
Harrison, William B.
Harrison, Battle
Harrison, Lawrence
Harper, James
Hawkins, John
Hayes, Thomas
Heth, John
Higgins, Peter
Higginbotham, Wm.
Hite, George
Hite, Isaac
Hite, Joseph
Hockaday, James
Hockaday, Philip
Hoffman, Philip
Hogg, Samuel
Holland, George
Holmes, T.
Holt, James
Holt, William
Hoomes, Thos. C.
Hooper, John
Howard, Vashael B.
Howell, Lewis
Hughes, Henry
Hughes, Jasper
Humphries, John
Hungerford, Thomas
Johnson, John
Johnson, Peter
Jolliff, John
Jones, Albrighton
Jones, Charles
Joynes, Reuben
Kays or Keyes, Robt.
Keith, Isiam
Keller, Abraham
Kennedy, James
Kennon, John

King, Elisha
Kirk, Robert
Lanier, Thomas
Langham, Elias
Lapsley, John
Lawson, Benjamin
Leigh, John
Lewis, Andrew
Lewis, E.
Lewis, Thomas
Linton, John
Lloyd, Edward
Long, Reuben
Lovell, James
Ludiman, John W.
Ludiman, Wm. I.
Lunsford, Lewis
McDowell, John
McGuire, William
McNutt, James
Mann, David
Manning, Lawrence
Marks, Isaiah
Martin, Thomas
Marston, John
Massenburgh, John
Maury, Abraham
Meade, William
Meanly, John
Meriwether, James
Meriwether, James
Meriwether, David
Mensier or Menzies,
    George
Micon, Henry
Miller, David
Miller, Javan
Miller, Thomas
Mitchell, Robert
Mills, John
Montgomery, James
Moon, Jacob

Moore, Jacob
Moore, John
Moore, William
Morgan, Spencer
Morton, James
Mosely, Benjamin
Mosely, Benjamin
Mountjoy, Alvin
Moxley, Rodham
Moxley, William
Nelson, John
Nelson, Roger
Noland, Pierce
Norwell, George
Norwell, Lipscomb
Oliver, William
Owens, Richard M.
Painter or Pointer,
    William
Parks, James
Parker, Nicholas
Parrott, Joseph
Payne, Joseph
Payne, Josiah
Payne, William
Pearson, Thomas
Perkins, Archelaus
Perry, John
Pettus, Samuel O.
Peyton, Dade
Peyton, Valentine
Porter, William
Porter, William
Powell, Peyton
Powell, Seymore
Powell, Thomas
Power, Robert
Price, William
Pride, William
Pugh, Joseph
Pugh, Willis
Pullen, William

Pyle, William	Smith, Nathan	Tyler, Nathaniel
Quarles, John	Smith, Obadiah	Vanderwall, Marks
Quarles, John	Smith, W.	Vanmeter, Joseph
Quarles, Robert	Smith, William	Vaughan, Claiborne
Quarles, Thomas	Smith, Wm. Sterling	Vaughan, John
Ralph, Ephraim	Southall, Stephen	Vawter, William
Randolph, William	Spencer, John	Vowles, Charles
Rankin, Robert	Spitfathom, John	Vowles, Henry
Read, Clement	Starke, Richard	Walker, David
Rhea, Matthew	Starke, William	Walker, Levin
Rice, Nathaniel	Steele, John	Walker, William
Richardson, Walter	Steele, William	Wallace, Adam
Ricketts, Nicholas	Stephens, William	Wallace, David
Robbins, John	Stephenson, F.	Wallace, Henry
Robinson, John	Stewart, Charles	Wallace, William B.
Roberts, John	Stith, John	Waring, Henry
Robertson, William	Stockley, Charles	Washington, Geo. A.
Rodes, ———	Stuart, Philip	Webb, Isaac
Rogers, Andrew	Sturdivant, John	Weshurts, Thomas
Rudder, Epaproditus	Suttle or Settle,	Westfall, Cornelius
Russell, Albert	Strother	Whitaker, William
Russell, Charles	Taliaferro, Nicholas	White, John
Russell, John	Tannehill, Josiah	White, John
Saunders, William	Tatum, Henry	White, Thomas
Saunders, Joseph	Tatum, Zachariah	White, William
Savage, Joseph	Taylor, Richard	Whiting, B.
Scarborough, John	Taylor, Thornton	Whiting, Francis
Scott, Charles	Tebbs, Thomas	Williams, David
Scott, John	Thompson, James	Williams, Edward
Scott, John Eppes	Thompson, John	Willis, Henry
Scott, Walter	Throckmort'n,Albion	Wilson, J.
Sears or Sayers,Thos.	Tibbs, John	Wilson, Willis
Selden, Samuel	Tompkins, Bennett	Winlock, Joseph
Shackleford, John	Tompkins, Daniel	Winston, William
Shackleford, William	Towner, John	Wisham, John
Slaughter, John	Trabue, John	Woolsey, M. L.
Slaughter, Lawrence	Travis, Edward	Warsham, Richard
Smith, Edward	Triplett, George	Warsham, William
Smith, Francis	Triplett, Hedgman	Yancey, John
Smith, James	Triplett, William	Yarborough, Charles
Smith, John	Tutt, Charles	Young, Robert
Smith, Jonathan	Tyler, John	

6

ENSIGNS.

Armistead, William
Arthur, Barnabas
Ball, Daniel
Barbour, James
Barksdale, John
Baylis, Henry
Berry, William
Berwick, James
Bunbury, William
Carey, Samuel
Coleman, John
Darby, Nathaniel
Delaplane, James
Eskridge, George
Eustace, John
Foster, John

Gibson, John
Giles, John
Gray, Francis
Green, Gabriel
Greenway, George
Herbert, Thomas
Hite, Isaac
Hughes, Henry
Hughes, Pratt
Jeffries, Isaac
Lee, John
Mills, John
Morgan, John
Morgan, Spencer
Phillips, James
Phillips, Samuel

Pritchard, Rees
Pugh, Willis
Quarles, William P.
Robertson, William
Sayers, Thomas
Scott, John
Slaughter, Robert
Slaughter, William
Smith, Francis
Spencer, William
Tompkins, Henry
Turner, John
Wallace, James
Walker, John
Williams, Edward

CORNETS.

Ball, Burgess
Carrington, Clement
Digges, Cole

Fitzhugh, William
Harrison, William
Hughes, Jasper
Perry, Edward

Scott, Charles
Worsham, William
Yancey, Leighton

OTHER OFFICERS.

(Rank not known, but probably mostly Ensigns and Cornets.)

Ballard, William
Bailey, John
Bennett, William
Blanden, Seth
Boush, Charles
Brown, John
Brittain, John
Bradley, Christopher
Callender, Eleazer
Calvert, Joseph
Claiborne, Richard
Cotterill, William.
Coke, Calvin
Dicklawman, Chris.
Dobson, Robert

Fleet, Henry
Goodwin, Dinwiddie
Green, Samuel Ball
Gray, Godfrey
Harcum, Rodham
Harvey, John
Henderson, David
Hoomes, Isaac
Hoffler, William
Howell, Vincent
James, Michael
Jennings, John
Jones, Lewis
Jones, Lewis
Kautzman, John

Kearney, John
Lane, James
Larty, John
Lewis, Stephen
Lightburn, Richard
Livingston, Justice
Lilley, Thomas
Longworth, Burgess
Longsford, William
Markham, James
Mazaret, John
McClung, Walter
McElhaney, John
McMahon, William
McWilliams, Joshua

Moore, Elson	Rust, Benjamin	Taylor, Benjamin
Montague, Richard	Rydman, John	Tompkins, Christ.
Muir, John	Saunders, Celey	Tupman, John
Nuttall, Iverson	Savage, Nathaniel	Volluson, Armand
Parker, William H.	Shearman, Martin	Waddy, Sharpleigh
Peyton, George	Singleton, Joseph	Wilson, Willis
Powell, Francis	Smart, Richard	Wilson, Willis
Quarles, Robert	Stribling, Erasmus	Winston, Benjamin
Renner, John	Stott, William	Williams, Jarret
Robins, John	Summerson, Gavin	Wright, Wescott

NON-COMMISSIONED OFFICERS AND PRIVATES.

Aaron, William	Barrett, John	Branham, John
Adams, Thomas	Basey, William	Branham, William
Adeson, John	Baughan, William	Brash or Banks,
Aikins, David	Baumgartner, Henry	James
Aldridge, John	Beall, Nathaniel	Brent, John
Alfred, Jacob	Beasley, Cornelius	Brice, John
Allen, John	Becks, Christopher	Britton, Isham
Allen, William	Bedinger, Daniel	Broadus, Richard
Anderson, Charles	Bell, James	Brook, Nathanial
Anderson, Jesse	Bell, William	Brooke, George
Anderson, John	Beltcher, George	Brooker, Richardson
Andrews, William	Bennett, John	Brown, John
Arbuckle, William	Bennett, Thomas	Brown, Robert
Armond, Peter	Berkley, William	Bridges, John
Armstrong, John	Bibbe, Samuel	Brittain, Samuel
Arnold, John	Bigbee, William	Bruce, George
Askew, James	Bird, Thomas	Bryant, John
Baptiste, John	Blackson, P.	Bryant, William
Bagwell, Thomas	Blair, Robert	Bryson, Mercer
Bailey, Isme	Blair, Samuel	Bruce, Robert C.
Bailey, James	Bohannon, Joseph	Burek, Samuel
Baldwin, James	Bolling, Jeremiah	Burk, John
Ballard, Charles	Boniface, William	Button, Harmon
Barbee, Daniel	Booth, James	Calvert, Reuben
Barbee, Joshua	Booze or Bose, John	Cardwell, John
Barbee, William	Borne, Jesse	Carter, Nicholas
Barber, John	Bowen, Henry	Carter, Robert
Barker, Charles	Bowman, John	Carter, William
Barnes, Margaret	Brady, Joseph	Chambers, David
Barr, John	Brady, Michael	Champ, William

Chaffin, Stanley
Clark, Henry
Clark, Hezekiah
Clark, William
Chapman, Thomas
Carpenter, Christ.
Casaday, James
Case, John
Case, William
Cash, Warren
Cassell, William
Cave, James
Cavender, Joseph
Chinowith, John
Chevers, John
Cole, Samuel
Colfrey, Charles
Coleman, Samuel
Chrisholm, George
Cockrell, Presley
Collins, John
Collins, William
Compton, Augustine
Connor, Terence
Conory, William
Cornelius, Josiah
Cook, James
Cosby, Sydnor
Crawford, Robert
Crawford, Thomas
Crosby, Jesse
Crouch, Robert
Custard, George
Cowherd, James
Coleman, Joseph
Dannakin, Daniel
Davis, Jeremiah
Davis, Presley
Davis, Thompson
Dawson, Francis
Dean, Joseph
Death, William

Dedman, Samuel
Demasters, Edward
Demus, James
Demsey, John
Dickens, James
Dillon, Jesse
Dishman, James
Dixon, Anthony
Dixon, Thomas
Dobbs, Nathaniel
Doland, John
Doran, Terence
Dorin, Terence
Dougherty, Patrick
Downing, ———
Draper, Robert
Drummond, Alex.
Drummond, David
Drummond, William
Dudley, Robert
Dugan, Robert
Duke, Henry
Durham, James
Eakins, Samuel
Edwards, John
Edwards, Richard
Emmins, William
Ermine, Leonard
Eskridge, George
Estes, Elisha
Evans, Joseph
Everheart, Lawrence
Ewell, Thomas
Extine, Leonard
Faint, George
Faint, Philip
Farmer, Jesse
Farrell, John
Fautz, Valentine
Feagle, Michael
Fear, Jacob
Fennegan, Patrick

Figgins, John
Finley, Archibald
Fitzpatrick, Joseph
Fitzsimmons, Thos.
Flaugherty, James
Fleppo, Joseph
Flinn, Osborne
Floyd, William
Forbus, William
Forrester, John
Fox, Lewis
French, Thomas
Friskell, George
Gardner, Caswell
Garnett, Anthony
Gassaway, John
Gesner, John
Gibbs, William
Gibes, James
Gimbo, William
Glass, Isaac
Glasser, Patrick
Glenn, Samuel
Gold, Michael
Gray, Benjamin
Green, Charles
Green, John
Gregory, Nathaniel
Gregory, Walter
Grigg, Matthew
Grimes, George
Grissett or Grissell,
    Joel
Groves, Thomas
Gunner, James
Hagerty, Nichols
Halfpenny, John
Hamilton, James
Hardin, John
Harris, Richard
Harrison, John
Harvie, Richard

Haynes, William	Kerr, James	Means, John
Hefferlin, John	Kidd, William	Mentor, Ebenezer
Henning, George	Lahaw, David	Mitchell, James
Herbert, William	Lahaw, Jeremiah	Mitchell, John
Hicks, James	Law, James	Mitchell, Thomas
Hines, James	Laws, John	Money, Isaac
Hodgkins, Samuel	Lear, George	Moody, William
Holand, Drury	Leach, Valentine	Moore, Nicholas
Holmes, James	Lee, John	Morehead, Charles
Hooks, William	Leer, John	Morgan, Charles
Hooper, Walter	Leigh, John	Morgan, James
Hough, Thomas	Leman, Dedrick	Moxley, George
Howard, James	Lemman, Samuel	Mullen, Anthony
Hughes, Joseph	Lent, William	Murphy, John
Hunt, James	Lipscomb, Major	Murphy, Michael
Hyslop, Smith	Lipscomb, Thomas	Murrick, John
Irby, William	Lively, Goodrell	Nash, Harman
Isan, George	Lucas, Samuel	Neal, George
Jacobs, John	McCain, Thomas	Nelmes, Charles
Jacobs, Roley	McCall, Samuel	Noel, Archelaus
Jacobs, William	McCartney, Peter	Noel, Richard
Jackson, Edward	McCraw, Francis	Norris, Bazabeel
Jarvis, Francis	McDonald, Terence	Norwell, Aquilla
Jefferies, Gowan	McDonald, William	Obannon, William
Johnson, John	McDorman, David	Obrean, James
Johnson, Moses	McDowell, John	Oram, Henry
Johnson, Samuel	McIntosh, Alexander	Overstreet, John
Jones, Holmes	McKay, Eneas	Palmer, William
Jones, Joel	McKinsey, Alexander	Parker, Jeremiah
Jones, John	McKnight, William	Parkerson, John H.
Jones, Richard	McLardy, Alexander	Parsley, Thomas
Jones, Robert	McNoley, Michael	Paul, Edward
Jones, Thomas	Madder, Martin	Payne, John
Jones, Zachariah	Maddox, Claiborne	Perry, William
Jourdain, John	Mancham, Henry	Peterson, Conrad
Kains, Michael	Marshall, Henry	Petrie, Alexander
Keen, John	Marshall, Richard	Peyton, James
Kelly, Peter	Marshall, Thomas	Phillips, John
Kendall, Jeremiah	Martin, Thomas	Pierson, Charles
Kendrick, David	Mason, Owen	Piles, William
Kennon, Thomas	Massie, John	Plodd, John
Kenny, Joseph	Mead, John	Poe, John

Poe, William
Polly, William
Pool, Robert
Pope, William
Potts, John
Powers, William
Powler, William
Price, David
Price, John
Priddy, Richard
Pritchard, James
Pritchett, George
Pugh, Lewis
Puntten, Henry
Rains, Robert
Ralls, Nathaniel
Rankins, James
Ratcliff, Francis
Ray, Thomas
Raynolds, William
Rawlins, Moses
Redwood, John
Reatley, James
Rice, John
Rice, William
Riley, John
Ritchie, Abraham
Ritchie, William
Ritchison, John
Roberts, George
Roberts, John
Robertson, James
Robertson, John
Robinson, George
Robinson, James
Robinson, William
Rock, William
Roundtree, Samuel
Rose, Jesse
Russell, Jeffrey
Russell, William
Rutherford, Julius
Ryalls, James
Ryan, George

Ryland, John
Sanders, Daniel
Sanders, Thomas
Saxton, John
Sergeant, James
Scott, Drury
Scott, John
Scroggins, Ephraim
Scroggins, John
Self, Larkin
Sellers, Michael
Shackleford, Henry
Shackleford, M.
Sharp, Josiah
Shelton, David
Shields, James
Shoope, John
Shores, Thomas
Shull, John
Simmons, Bryant
Skinner, Henry
Slaughter, N.
Smith, George
Smith, Minor S.
Smith, William
Smock, Jacob
Soles, William
Solomon, George
Spence, Henry
Spruce, John
Stafford, David
Steith, Daniel
Stephens, John
Stewart, Philip
Stewart, Robert
Stockdell, John
Stokes, Edward
Strotherd, Thomas
Sudduth, William
Sudthard, John
Taylor, William
Terrill, Edmund
Tharp, Elkanah
Timmons, John

Todd, Robert
Tomlin, William
Townsend, Ewell
Tracy, Solomon
Trapp, Vincent
Treackle, Dawson
Treackle, John
Triplett. Nathaniel
Turk, Robert
Turner, David
Tyler, Benjamin
Vann, Henry
Walden, George
Wallerson, Robert
Walters, Tillman
Ware, Lawrence
Wasser, Daniel
Waterfield, Peter
Wayland, Joshua
Weaver, John
Webber, Philip
Welch, John
Welch, Patrick
Whistler, Sawney
Whitsell, Jacob
Williams, James
Williams, John
Williams, Reuben
Wilson, James
Wilson, John
Wimbush, John
Winifree, John
Winkfield, James
Winter, George
Wise, Samuel
Wofter, John
Wolf, Andrew
Wood, Hugh
Wooten, Thomas
Wyatt, Thomas
Yates, Anthony
Yeager, Henry
Zimmerman, William

Illinois Regiment.

A List of the Officers, Non-Commissioned Officers, and Privates of " The Illinois Regiment," who, under the command of General George Rogers Clark, in an unparalleled campaign, achieved the Conquest of the Northwest (from which the States of Ohio, Indiana, Illinois, Michigan, and Wisconsin were formed), and held it for the United States.

(Republished by permission of the Virginia Magazine of History and Biography.)

BRIGADIER-GENERAL.

Clark, George Rogers

LIEUTENANT-COLONEL.

Montgomery, John

MAJORS.

Quirk, Thomas   Slaughter, George

CAPTAINS.

Bailey, John
Brashear, Richard
Chaplin, Abraham
Fields, Benjamin
George, Robert

Gerault, John
Kellar, Abraham
McCarty, Richard
Pereault, Michael
Roberts, Benjamin

Rogers, John
Taylor, Isaac
Thomas, Mark
Todd, Robert
Williams, John

CAPTAIN - LIEUTENANT.

Harrison, Richard

LIEUTENANTS.

Clark, Richard
Clark, William

Merriweather, James
Montgomery, James
Roberts, William

Robertson, James
Williams, Jarret

ENSIGNS.

Asher, William   Slaughter, Lawrence

CORNET.

Thurston, John

15

"CROCKETT'S REGIMENT."

LIEUTENANT-COLONEL.

Crockett, Joseph

MAJOR.

Walls, George

SURGEON.

Greer, Charles

CAPTAINS.

Chapman,Jno.(killed)	Kerney, John	Tipton, Abraham
Cherry, William	Kinley, Benj. (died)	Young, Thomas
	Moore, Peter	

ENSIGNS.

Daring, Henry   Green, Samuel Ball   McGavock, Hugh

QUARTERMASTER.

Crutcher, Henry

SERGEANT-MAJOR.

Durst, Daniel

MUSICIANS.

Connolly, Thomas, fifer   Lovell, Richard, drummer
Poores, Arthur, fifer

MATROSSES.

Hopkins, Richard   Hupp, Philip

GUNNERS.

Harrison, James	Morgan, Charles	Oakley, John
Leney, Thomas	(also Sergeant)	Smith, Josiah
McGann, John	Mulby, William	

SERGEANTS.

Allen, Samuel	Burne, Pierre	Frazier, Abraham
Andree, John	Bush, William	Goodloe, Henry
Ballard, Bland	Campbell, George	Green, John
Biron, J. B.	Carbine, Henry	Hazard, John
Bland, Shadrach	Clark, Andrew	Hicks, David
Blearn, David	Crump, William	Jameison, Thomas
Bolton, Daniel	Davis, James	Joines, John
Breeden, John	Denton, Thomas	Keller, Isaac
Brossard, Pierre	Dewett, Henry	Laventure, J.
Brown, Collin	Drumgold, James	Marr, Patrick
Brown, James	Elms, William	Mason, Charles

Mathews, Edward
Moore, John
Munroney, William
Murray, Thomas
Parker, Edward
Perie, William
Pittman, Buckner
Portwood, Page
Ranger, J. B.

Rice, John
Richards, Lewis
Roberts, Benjamin
Robertson, John
Ross, James
Ross, John
Slaughter, John
Soverims, Ebenezer
Stephenson, John

Trent, Beverly
Villiers, Francis
(killed)
Walker, John
White, Randolph
Wilson, John
Workman, Conrad
Young, John

CORPORALS.

Ballard, James
Baxter, James
Blein, Pierre
Cameron, James
Hawkins, Samuel

Huin, William
Miller, Abraham
(killed)
Pritchett or Pritcher,
William

Ross, Joseph
Shepherd, Peter
Sills, Samuel
Thompson, William

PRIVATES.

Abbott, sr., William
Abbott, jr., William
Adams, Francis
Allen, David
Allen, Isaac
Allen, sr., John
Allen, jr., John
Allery, Joseph
Alonton, Jacob
Anderson, John
Antier, Francis
Apperson, Richard
Ash, John
Asher, Bartlett
Back, John
Bailey, David
Ballard, Bland Wm.
Ballard, Proctor
Ballinger, James
Ballinger, Larkin
Barber, John
Barry, William
Bass, David
Beckley, William

Bender, Lewis (died)
Bender, Robert
Begraw, Alexander
Bell, William
Bentley, James
Bentley, John
Benton or Bernton,
Thomas
Berard, ——
Berry, William
Bingoman, Adam
Binkley, William
Bird, Samuel
Blackford, Samuel
Blair, John
Blanchor, Pierre
Blankenship, Henry
Boston, Travis
Boston, William
Bouche, John
Bowen, William
Bowing, Ebenezer
Bowman, Christian
Boyles, John

Brazer, Peter
Breeden, Richard
Bressie, Richard
Brown, Asher
Brown, Colin
Brown, James
Brown, John
Brown, Lewis
Brown, Low
Bryant, James
Burbridge, Jno. (died)
Burbridge,Wm.(died)
Burke, George
Burnett, Robert
Burney, Simon
Burris, John
Bush, Drewry
Bush, John
Bush, Thomas
Buskey, Francis
Butcher, Gasper
Butts,Wm. (prisoner)
Cabbage, Joseph
Cabassie, B.

Calvin, Daniel
Camp, Reuben
Campbell, John
Camper, Tilman
Campo, Lewis
Campo, Michael
Certain, Page
Chambers, Alexander
Chapman, Edward
Chapman, Richard
Chapman, William
Clairmont, Michael
Clarke, John
Clifton, Thomas
Cockran, George
Cockran, Edward
Cocles, Andrew
Coffee, Samuel
Cogar, Jacob
Cogar, Peter
Cohen, Dennis
Compera, Francis
Compera, Lewis
Conn, John
Conroy, Patrick
Contraw, Francis
Convance, Paul
Cooper, Christopher
Cooper, Ramsey
Coontz, Joseph
Corder or Corden, Jas.
Corneilla, Patrick
Corns, John
Coste, J. B. de
Cowan, Andrew
Cowan or Cowin, Jno.
Cowan, Mason
Cowdry, John
Cowgill, Daniel
Cox, James
Creze, Craze or Cruze,
    Noah

Crane, John S.
Crawley, John
Crossley, William
Cure, Jean Baptiste
Damewood, Boston
Dardy, Baptiste
Dardy, John
Darnell, Cornelius
Darnell, Cornelius
Davis, Joseph
Davis, Robert
Dawson, James
Dawson, James
Day, William
Decker, Jacob (died)
Deen, James
Deerand, P.
Deneichelle, Lewis
Detering, Jacob
Doherty, Edward
Doherty, Frederick
Doherty, John
Dolphin, Peter
Donovan, John
Donow, Joseph
Doud, Robert
Doyle, John
Dudley, Armistead
Duff, John
Dulhoneau, Pierre
Duncan, Archibald
Duncan, Benjamin
Duncan, Charles
Duncan, David
Duncan, Nimrod
Duncan, Samuel
Durrett, James
Dusablong, B.
Duselle, Mons.
Elms, James
Elms, John (died)
English, Robert

Estes, James
Evans, Charles
Evans, Stanhope
Fache, Lewis
Fair, Edmund
Favers, John
Fever, William
Field, Daniel (died)
Field, Lewis (prisoner,
Flandegan, Dominick
Floyd, Isham
Foster, Henry
Freeman, Peter
Freman, William
Gagnia, Pierre
Gaines, John
Gaines or Garner, Wm
Gallagan, Owen
Garrett, John
Gaskins, Thomas
Garuldon or Gauch-
    eon, Baptiste
George, John
Germain, J. B.
Gibbons, Samuel
Ginon, Frederick S.
Glass, Michael
Glenn, David
Godfrey, Francis
Gognia, Jacques
Gognia, Lewis
Gomier or Gaunia,
    Abraham
Goodwin, Amos
Goodwin, Edward
Goodwin or Goodam,
    William
Gordon, John
Graham, James
Gratiott, Jean
Green, James (died)
Greenwood, Daniel

Grimes, James
Grimshire, John
Grolet, sr., Francis
Grolet, jr., Francis
Guess, John
Gwinn, Wm. (died)
Hall, William
Hammett, Jas. (died)
Hardin, Francis
Harrison, James
Harrison, Richard
Hart, Miles
Hatcher or Hacker, John
Hatter, Christopher
Haut, Henry (killed)
Hawley, Richard
Hays, James
Hays, Thomas
Head, James
Heldebrand, James
Hendricks, Andrew
Heywood, Berry
Hico, sr., Peter
Hico, jr., Peter
Hicks, Mordecai (died)
Higgins, Barney
Hite, George
Hobbs, James
Holler, Francis
Hollis, Joshua
Holmes, James
Hooper, Thomas
Horn, Christopher
Horton, Adin
Houndsler, Charles
House, Andrew
Howell, Peter
Huffman, Jacob
Humphries, Samuel
Irby, David
Isaacs, John

Jarrell, James
Jewell, Charles
Jewell, John
Johnston, Edward
Johnston, John
Johnston, Samuel
Jones, David
Jones, Edward
Jones, John
Jones, Matthew
Kemp, Reuben
Kendall, William
Kennedy, David
Kerr, William
Key, George
Key, Thomas
Kidd, Robert
Kina, Christopher
Kincaid, James
King, George
King, Nicholas
Kirk, Thomas
Kirkley, James
La Bell, Charles
La Casse, Jacque
Lafaro, Francis
Lafarton, Francis
Laform, John
Laflour, Pierre
Lamarch, J. B.
Lamarch, Lewis
La Paint, Louis
Larose, Francis
Lasley, John
Lasout, Joseph
Lanbran, ———
Laughlin, Peter
Lavigne, Joseph
Laviolette, Baptiste
Laviolette, Louis
L'Enfant, Francis
Leney, John

Lenoy, Thos. (killed)
Levinston, George
Lewis, Benj. (killed)
Lewis, James
Lockhart, Archibald
Lockhert, Pleasant
Logan, Hugh
Long, William
Lunsford, Anthony
Lunsford, George
Lunsford, Mason
Luzader, Abraham
Lyon, Jacob
Lyons, John
McClain, Thomas
McClure, Patrick
McDaniel, Thomas
McDermott, Francis
McDonald, David
McDonald, James
McDonald, Thomas
McGuire, John
McIntosh, James
McKin, James
McKinney, John
McLockland, Charles
McMichaels, John
McMickle, John
McMullen, James
McQuiddy, Thomas
Maid, Ebenezer (killed)
Malbeff, Joseph
Malroof, Joseph
Mailone, J. B.
Marshall, William
Maisonville, Mons. de
Martin, Charles
Martin, Elijah
Martin, Pierre
Martin, Solomon
Maurisette, M.

Mayfield, Elijah
Mayfield, James
Mayfield, Isaac
Mayfield, Micajah
Meadows, Josiah
Merriweather, Wm
Miller, John
Missie, Bernard
Monet, J. B.
Montgomery, John
Montgomery, Wm.
Moore, John
Moore, Thomas
Moran or Mauran, Peter
Morris, Jacob
Morris, James (died)
Morris, William
Munam, Joseph
Munrony, Sylvester
Mummilly, Joseph
Murray, Edward
Murphy, John
Murshen, Nathaniel (died)
Mustache, ———
Nare, Conrad
Nash, Francis
Neal, John
Nelson, Enock
Nelson, John
Nelson, Moses
Newton, Peter
Oates, Samuel
Ofin, James
Oharro, Michael
Oliver, John
Oliver, Lewis
Oliver, Turner
Onslow, Charles
Osburn or Ozburn, Ebenezer

Owditt or Odett, Lewis
Pagan, David
Parisienne, Baptiste
Paroult, Peter
Panther, Joseph
Patterson, John
Patterson, William
Payne, Adam
Payne, William
Peaters, John
Peguin, Francis
Pellot, Charles
Peltier, Joseph
Penett or Penit, Josh'a
Penir, Jesse (killed)
Pepin, John (killed)
Petter, Joseph
Phillips, Henry
Pickens, Samuel
Potter, James
Potter, Ebenezer
Priest, Peter
Powell, Micajah
Pulford, John
Puncrass, Francis
Puncrass, Joseph
Pupin, M.
Purcell or Purseley, William
Rabey, Cader
Ramsey, James
Randal, Robert
Rector, John
Richards, Dick
Riley, Patrick
Roberts, Eliab
Roberts, Joseph
Robinson, Richard
Rogers, Joseph
Rollison, Wm (died)
Roy, Julien
Rubido, Francis(died)

Rubido, James
Ruddle or Riddle, Cornelius
Rushare, Francis
Russell, Benjamin
Rutherford, Larkin
Ryan, Andrew
Ryan, Lazarus
Savage, Bryan
Savage, Dominick
Scates, David
Searay, John
Seare, William
Sennitt, Richard
Setzser, John
Severidge, John
Shank, Jacob
Shank, John
Shannon, William
Sharlock, James
Shepherd, George
Ship, William
Shoemaker, Leonard
Siburn, Christopher
Sigonier, Francis
Sills, Samuel
Slack, William
Slaughter, George
Smith, David
Smith, Josiah
Smith, Joseph
Smith, Randal
Smithers or Smothers, John
Smock, Henry
Snellock, Thomas
Snow, George
Soverins, Ebenezer
Sowers, Frederick
Spencer, John
Spillman, James
Stephenson, John

Stephenson, Samuel
Stoball, Thomas
Sworden, Jonathan
Taliaferro, Richard C.
Taylor, Abraham
Taylor, Benjamin
Taylor, Edward
Taylor, James
Taylor, Thomas
Thomas, Edward
Thompson, James
Thoornington, Jos.
Tillis, Griffin
Tolley, Daniel
Tolley, John
Trantham, Martin
Triplett, Pettis
Tuttle, Nicholas
Tyler, William
Underhill, James

Veale, Peter
Villiard, Isaac
Voushiner, Thomas
Waddington, John
Waggoner, Peter
Walker, John
Wallace, David
Ward, Lewis
Ward, Thomas
Waters, Barney
Watkins, Samuel
Watlers, Lewis
Welton, Daniel
Wemate, ——
West, Benjamin
Wethers, Benjamin
Wheat, Jacob
Wheel, Jacob
Whit, Robert
Whitacre, David

White, John
White, Laden
White, Randal
White, William
Whitten, Daniel
Whitehead, Robert
Whitehead, William
Wilkerson, William
Williams, Daniel
Williams, George
Williams, John
Williams, Zachariah
Winson, Christopher
Wood, Charles
Wray, Thomas
Wray, Thomas
Wright, William
Yates, Isaac
Zimmerman, Fred'k
Zuckledz, William

The Virginia Navy.

List of Officers, Sailors, and Marines of the Virginia Navy in the American Revolution.

(By permission of the Virginia Magazine of History and Biography.)

COMMISSIONERS OF ADMIRALTY.

Hutchings, John	Travis, Champion	Whiting, Thomas
Nelson, Thomas	Webb, George	

COMMODORES.

Barron, James	Brooke, Walter	Boucher, ——

CAPTAINS.

Barrett, John	Greene, William	Skinner, William
Barron, Richard	Guthrie, Alexander	Stephens, ——
Boush, Goodrich	Harris, John	Sturdivant, Joel
Bright, Francis	Herbert, Thomas	Taylor, Richard
Calvert, Christopher	Ivey, William	Thomas, John
Calvert, John	Lilley, Thomas	Thompkins, Robert
Callender, Elieser	Markham, James	Towles, Samuel
Carr, Samuel	Parker, William H.	Travis, Edward
Cocke, James	Pasture, John	Underhill, William
Conway, Robert	Rogers, George	Watson, Johannes
Cooke, Robert	Rogers, John	Wilson, Willis
Deane, William	Sanford, Lawrence	Wright, Westcot
Elliott, George	Saunders, William	Younghusband, Isaac
	Saunders, Celey	

LIEUTENANTS.

Allen, Thomas	Chamberlayne, Byrd	Dougherty, James
Archer or Asher, John	Chamberlayne, Geo.	Elam, Robert
Barnett, Jonathan	Chamberlayne, Phil.	Field, Theophilus
Barron, Samuel	Chandler, Thomas	George, Jesse
Barron, William	Cheshire, John	Goffogan, Laban
Blaws, Robert	Christian, William	Gray, James
Boush, Charles	Crew, John	Gray, Robert
Cabell, Absalon	Cunningham, Wm.	Hamilton, John
Cannon, Jesse	Dale, Richard	Harris, John

22

Healey, Samuel Lightburne, Stafford Richardson, William
Herbert, Argyle Lipscomb, Daniel Roots, John
Herbert, Bascow or Lurty, John Ross, John
   Pascow Messeures, Francis Rust, Benjamin
Humphlett, Thomas Millener, Robert Saunders, Joseph
James, Michael Montague, Richard Servant, Richard
Jefferies, Aaron Morton, Edward Singleton, Joshua
Jones, Charles Parker, Richard Speake, Joseph
Jones, jr., Lewis Parker, William H. Steele, William
Kautzman, John Payne, Merryman Taylor, John
Lattimore, Edward Pettigrew, John Thrall, John
Larkins, David Pollard, Thomas Tompkins, Christ.
Lightburne, Henry Richards, John Watkins, James
Lightburne, Richard Richardson, Daniel Wonicutt, Edward

MASTERS.

Bennett, William Crane, James Moore, John
Bonnewell, Thomas Elliston, John Payne, John
Buckner, William Marshall, Joseph Tupman, John
Corbin, William Mercer, Isaac

MIDSHIPMEN.

Anderson, David Eskridge, Edwin Kent, Jesse
Ashby, Benjamin Eskridge, Samuel Lane, John
Ashley, Warren Fleet, Henry McWilliams, Joshua
Bloxom, Scarboro Foster, Peter March, William
Blundon, Seth Grant, Thomas Marshall, James
Bush, William Green, James Massenburg, Alex'r
Broadwater,Covingt'n Gordon, Churchill Masterton, Thomas
Brown, George Hall, Robert Mitchell, Richard
Brown, William Hall, Thomas Muir, John
Cannon, Luke Harcum, Henry Muse, Jesse
Capes, Beverly Harcum, Lott Neal, Presley
Chamberlayne, Edw. Harcum, Rhodam Nuttall, Iverson
Cook, Dawson Henderson, David Parker, Thomas
Cotrill, William Holt, Henry Patterson, John
Currell, James Howard or Hayward, Pierce, John
Curtis, James   Thomas Pope, William
Dawson, Thomas Hubbard, John Powell, Francis
Dove, James Hughlett, William Read, Francis
Elliott, Alexander Hughlett, John Robins, John
Epperson, Richard Kennon, Hawson Saunders, Richard

Shearman, Martin
Stubbs, John
Stott, William
Strother, Benjamin
Summerson, Gavin
Taylor, Benjamin

Taylor, John
Triplett, Reuben
Turpin, John
Tutt, James
Tyler, Henry
Waddy, Shepleigh
Washington, ——

Webb, Francis
Willis, Henry
Wilson, John
Wilson, Joseph
Wilson, Samuel
Wray, George

SURGEONS.

Bell, William Smith
Brown, David
Carter, William
Chaplain, Benjamin
Cheeseman, Thomas
Christie, William
Grear, Charles

Griffin, Corbin
Harris, Simon
Hunter, George
Johnston, William
Livingston, Justice
McClurg, Walter
McNickal, John
Pell, Joseph F.

Pitt, John
Reynolds, John
Riddle, George
Russell, James
Sharpless, John
Snead, Robert
Swoope, John

SURGEONS' MATES.

Banks, James
Britain, John
Cary, Hansford
Chowning, William
Dobson, Robert

Ferguson, Robert
Gibson, John
Jennings, John
Landrum, Thomas
Lyons, John

Marshall, Janifer
Murray, David
Roe, William
White, William

OFFICERS OF MARINES.
CAPTAINS.

Allison, John
Arell, John
Carr, Samuel
Cocke, John Catesby
Dick, Alexander

Foster, James
Hamilton, Thomas
Hanway, John
Jones, Gabriel
Lee, John

Madison, Gabriel
Merewether, Thomas
Mitchell, William
Peers, Valentine
Pollard, Benjamin

LIEUTENANTS.

Bush, Charles
Brown, Windsor
Burkhead or Bank-
    head, James
Davis, John R.

Graves, Richard C.
Hogg, Richard
Merewether, James
Moody, James
Payne, William
Quarles, James

Reynolds, John
Shields, John
Stratton, Henry
Valentine, Jacob
Waller, Edmund

WARRANT OFFICERS OF THE NAVY.

PILOTS.

Ballard, William	Goffigon, Peter	Webb, Robert
Bird, Levin	Parrish, John	Williams, John
Butler, Thomas	Terrant, Cæsar	Williamson, John

COXSWAIN.

Simpson, Hancock

GUNNERS.

Allman, William	Crabb, John	Loyd, Morris
Amands, Ambrose	Gibson, James	Lumber, William
Barnett, Artaxerxes	Gibson, John	Mears, Bartholomew
Broadwater, John	Green, William	Rydman, John
Burk, James	House, William	White, John
Cook, William	Longwith, Burgess	

GUNNERS' MATES

Dounton, William	Lumber, Thomas	Revel, John

CARPENTERS.

Burk, John	Evans, Philip	Herbert, Thomas
Cropper, John	Flint, John	Moss, Starke
Doggett, George	Green, William	White, Jacobus

CARPENTERS' MATES.

Bartee, Samuel	Lavis, Matthew	Tatum, Thomas
	Melson, Levin	

MASTERS-AT-ARMS.

Lacy, Edmund   Simpson, Salathel

BOATSWAINS.

Bully, John	Evans, William	Taylor, John
Chiles, John	Jennings, Michael	Walters, Isaac
Clements, John	Lang, Alexander	Wharton, John
	Phillips, Jacob	

BOATSWAINS' MATES.

Johnston, Joshua	Stott, William	Taylor, Jabez

7

MASTERS' MATES.

Ashley, William   Jones, Lewis   Smart, Richard
Dunford, William   Murray, David

PAYMASTER.

Tucker, Silas

QUARTERMASTERS.

Bailey, Laban   Chaine, Shadrach   Price, Ebenezer
Broadwater, James   Griggs, William   Warrington, Stephen

STEWARDS.

Frazier, Thomas   Fields, John   Lovewell, William
Ferguson, Robert   Hinton, Spencer   Lowell, Thomas
                     Hughlett, Garrett

ARMORER.

Saulsberry, Moses

CLERKS.

Lucas, William   Opie, George H.

SEAMEN.

Abraham (a negro)   Bond, James   Brumley, William
Alexander, George   Boston (a negro)   Budd, Thomas
Anderson, Luke   Boston, Thomas   Buker, John
Anderson, Nathaniel   Boush, Daniel   Burns, Christopher
Andrews, William   Boush, George   Bush, Samuel
Apperson, Richard   Boush, Jack   Byrd, Frederick
Ashburn, Thomas   Boush, James   Carter, George
Badger, Jesse   Boush, Wilson   Carter, Philip
Bailey, James   Bottom, John   Caser, Terence
Bailey, John   Bowen, John   Casity, William
Bailey, Robert   Bowing, Joshua   Cassity, John
Bailey, Southey   Bowman, Chris.   Chandler, Thomas
Bailey, Thomas   Boyd, Augustine   Channing, William
Banks, James   Brent, Hugh   Charles, Moore
Bartee, William   Brent, John   Claiborne, Nath.
Bennett, Elias   Brent, Richard   Clairborne, Thomas
Bess, John   Brown, John   Cleverius, John
Bishop, Joshua   Brown, William   Coats, Edney
Bloxham, Stephen   Brumley, Philip   Coats, Jesse

Coats, John
Coats, Raleigh
Coats, Thomas
Coats, William
Coleman, John
Cooke, William
Cooper, Henry
Cooper, jr., William
Corbett, Clem.
Cottrell, Thomas
Cox, Anthony
Cox, Edward
Crowder, Joshua
Currell, James
Currell, Spencer
Currell, Thomas
Daniel (a negro)
Denby, William
Denby, Willis
Dobson, Robert
Doghead or Doggett, Reuben
Drake, Augustine
Driver, John
Dudley, John
Dunton, Severn
Dyes, Richard
Dykes, John
Edgcomb, Thomas
Edwards, Ellis
Evans, John
Fandry, John
Fendla, John
Fisher, Isaac
Fisher, William
Flint, Thomas
Fortune, Gabriel
Fortune, James
Forrest, William
Freshwater, Wm. E.
Gaskins, Thomas
Gaston, Benjamin

George, Brister
George, Daniel
George, Samuel
George, Samuel
George, William
Gibbs, James
Gill, Cuthbert
Glass, Thomas
Grant, Thomas
Groton, Charles
Grymes, Joseph
Gunter, John
Hail, Edward
Hamminson, Wm.
Harcum, Elisha
Harman, Curtis
Haw, Peter
Haywood, Richard
Haywood, Thomas
Hearn, Francis
Hill, John
Hobday, Francis
Hodges, Joseph
Hogdon, Matthew
Hubbard, Jesse
Humphreys, James
Hunt, John
Hunter, Thomas
Hutcheson, William
Innis, Levi
James, Christopher
Jenkins, Richard
Jennings, James
Jeter, Clem.
Joab, Moses
Johnson, Isaiah
Johnson, Joshua
Johnson, William
Jones, Charles
Jones, Robert
Kent, Joshua
Lane, Thomas

Lee, James
Lewis, Charles
Lewis, Daniel
Litchfield, Thomas
Lucas, James
Mairs, Thomas
Mailey, James
Malone, Jeremiah
Maltimore, James
Marriner, Levin
Marshall, Joseph
Marshall, Kingston
Mason, Abel
Mason, John
Miles, William
Mills, John
Mitchell, Thomas
Moore, Charles
Moore, Lot
Mott, James
Murden, Edward
Nelms, Mendeth
Nicholson, John
Nicken, Edward
Nicken, Hezekiah
Northup, Joseph
Northup, Stephen
Nutall, John
Oats, William
Oldham, Samuel
Overstreet, John
Owen, John
Palmer, Thomas
Paradise, Merritt
Parker, George
Peaters, Solomon
Peter (a negro)
Pettigrew, Abel
Pettigrew, Edward
Pettigrew, Richard
Piper, William
Pluto (a negro)

Pope, Joseph	Smith, James	Tunnell, James
Pope, Thomas	Spann, Thomas	Tunnell, William
Pope, Thomas	Spratt, James	Walker, John
Powell, Samuel	Stanback, Littleberry	Wallace, Roger
Powers, Jacob	Stephens, Joseph	Ward, John Wyatt
Pritchett, George	Stephens, William	Warrington, James
Procure, Thomas	Stuart, Francis	Waterman, James
Prosser, John	Sympson, Hammock	Watkins, James
Pumroy, Esau	Sympson, Salathiel	Watson, Castilio
Purcell, Charles	Tailor, Jesse	Weaver, Elijah
Ransom, Augustine	Tankersley, Benj.	Welch, Patrick
Ransom, Thomas	Tankersley, John	White, Gillen
Rawley, James	Tate, Jesse	White, John
Richardson, Solomon	Taylor, Airs	White, John
Richardson, William	Taylor, Daniel	Whitehurst, Samuel
Riggs, William	Taylor, Thomas	Wilders, James
Roberts, George	Taylor, Thomas	Wiles, Reuben
Romas, Adam	Thatcher, William	Will (a negro)
Rudd, James	Thatcher, William	Willis, James
Rudd, John	Thomas, James	Willis, William
Saunders, Joseph	Thomas, Humphrey	Wilson, Henry
Schofield, Robert	Thompson, James	Wilson, John
Schofield, William	Timberlake, Richard	Wilson, Samuel
Scott, John	Tom (a negro)	Winbrough, Eburn
Scott, William	Tomlinson, John	Wood, John
Sheerman, Martin	Tomlinson, William	Wood, Philip
Skinner, Elisha	Tully, Matthew	Wood, Thomas

Roll of Citizens of Kentucky

Who were granted pensions for services in the Revolutionary War, under the various Pension Acts up to 1832. Compiled by Anderson C. Quisenberry, from the report of the Secretary of War to Congress in 1835 on the Pension Establishment of the United States, to which is appended additional names, from Collins' History of Kentucky, of persons drawing Revolutionary Pensions in 1840.

NOTE.—The first date is that on which the pensioner was placed on the roll; the second date shows when the pension began.

ADAIR COUNTY.

PENSIONERS UNDER THE ACT OF MARCH 18, 1818.

Caldwell, William, private, ... Virginia line
    July 20, 1819; January 22, 1819; $96. Age 66. Died July 5, 1825.

Cooper, Leighton, private, ... Virginia line
    July 29, 1831; July 27, 1831; $96. Age 77.

Jones, Charles, private, ... Virginia line
    February 14, 1831; February 8, 1831; $96. Age 71.

Lawless, Augustin (*alias* Austin), private, ... Virginia line
    December 15, 1825; October 15, 1825; $96. Age 82.

Mosby, William, private, ... Virginia line
    February 1, 1819; September 7, 1818; $96. Age 80.

Miller, John, sergeant, ... Virginia line
    April 9, 1821; October 5, 1818. Age 79.

Ross, John, private, ... Virginia line
    May 25, 1829; April 8, 1829; $96. Age 77.

Tucker, William, lieutenant, ... Virginia line
    December 9, 1820; June 1, 1818; $240. Age 77. Died May 23, 1829.

Townsend, John, private, ... Virginia line
    December 22, 1827; October 6, 1827; $96. Age 73.

Weir, Joseph, private, ... Pennsylvania line
    February 1, 1819; October 5, 1818; $96. Age 75.

Warmack, William, private, ... Maryland line
    March 18, 1824; $96. Age 72.

PENSIONERS UNDER THE ACT OF JUNE 7, 1832.

(All pensions under this Act began March 4, 1831.)

Aarons, Abraham, private, ... Virginia line
    April 12, 1833; $40. Age 75.

Atkinson, Joshua, private, ... Virginia line
    June 7, 1833; $30. Age 79.

Armstrong, Henry, private, ... Virginia line
    November 12, 1833; $30. Age 80.

Bailey, Elisha, private, ... Virginia line
    September 23, 1833; $26.66. Age 70.

Busby, Robert, private, ... Virginia line
    April 2, 1834; $80. Age 75.

Bettsworth, Charles, corporal, ... not stated
    August 22, 1833; $58.33. Age 76.

Cooper, John, private, ... North Carolina line
    November 6, 1832; $80. Age 100.

Cochran, Thomas, private, ... Georgia line
    February 8, 1832; $80. Age 74.

Conover, Levi, private, ... New Jersey line
    October 12, 1833; $80. Age 77.

Elliott, Alexander, midshipman, ... Virginia navy
    October 11, 1833; $144. Age 71.

Greider, sr., John, private, ... Virginia line
    April 1, 1833; $80. Age 73.

Holladay, Zacharias, drummer, ... Virginia line
    July 15, 1833; $88. Age 72.

Hopkins, William, private, ... Virginia line
    January 28, 1834; $80. Age 70.

Hurt, William, private, ... Virginia line
    March 21, 1834; $50. Age 77.

Ingram, Jeremiah, private, ... Virginia line
    February 28, 1833; $80. Age 75.

Irvine, James, private, ... Virginia line
    October 12, 1833; $46.66. Age 78.

James, William, private, ... North Carolina line
    August 17, 1833; $40. Age 76.

Miller, sr., Joseph, private, ... Virginia line
    December 28, 1832; $73.33. Age 81.

McKinney, William, private, ... Virginia line
    February 2, 1833; $80. Age 76.

Moore, Charles, private, ... North Carolina line
    August 21, 1833; $33.33. Age 74.

McGlassen, Matthew, private, ... Virginia line
    February 7, 1834; $60. Age 79.

Rogers, sr., William, private, ... Virginia militia
 May 31, 1833; $63.33. Age 86.
Royse, Solomon, private, ... North Carolina line
 August 21, 1833; $80. Age 70.
Staples, Isaac, private, ... Virginia militia
 November 6, 1832; $33.33. Age 72.
Smith, Moses, private, ... North Carolina State troops
 June 17, 1833; $80. Age 72.
Smith, 2d, John, private, ... North Carolina line
 June 17, 1833; $80. Age 79.
Smith, James, sergeant and private, ... Maryland militia
 October 12, 1833; $36.66. Age 79.
Skaggs, Archibald, private, ... Maryland militia
 July 10, 1834; $25. Age 74. Dead.
Trabue, Daniel, com. and private, ... Virginia militia
 December 26, 1832; $260. Age —.
Winfrey, Philip, private, ... Virginia line
 April 9, 1833; $20. Age 71.
White, Thomas, private, ... Virginia line
 August 21, 1833; $21.12. Age 71.
Young 2d, William, private, ... North Carolina militia
 April 1, 1833; $80. Age 74.

PENSIONERS UNDER THE ACT OF MAY 15, 1828.

Biggs, John, matross, ... Harrison's artillery
 February 28, 1829; March 3, 1826; $100. R. A. Buckner, Agent.
Hamilton, John, sergeant, third regiment, ... Maryland line
 February 24, 1829; March 3, 1826; $120. R. A. Buckner, Agent.

PENSIONERS IN THE COUNTY IN 1840.
(Collins' History of Kentucky, Vol. I, p. 5.)

Ellis, Samuel, age 79. Montgomery, John, age 78.
Total for the County, 48.

ALLEN COUNTY.

PENSIONERS UNDER THE ACT OF MARCH 18, 1818.

Johnson, Robert, private, ... Virginia line
 February 26, 1818; June 26, 1818; $96. Age 60. Suspended by Act
 May 1, 1820.
Morrison, Hugh, private, ... Virginia line
 Sept. 15, 1820; May 18, 1820; $96. Age 69. Died Dec. 23, 1823.
Richey, John, private, ... Maryland line
 April 4, 1826; July 19, 1825; $96. Age 80.

Tiffany, Walter, private, ... Connecticut line
    October 2, 1819; August 3, 1819; $96. Age 65. Transferred from
    West Tennessee Agency September 4, 1825. Died April 1, 1826.

Weaver, John, private, ... Virginia line
    May 1, 1820; August 18, 1818; $96. Age 78.

PENSIONERS UNDER THE ACT OF JUNE 7, 1832.

(All began March 4, 1831.)

Alexander, James R., private and sergeant, . . Maryland militia
    July 25, 1834; $103.33. Age 77.

Brook, John, private, ... Virginia line
    May 29, 1833; $40. Age 79.

Borders, Peter, private and sergeant, ... North Carolina line
    September 25, 1833; $91.65. Age 78.

Brunson, Stout, private and sergeant, . . . Pennsylvania line
    April 29, 1834; $80. Age 78.

Durham, John, private, ... Virginia militia
    January 28, 1834; $20. Age 73.

Gibson, John, private, ... Virginia line
    July 18, 1833; $26.66. Age 73.

Gatewood, John, private, ... Virginia line
    August 17, 1833; $45.43. Age 74.

Hains, Christopher, private, ... Virginia line
    February 18, 1833; $80. Age 74.

Heeter, George, private, ... Maryland militia
    February 18, 1833; $21.65. Age 82.

Hatler, Michael, private, ... Virginia line
    July 15, 1833; $21.55. Age 74.

Harrison, Richard, private, ... North Carolina militia
    September 24, 1833; $20. Age 70.

Moore, Wilson, private, ... Virginia line
    July 15, 1833; $76.66. Age 76.

Merrit, Stephen, private, ... North Carolina militia
    October 18, 1833; $30. Age 72.

McElroy, John, private, ... South Carolina militia
    October 18, 1833; $80. Age 73.

Pickford, Daniel, private, ... Virginia militia
    August 17, 1833; $23.22. Age 73.

Poe, Benj., private of infantry and cavalry, . North Carolina line
    December 28, 1833; $47.50. Age 85.

Sherry, William, private, ... North Carolina militia
    November 10, 1832; $30. Age 86.

Stovall, George, private, ... Virginia militia
    May 18, 1833; $30. Age 72.

Smith, 2d, Samuel, private, ... Virginia militia
    May 18, 1833; $30. Age 71.
Wright, Jarrett, corporal, ... Virginia line
    November 12, 1833; $80. Age 76.
Williamson, James, private of cavalry and infantry, Virginia line
    March 3, 1834; $99.42. Age 81.
Warden, Elisha, private, ... Virginia militia
    April 14, 1834; $21.21. Age 73.

Total for the County, 27.

ANDERSON COUNTY.

PENSIONERS UNDER THE ACT OF MARCH 18, 1818.

Atkins, Edward, private, ... Virginia line
    July 15, 1819; September 7, 1818; $96. Age 77.

PENSIONERS UNDER THE ACT OF JUNE 7, 1832.
(All began March 4, 1831.)

Boston, Reuben, private, ... Virginia line
    February 1, 1833; $50. Age —.
Cowgill, Ralph, private, ... Virginia State troops
    February 3, 1833; $80. Age —.
Franklin, Stephen, private, ... North Carolina line
    February 7, 1834; $40. Age 72.
Jordan, George, private, ... Virginia militia
    April 12, 1833; $80. Age 78.
McGuire, James, private, ... Virginia line
    June 5, 1820; February 7, 1820; $96. Age 87. Dropped under Act of
    May, 1820. Installed on roll under Act of June 7, 1832, at $80.
Mills, Menan, private, ... Virginia militia
    January 10, 1834; $20. Age —.
Penny, John, private, ... Virginia State troops
    November 28, 1832; $80. Age 75.
Petty, Rodham, private, ... Virginia militia
    September 26, 1833; $48.33. Age 82.
Pollard, William, private, ... Virginia militia
    October 31, 1833; $36.66. Age 72.
Slayden, John, private, ... Virginia militia
    December 1, 1832; $60. Age 72.
Searcy, Richard, private, ... Virginia militia
    December 23, 1833; $80. Age 75.
Warford, Benjamin, private, ... North Carolina militia
    February 1, 1833; $80. Age —.
Watson, 2d, John, private, ... Virginia militia
    February 7, 1834; $60. Age 74.

PENSIONERS UNDER THE ACT OF MAY 15, 1828.

Wallace, William B., lieutenant, . . . First regiment of artillery
July 16, 1828; $400.

REVOLUTIONARY PENSIONERS LIVING IN THE COUNTY IN 1840.
(Collins, Vol. I, p. 5.)

Robertson, James, age 86.   Hawkins, Jane, age 77.
Hill, Ann, age 75.
Total for the County, 18.

BARREN COUNTY.

PENSIONERS UNDER THE ACT OF MARCH 18, 1818.

Brownlee, John, private, ... Virginia line
September 6, 1819; May 29, 1818; $96.   Age 75.

Boon, Elisha, private, ... North Carolina line
October 4, 1819; February 3, 1819; $96.   Age 80.   Transferred from
North Carolina September 4, 1824.

Downing, Samuel, private, ... Maryland line
May 8, 1820; November 15, 1819; $96.   Age —.

Forrester, John, private, ... Virginia line
January 10, 1821; June 16, 1818; $96.   Age 81.

Foster, John, private, ... Virginia line
May 6, 1825; February 22, 1825; $96.   Age 79.

Kelly, John, private, ... Virginia line
April 10, 1822; August 11, 1818; $96.   Age —.   Died Dec. 31, 1822.

Luckett, Samuel, sergeant, ... Maryland line
June 4, 1819; May 12, 1818; $96.   Age 71.   Died August 22, 1828.

Scott, Francis, private, ... Virginia line
July 11, 1821; July 15, 1818; $96.   Age 76.

PENSIONERS UNDER THE ACT OF JUNE 7, 1832.
(Beginning March 4, 1831, unless otherwise stated.)

Arnett, David, private, ... Virginia line
January 28, 1833; $20.   Age 82.

Beavers, John, private, ... Virginia militia
November 6, 1832; March 4, 1832; $60.   Age 72.

Bagley, John, sergeant, ... Virginia line
January 28, 1833; March 4, 1832; $120.   Age 73.

Bailey, Callow, private, ... Virginia line
May 11, 1833; March 4, 1832; $60.   Age 84.

Boyd, William, private, ... North Carolina militia
May 30, 1833; March 4, 1832; $80.   Age 80.

Bell, William, private, ... Virginia militia
     June 7, 1833; March 4, 1832; $24.66. Age 79.

Bibb, James, private and sergeant, ... Virginia militia
     July 15, 1833; March 4, 1832; $73.38. Age 80.

Bailey, Richard, private, ... Virginia line
     July 15, 1833; March 4, 1832; $46.66. Age 70.

Burch, John, private, ... Virginia militia
     August 24, 1833; March 4, 1832; $80. Age 76.

Buford, Simeon, ensign and private, ... Virginia line
     August 24, 1834; March 4, 1832; $116.66. Age 77.

Carter, Henry, private, ... Virginia line
     January 28, 1833; $80. Age 82.

Coleman, Thomas, private, ... Virginia militia
     February 18, 1833; $80. Age 69. Died August 17, 1832.

Carter, Philip, private, ... Virginia militia
     May 31, 1833; $48.66. Age 68.

Cole, John, private, ... Maryland militia
     October 11, 1833; $40. Age 81.

Craig, William, private, ... Virginia militia
     November 28, 1833; $30. Age —.

Denton, David, private, ... Virginia line
     January 28, 1833; $80. Age 79.

Depp, William, private, ... Virginia militia
     September 26, 1833; $21.33. Age 73.

Dishman, William, private, ... Virginia State troops
     December 24, 1833; $80. Age 79. Died December 4, 1833.

Elmore, John, private of cavalry, . . . North Carolina militia
     November 6, 1832; $26.22. Age 75.

Frogget, William, private, ... Virginia line
     January 28, 1833; $100. Age 74.

Fulcher, Richard, corporal and private, ... Virginia line
     August 17, 1833; $33.22. Age 78.

Goodin, Lewis, private, ... Virginia line
     October 22, 1832; $80. Age 73.

Gibson, John, private of artillery, ... Virginia line
     January 28, 1833; $100. Age 78.

Gorin, John, sergeant, corporal, and private, . . Virginia militia
     July 15, 1833; $30.88. Age 71.

Green, Thomas, private, ... Virginia militia
     August 17, 1833; $32.22. Age 73.

Hiser, John, private, ... Pennsylvania militia
     January 28, 1833; $50. Age 74.

Huffman, Ambrose, ... Virginia militia
     January 28, 1833; $60. Age 80.

Hill, Clem, ... Virginia militia
    March 1, 1833; $60. Age 77.

Hamilton, Abner . . . . Virginia militia
    April 2, 1833; $30. Age 72.

Hughes, Absalom, private and sergeant, ... Virginia militia
    May 30, 1833; $63.33. Age 79.

Harris, William, private, ... Virginia militia
    November 28, 1833; $36.66. Age 79.

Higdon, Joseph, corporal and private of cavalry, Virginia militia
    January 13, 1834; $110. Age 75.

Hunt, Jonathan, private, ... North Carolina militia
    April 3, 1834; $24.44. Age 74.

Jameson, John, private, ... Virginia line
    October 11, 1833; $80. Age 71.

Jones, Richard, private, ... Virginia militia
    October 18, 1833; $26.66. Age 89.

Lynn, Israel, private, ... North Carolina militia
    January 28, 1833; $21.12. Age 75.

Larrance, Rodham, private, ... Virginia militia
    July 29, 1833; $20. Age 72.

Murrell, sr., Samuel, ensign, ... Virginia line
    January 28, 1833; $80. Age 78.

McGuire, Daniel, private, ... New Jersey line
    January 28, 1833; $63.33. Age 75.

Martin, Benjamin, private, corporal, and sergeant, . Virginia line
    May 11, 1833; $77. Age 75.

McGinness, Andrew, drummer, ... Virginia line
    September 24, 1833; $84. Age 79.

Nevill, James, private, ... Virginia militia
    June 20, 1834; $22.88. Age 92.

Priest, Peter, private, ... Virginia line
    November 25, 1833; $80. Age —.

Peers, William, mariner, ... Virginia navy
    May 6, 1834; $80. Age 74. Died May 29, 1833.

Robinson, James, private, ... Virginia line
    January 28, 1833; $80. Age 73.

Renfro, John, drummer, and private of infantry
    and cavalry, ... Virginia militia
    May 30, 1833; $39.33. Age 74.

Roberts, Thomas, private and sergeant, ... Virginia line
    July 15, 1833; $46.25. Age 71.

Reynolds, Nathaniel, private, ... Virginia militia
    September 28, 1833; $23.33. Age 72.

Spillman, James, private, ... Virginia militia
    November 6, 1832; $80. Age 71.

Smith, Thomas, private, ... South Carolina militia
  November 9, 1833; $26.66. Age 73.
Smith, Frederick, private and captain, ... Virginia line
  November 3, 1832; $160. Age —.
Terry, Thomas, private, ... Virginia line
  January 28, 1833; $80. Age 73.
Woodson, Samuel, private, ... Virginia line
  November 6, 1832: $33.33. Age 73.
Watson, John, private, ... Virginia line
  August 6, 1833; $60. Age 71.
Wade, Obadiah, private, ... Virginia militia
  January 28, 1833; $60. Age 71.

PENSIONERS UNDER THE ACT OF MAY 15, 1828.

Goodman, Thomas, matross, ... Harrison's artillery
  November 25, 1828; March 3, 1826; $100. Thomas Underwood,
  agent. Transferred from Henrico County, Virginia.

REVOLUTIONARY PENSIONERS LIVING IN THE COUNTY IN 1840.
(Collins, Vol. I, p. 5.)

Cosby, John, age 99.   Huffman, Ambrose, age 86.
Duff, John, age 80.   Sanders, Philemon, age 78.
Goodman, Thomas, age 77.   Key, Sarah, age 78.

Total for the County, 70.

BATH COUNTY.

PENSIONERS UNDER THE ACT OF MARCH 18, 1818.

Ashley, Thomas, private, ... Virginia line
  September 10, 1819; June 17, 1818; $96. Age 81.
Birch, John, private, ... Pennsylvania line
  August 1, 1821; June 15, 1818; $96. Age 81.
Deskins, Daniel, private, ... Virginia line
  April 10, 1819; June 17, 1818; $96. Age 74.
Fasbrook, John, private, ... Pennsylvania line
  November 26, 1819; June 17, 1818; $96. Age 104.
Gorrell, John, private, ... Pennsylvania line
  March 10, 1819; June 17, 1818; $96. Age 70.
Griffin, Gordon, private, ... Pennsylvania line
  November 15, 1820; June 17, 1818; $96. Age 80.
Hines, James, private, ... Virginia line
  February 13, 1819; July 10, 1818; $96. Age 80. Died Feb. 4, 1830.

Hasty, John, private, ... Virginia line
    February 12, 1819; July 15, 1818; $96. Age 73. Died Feb. 2, 1826.
Love, Mark, private, ... South Carolina line
    Sept. 15, 1819; June 22, 1819; $96. Age 68. Died Nov. 30, 1831.
Mulberry, James, private, ... Virginia line
    April 9, 1819; June 17, 1818; $96. Age 79.
Moore, Michael, private, ... Virginia line
    April 7, 1819; June 17, 1818; $96. Age 74.
Purvis, William, private, ... Virginia line
    April 9, 1819; July 17, 1818; $96. Age 77. Dropped under act of
    May 1, 1820. Restored August 17, 1826.
Petit, Matthew, private, ... Pennsylvania line
    April 6, 1819; June 17, 1818; $96. Age 74.
Sorrell, Elias, private, ... Virginia line
    April 9, 1819; June 17, 1818; $96. Age 71. Died July 9, 1825.

PENSIONERS UNDER THE ACT OF JUNE 7, 1832.
(Began March 4, 1831.)

Botts, Moses, private, ... Virginia line
    March 6, 1833; $40. Age 84.
Bromigin, Jarvis, private, ... Virginia militia
    December 21, 1833; $20. Age 72.
Collins, Joshua, private, ... Virginia line
    September 2, 1833; $80. Age 77.
Jameson, William, private, ... Virginia line
    March 6, 1833; $26.66. Age 75.
Kearnes, William, private, ... Virginia militia
    December 2, 1833; $80. Age 77.
Nelson, Moses, private, ... North Carolina line
    April 9, 1833; $80. Age 76.
Parker, Edward, sergeant, ... Virginia State troops
    April 9, 1833; $120. Age 80.
Rice, Holman, private and captain, ... Virginia line
    July 14, 1819; $240. Age 76. Increased to $480 April 12, 1833.
Smallwood, Beane, private, ... Virginia line
    October 31, 1823; $80. Age 76.
Thomas, Richard, private, ... North Carolina line
    March 21, 1833; $80. Age 76.

PENSIONERS UNDER THE ACT OF MAY 15, 1828.

Triplett, sr., Thomas, captain, ... Virginia line
    October 31, 1831; March 3, 1826; $480. Died February 28, 1833.
    Agents: Thomas Triplett, jr., W. T. Barry, Richard M. Johnson,
    H. Daniel, and M. Harrison. Betsey H. Triplett, widow.

REVOLUTIONARY PENSIONERS LIVING IN THE COUNTY IN 1840.
(Collins, Vol. I, p. 5.)

Boyd, William, age 74.   McElhany, James, age 80.
Linam, Andrew, age 81.   Sims, John, age 79.

Total for the County, 29.

BOONE COUNTY.

PENSIONERS UNDER THE ACT OF MARCH 18, 1818.
(All began March 4, 1831.)

Allen, Isham, private, ... Virginia line
   October 21, 1823; September 24, 1823; $96. Age 70.
Burns, James, private, ... Pennsylvania line
   May 13, 1819; June 15, 1818; $96. Age 80.
Beech, Asa, private, ... Connecticut line
   April 15, 1819; August 6, 1818; $96. Age 84.
Butler, Richard, private, ... New Jersey line
   January 4, 1823; October 2, 1820; $96. Age 70. Died Jan. 31, 1826.
Bruner, Jacob, private, ... New Jersey line
   January 22, 1824; November 13, 1823; $96. Age 73.
Brady, William, private, ... South Carolina line
   April 6, 1826; December 19, 1825; $96. Age 76.
Barlow, Joseph, private, ... Virginia line
   September 6, 1830; January 1, 1828; $96. Age 74.
Hayden, Jeremiah, private, ... Virginia line
   July 7, 1819; May 5, 1818; $96. Age 72.
McPherson, Alexander, private, ... Pennsylvania line
   April 21, 1819; September 26, 1818; $96. Age 82. Dropped May
   22, 1829; restored December 26, 1829. Died November 18, 1832.
Reed, Zachariah, private, ... Georgia line
   June 8, 1820; February 1, 1819; $96. Age 57. Suspended under
   Act May 1, 1820.
Stribling, Samuel, private, ... Virginia line
   July 7, 1819; May 5, 1818; $96. Age 92.
Taylor, John, private, ... Maryland line
   May 21, 1819; April 22, 1818; $96. Age 84.
Vance, Thomas, private, ... New Jersey line
   November 23, 1818; August 4, 1818. Age 73.

PENSIONERS UNDER THE ACT OF JUNE 7, 1832.
(Beginning March 4, 1831.)

Aldridge, William, private, ... Maryland militia
   January 10, 1823; $20. Age 77.
Bridges, John, private, ... Virginia line
   May 10, 1823; $96. Age 78. Raised to $100 March 4, 1831.

Craig, John H., private and quartermaster-general, Virginia line
June 10, 1823; $123.33. Age 77.
Clarkson, David, private, ... Virginia line
January 19, 1833; $40. Age 72. Died November 15, 1833.
Golding, William, private, ... Virginia line
December 7, 1833; $80. Age 75.
Gaff, David, private, ... Virginia line
March 14, 1834; $80. Age 80.
Hamilton, William, private, ... Virginia line
December 10, 1833; $46.66. Age 94. Dead.
Johnson, Cave, private, ... Virginia line
December 5, 1833; $40. Age 73.
Kay, James, private, ... Virginia line
June 18, 1833; $80. Age 75. Died July 12, 1833.
Kennedy, Joseph, private, ... Virginia militia
December 7, 1833; $23.33. Age 71.
Pratt, Jacob, adjutant and captain, ... New Jersey line
November 5, 1832; $351.24. Age 87.
Rouse, Samuel, private, ... Virginia militia
December 4, 1832; $20. Age 84.
Rouse, Jacob, private, ... Virginia militia
January 10, 1833; $33.33. Age 76.
Ross, Alexander, private, ... Virginia militia
April 25, 1833; $40. Age 74.
Ruddeel, James, private, ... Virginia militia
October 2, 1833; $80. Age 76.
Swindle, John, private, ... Virginia militia
January 17, 1833; $20. Age 82.
Smither, William, private, ... Virginia militia
April 25, 1833; $30. Age 79.
Stephenson, James, private, ... New Jersey line
June 12, 1833; $80. Age 79.
Vest, George, private, ... Virginia line
January 19, 1833; $63.33. Age 81.

REVOLUTIONARY PENSIONERS LIVING IN THE COUNTY IN 1840.

(Collins, Vol. I, p. 5.)

Brumback, Peter, age 87.   Hubbell, Richard, age 74.
Steers, Hugh, age 81.   Tomlinson, John, age 81.
Alexander, Jerusha, age 86.

Total for the County, 38.

BOURBON COUNTY.

PENSIONERS UNDER THE EARLY INVALID ACTS.

Campbell, William, sergeant, ... Revolutionary army
March 4, 1789; September 27, 1789; $30. Raised to $76.80. Transferred from Pennsylvania September 4, 1820.

Kindrick, Benjamin, private, ... Revolutionary army
January 1, 1786; June 1, 1786; $40. Raised to $64 March 4, 1820, and to $96 July 7, 1829. Died June 12, 1830.

PENSIONERS UNDER THE ACT OF MARCH 18, 1818.

Batterton, Samuel, private, ... Virginia line
May 7, 1819; August 11, 1818; $96. Age 76. Died June 12, 1833.

Barbey, Elijah, private, ... Virginia line
April 15, 1819; August 14, 1818; $96. Age 76. Died April 24, 1833.

Bates, Thomas, private, ... Virginia line
August 11, 1819; May 19, 1818; $96. Age 79.

Busby, James, private, ... Virginia line
January 6, 1819; May 25, 1818; $96. Age 78.

Cockerel, Peter, private, ... Virginia line
April 16, 1819; August 22, 1818; $96. Age 75.

Dawson, William, private, ... Pennsylvania line
May 22, 1819; July 2, 1818; $96. Age 96.

Drebuler, John, private, ... Maryland line
June 7, 1819; August 11, 1818; $96. Age 83.

Humphries, Joseph, private, ... Pennsylvania line
September 21, 1819; May 25, 1818; $96. Age 66.

Jameison, John, private, ... Virginia line
July 1, 1820; December 8, 1819; $96. Age 82.

Kendrick, Benson, private, ... Virginia line
June 23, 1819; May 29, 1818; $96. Age 76.

Kelly, Thomas, private, ... Pennsylvania line
October 2, 1819; May 10, 1818; $96. Age 84. Died Dec. 30, 1822.

Miller, John, private, ... South Carolina line
February 15, 1819; June 17, 1818; $96. Age 73. Died Aug. 23, 1825.

Pritchett, James, private, ... Virginia line
February 13, 1819; July 16, 1818; $96. Age 58. Dropped Act May 1, 1820.

Pater, Robert, private, ... Pennsylvania line
April 15, 1818; April 1, 1818; $96. Age 76. Died January 25, 1826.

Raine, Nathaniel, private, ... Virginia line
June 5, 1820; November 22, 1819; $96. Age 77.

Stoker, Edward, private, ... Virginia line
April 14, 1819; June 17, 1818; $96. Age 77.

8

Terrill, John, private, ... Pennsylvania line
    July 2, 1819; August 29, 1818; $96. Age 81.
Talbott, Isham, private, ... Virginia line
    July 18, 1823; May 13, 1823; $96. Age 75.
Whittington, John, private, ... Delaware line
    September 6, 1819; January 15, 1819; $96. Age 86. Died September 9, 1822.
Williams, Benjamin, private, ... Maryland line
    September 6, 1819; August 12, 1818; $96. Age 72.

PENSIONERS UNDER THE ACT OF JUNE 7, 1832.
(Began March 4, 1831.)

Ament, Philip, private, ... Pennsylvania militia
    July 10, 1834; $53.33. Age 79.
Breast, John, private, ... Virginia line
    December 18, 1832; $60. Age 74.
Branham, William, corporal, ... Virginia militia
    December 5, 1832; $66. Age 71.
Bowels, Samuel, private, ... Delaware line
    March 16, 1833; $80. Age 84.
Corbin, Lewis, private and sergeant, ... Virginia militia
    June 17, 1833; $76.66. Age 79.
Clinkenbeard, Isaac, private, ... Virginia line
    March 4, 1834; $36.66. Age 75.
Davis, James, private, ... Virginia line
    May 11, 1833; $30. Age 72.
Doudon, Clementius, sergeant and private, Pennsylvania militia
    July 23, 1833; $41.66. Age 72.
Edwards, George, private, ... North Carolina militia
    January 9, 1834; $20. Age 72.
Endicott, Moses, private, ... North Carolina militia
    April 14, 1834; $40. Age 74. Died April 24, 1834.
Forgueran, Peter, private, ... Virginia militia
    May 3, 1833; $30. Age 85.
Forgey, Hugh, private, ... Pennsylvania militia
    December 28, 1833; $40. Age $80.
Harris, William, private and sergeant, ... Virginia militia
    October 26, 1836; $51.60. Age 89.
Hill, Robert, private, ... Virginia militia
    May 11, 1833; $66.66. Age 77.
House, Andrew (Hawes), private, ... Pennsylvania militia
    July 10, 1834; $21.66. Age 86.
Hays, Thomas, private, ... Maryland militia
    December 23, 1833; $41.66. Age 72.
Jameson, David, ... Virginia line
    October 19, 1832; $80. Age 78.

Jackson, Joseph, private, ... Virginia line
November 1, 1832; $80. Age 77.
Jones, Thomas, private, ... Virginia militia
May 11, 1833; $40. Age 77. Died July 1, 1833.
Lander, Charles, sergeant, ... Virginia line
April 1, 1833; $120. Age 79. Died August 15, 1833.
Lockwood, Samuel, private, ... Delaware militia
May 7, 1833; $80. Age 78.
Luckey, Robert, private, ... Virginia militia
April 28, 1834; $66.66. Age 74.
McCloud, John, private, ... Virginia line
May 11, 1833; $33.33. Age 94.
McDowell, Daniel, ... Virginia militia
May 31, 1833; $40. Age 82.
Patton, William, private of cavalry, ... North Carolina line
November 5, 1832; $32.50. Age 75.
Rogers, Thomas, private, ... Virginia militia
April 12, 1833; $26.66. Age 80.
Shropshire, Abner, private, ... Virginia militia
January 26, 1833; $43.33. Age 73.
Shaw, Thomas, ... Pennsylvania militia
April 16, 1833; $43.33. Age 81.
Speaks, Hezekiah, private, ... Maryland militia
October 11, 1833. Age 76.
Stipp, John, ... Pennsylvania militia
October 31, 1833; $20. Age 86.
Stevens, Joseph L., private, ... Virginia militia
February 4, 1834. Age 70.
Wheley, Benjamin, sergeant and captain, Virginia State troops
August 7, 1833; $240. Age 74.

PENSIONERS UNDER THE ACT OF MAY 15, 1828.

Pritchard, James, dragoon, . . . Colonel Washington's cavalry
January 8, 1829; March 3, 1826; $100.
Wilmott, Robert, lieutenant, ... Harrison's artillery
January 8, 1829; March 3, 1826; $400.

REVOLUTIONARY PENSIONERS LIVING IN THE COUNTY IN 1840.
(Collins, Vol. I, pp. 5, 6.)

Bell, Archibald, age 84.   Scott, sr., William, age 67.
Bryan, George, age 82.   Smith, Michael, age 88.
Harris, Nathaniel, age 81.   Towles, Henry, age 54.
Hennis, Benjamin, age 80.   Wigginton, Henry, age 84.
Edward McConnell, age 68.   Wilson, Henry, age 84.
Total for the County, 66.

BRACKEN COUNTY.

PENSIONERS UNDER THE ACT OF MARCH 18, 1818.

Dean, Michael, private, ... Virginia line
    March 18, 1819; November 2, 1818; $96. Age 94.
Dilman, Andrew, private, ... Virginia line
    November 15, 1820; October 5, 1818; $96. Age 67.
Franklin, Joseph, private, ... Virginia line
    March 18, 1819; May 11, 1818; $96. Age 73. Died Dec. 30, 1829.
Jaco, William, private, ... Virginia line
    August 2, 1821 ; July 13, 1818; $96. Age 98.
Morris, Nathaniel G., captain, ... Virginia line
    March 18, 1819; May 4, 1818; $240. Age 76. Died Sept. 15, 1824.
Moore, Thomas, private, ... Virginia line
    March 18, 1819; Nov. 2, 1818; $96. Age 84. Died Aug. 18, 1825.
Maines, George, private, ... Virginia line
    Dec. 16, 1828; Nov. 16, 1828; $96. Age 84. Died Nov. 9, 1833.
Thomas, John T., private, ... Lee's legion
    March 18, 1819; May 4, 1828; $96. Age 74.

PENSIONERS UNDER THE ACT OF JUNE 7, 1832.
(Began Mach 4, 1831.)

Arbuckle, James, private, ... Virginia State troops
    May 12, 1834 ; $30. Age 72.
Black, Rudolph, private, ... Virginia militia
    January 30, 1834 ; $20. Age 72.
Hamilton, John, private, ... Pennsylvania line
    January 8, 1834; $53.33. Age 69.
Henderson, Benjamin, private, ... North Carolina militia
    January 8, 1834; $23.33. Age 76.
King, John, private, ... Pennsylvania line
    August 21, 1833; $46.66. Age 73.
King, William, private, ... Virginia militia
    October 31, 1833; $20. Age 71.
Kendall, Aaron, private, ... North Carolina militia
    January 4, 1834; $30. Age 75.
Morris, Jacob, private, ... New Jersey militia
    May 29, 1834 ; $20. Age 62.
Miranda, Samuel, private, ... Pennsylvania militia
    February 12, 1834 ; $20. Age —. Died November 6, 1833.
Owens, William, private, ... Virginia militia
    February 18, 1833 ; $20. Age 71.
Rice, Philip, musician and sergeant, ... Virginia militia
    December 20, 1833 ; $67. Age 75.

Sergeant, William, private, ... Maryland line
     June 6, 1834; $23.33. Age 74.
Tucker, John, private, ... Maryland line
     July 9, 1833; $80. Age 88.
Taylor, Bartholomew, private, ... Maryland militia
     June 17, 1834; $20. Age 79.

PENSIONERS UNDER THE ACT OF MAY 15, 1828.

Kimmer, Nicholas, corporal, Fourth Regiment Pennsylvania line
     October 6, 1828; March 3, 1826; $88. Transferred to Fayette
     County, Indiana.
Robinson, William, sergeant, . . Bull's Pennsylvania Regiment
     September 10, 1828; March 3, 1826; $120. Died February 15, 1835.

Total for the County, 24.

BREATHITT COUNTY.
(County formed after 1835.)

REVOLUTIONARY PENSIONERS LIVING IN THE COUNTY IN 1840.
(Collins, Vol. I, p. 6.)

Bowling, Jesse, age 82.   Bush, Drury, age 82.
Turner, Roger, age 83.

Total for the County, 3.

BRECKINRIDGE COUNTY.

PENSIONERS UNDER THE ACT OF MARCH 18, 1818.

Bassam, Obadiah, private, ... Virginia line
     April 14, 1819; July 25, 1818; $96. Age 74.
Dehaven, Edward, private, ... Pennsylvania line
     October 26, 1832; March 12, 1818; $96. Age 82.
Fate, Samuel, private, ... Pennsylvania line
     October 3, 1818; June 27, 1818; $96. Age 64.
Goatley, John, private, ... Virginia line
     September 9, 1819; July 25, 1818; $96. Age —.
Pullen, George, private, ... Virginia line
     September 9, 1819; July 25, 1818; $96. Age 75.
Weatherhall, Jacob, private, ... Virginia line
     February 15, 1820; October 23, 1818; $96. Age 75.
Wells, James, private, ... Virginia line
     January 16, 1822; April 20, 1819; $96. Age 74.

PENSIONERS UNDER THE ACT OF JUNE 7, 1832.
(Began March 4, 1831.)

Allgood, John, private, ... Virginia militia
     March 4, 1834; $21.33. Age 76.

Bramblett, James, private and corporal, ... Virginia militia
    May 11, 1833; $25.50. Age 70.

Fantress, Valentine, private, ... Virginia line
    December 5, 1832; $80. Age 74.

Gough, Ignatius, private, ... Virginia line
    October 18, 1833; $80. Age 81.

Hutchinson, Joseph, ... Virginia militia
    April 12, 1833; $20. Age 77.

Hashfield, Henry, ... Pennsylvania militia
    May 31, 1833; $26.66. Age 76.

Hoskinson, Charles, private, ... Maryland militia
    August 21, 1833; $26.66. Age 75.

Kincheloe, Thomas, sergeant, ... Virginia militia
    December 2, 1833; $35. Age 72.

Miller, Barney, private, ... Virginia militia
    August 21, 1833; $23.33. Age 69.

Mason, Joseph, private and sergeant, ... Virginia militia
    August 21, 1833; $36.54. Age 77.

Paul, George, private, ... Virginia militia
    August 21, 1833; $23.33. Age 68.

Parks, Samuel, private, ... New York militia
    December 23, 1833; $40. Age 75.

Reed, George, private, ... Maryland militia
    August 21, 1833; $20. Age 85.

Robertson, James, private, ... North Carolina militia
    March 14, 1834; $20. Age —.

Sharp, sr., Samuel, private, ... North Carolina militia
    August 21, 1833; $36.66. Age 85.

Seaton, George, sergeant and private, ... Virginia militia
    October 21, 1833; $78.33. Age 79.

Thornhill, William, private, ... Virginia militia
    March 5, 1834; $26.66. Age 77.

Wilkerson, Francis, private, ... North Carolina militia
    April 9, 1833; $36.66. Age 73.

PENSIONERS UNDER THE ACT OF MAY 15, 1828.

Goatley, John, dragoon, ... Washington's cavalry
    September 11, 1828; March 3, 1826.

REVOLUTIONARY PENSIONERS LIVING IN THE COUNTY IN 1840.
(Collins, Vol. I, p. 6.)

Pullin, George, age 81.   Wells, James, age 77.

Total for the County, 28.

BULLITT COUNTY.

PENSIONERS UNDER THE ACT OF MARCH 18, 1818.

Buzan, John, private, ... Virginia line
September 17, 1819; July 21, 1819; $96. Age 79.

Cornwell, William, private, ... New York line
October 2, 1819; July 23, 1819; $96. Age 73.

Edens, John, private, ... South Carolina line
February 10, 1819; Sept. 21, 1818; $96. Age 77. Died Jan. 23, 1826.

Field, Henry, private, ... Virginia line
February 10, 1819; May 12, 1818; $96. Age 74. Died May 27, 1823.

Goldsmith, John, private, ... Virginia line
July 30, 1825; July 4, 1825; $96. Age 68. Died October 30, 1825.

Hubbard, Eppa, sergeant, ... Virginia line
March 14, 1820; March 27, 1819; $96. Age 73. Died Sept. 12, 1830.

Johnson, Isaac, private, ... Virginia line
August 28, 1819; June 1, 1818; $96. Age 85. Died October 21, 1833.

Isbell, Henry, private, ... Virginia line
August 13, 1818; June 1818; $96. Age 75.

Langsdon, Charles, private, ... Virginia line
May 6, 1820; September 24, 1819; $96. Age 72.

Lloyd, Joseph, private, ... Virginia line
July 30, 1825; July 4, 1825; $96. Age 73.

McMannis, Charles, private, ... Virginia line
September 9, 1819; July 9, 1819; $96. Age 69. Died Jan. 31, 1828.

PENSIONERS UNDER THE ACT OF JUNE 7, 1832.
(Began March 4, 1831.)

Bishop, Lawrence, private, ... Pennsylvania militia
September 9, 1833; $20. Age 71.

Cardwell, William, private, ... Virginia line
March 15, 1834; $100. Age 74.

Chappell, William, private, ... Virginia militia
October 18, 1833; $50. Age 74.

Hubbs, Jacob, private, ... Virginia militia
March 2, 1833; $36.66. Age 72.

Hornbeck, Samuel, private, ... Virginia militia
September 9, 1833; $20. Age 71.

Miles, Jesse, private, ... Virginia militia
September 28, 1833; $30. Age 71.

Miller, John, private, ... Virginia militia
June 6, 1834; $30. Age 85.

Northern, Reuben, private, ... **Virginia** militia
December 26, 1833; $20. Age 75.

Rowland, Samuel, private, ... New Jersey State troops
    October 21, 1833; $63.33. Age 76.
Saunders, Joseph, lieutenant, ...Virginia line
    November 14, 1832; $320. Age 78.
Stringer, John, private, ...Virginia militia
    March 2, 1833; $43.33. Age 79.
Skinner, Isaac, private, ...Virginia militia
    August 9, 1833; $23.33. Age 74.
Spencer, William, private, ...Virginia militia
    July 1, 1834; $80. Age 73.
Webb, Augustin, sergeant, ... Virginia State troops
    March 2, 1833; $60. Age —.
Wright, Elijah, private, ... Pennsylvania State troops
    September 2, 1833; $28.33. Age 78.

REVOLUTIONARY PENSIONERS LIVING IN THE COUNTY IN 1840.
(Collins, Vol. I, p. 6.)

Humphrey, John, age 77.   Pilkenton, Larkin, age 70.
Total for the county, 28.

BUTLER COUNTY.

PENSIONERS UNDER THE ACT OF MARCH 18, 1818.

Brown, Peter, private, ...Virginia line
    March 5, 1819; April 12, 1818; $96. Age 69. Died Sept. 20, 1833.
Lindsay, Abraham, private, ...Virginia line
    December 10, 1827; July 28, 1827; $96. Age —.

PENSIONERS UNDER THE ACT OF JUNE 7, 1832.
(Began March 4, 1831.)

Busby, William, private, ... North Carolina militia
    June 6, 1833; $60. Age 72.
Borah, Jacob, private, ... Pennsylvania militia
    January 28, 1834; $20. Age 69.
Cook, John, private, ...Virginia line
    January 15, 1833; $30. Age 72.
Carson, Thomas, private, ... Virginia State troops
    April 2, 1833; $80. Age 74.
Kuykendall, Matthew, priv. of inf. and cavl., South Carolina line
    August 17, 1833; $50. Age 76.
Lawrence, Thomas, sergeant, ...Virginia line
    November 3, 1832; $120. Age 73.
Porter, John, private and sergeant, ...Virginia militia
    April 2, 1833; $110. Age 75.

Scholfield, Jesse, private, ... Connecticut line
May 29, 1833; $80. Age 77.

Sharp, 2d, John, private, ... Virginia militia
January 28, 1834; $20. Age 75.

Whittaker, Mark, private, ... North Carolina line
May 29, 1833; $20. Age 84.

Warnack, Abner, private, ... North Carolina militia
August 17, 1833; $24.44. Age 70.

PENSIONER UNDER THE ACT OF MAY 15, 1828.

Porter, William, lieutenant, ... Virginia line
November 29, 1828; March 3, 1836; $320. Died July 8, 1828.

REVOLUTIONARY PENSIONERS LIVING IN THE COUNTY IN 1840.

Beasley, William, age 78.　　　Sowell, John, age 81.
Clark, John, age 103.

Total for the County, 17.

CALDWELL COUNTY.

PENSIONERS UNDER THE ACT OF MARCH 18, 1818.

Cartwright, Justinian, sergeant, ... Virginia line
June 5, 1819; April 27, 1819; $96. Age 73. Died Sept. 27, 1832.

Farmer, William, private, ... North Carolina line
September 28, 1818; August 24, 1818; $96. Age —.

Freeman, Aaron, private, ... North Carolina line
Oct. 29, 1819; July 26, 1819; $86. Age 77. Died Nov. 26, 1821.

Gholson, William, sergeant, ... Virginia line
September 18, 1819; May 25, 1818; $96. Age 76.

Jennings, James, private, ... South Carolina line
May 28, 1819; November 24, 1818; $96. Age 79.

Lyon, Matthew, lieutenant, ... New Hampshire line
April 20, 1819; August 24, 1818; $240. Age 85. Died Aug. 1, 1822.

Porter, William, lieutenant, ... Virginia line
Aug. 2, 1820; Aug. 24, 1820; $240. Age 71. Died Jan. 6, 1828.

Thomas, Henry, private, ... Virginia line
November 24, 1818; May 26, 1818; $96. Age 77. Transferred from
West Tennessee.

Veach, Elijah, private, ... Virginia line
June 30, 1818; May 25, 1818; $96. Age 79.

Williams, Thomas, private, ... Delaware line
June 28, 1819; Sept. 29, 1818; $96. Age 84. Died June 17, 1825.

Waterfield, Peter, private, ... Virginia line
January 10, 1828; December 17, 1827; $96. Age 73.

PENSIONERS UNDER THE ACT OF JUNE 7, 1832.

(Began March 4, 1831.)

Ashurst, William, private, ... Virginia militia
March 13, 1833; $20. Age 72.

Armstrong, William, private, ... North Carolina line
February 24, 1834; $43.33. Age 81.

Blackburn, William, private, ... Virginia militia
March 13, 1833; $95. Age 77.

Beck, Thomas, private, ... Maryland line
December 2, 1833; $36.66. Age 70.

Blick, John, private, ... Virginia State troops
December 9, 1833; $20. Age 72.

Cooper, Tracy, midshipman, ... Pennsylvania navy
March 13, 1833; $108. Age 69.

Calvert, Spencer, sergeant and private, ... Virginia line
August 22, 1833; $41.66. Age 73.

Clinton, James, private and lieutenant, ... Virginia line
October 11, 1833; $183.33. Age 72.

Dunn, Joseph, private of infantry and cavalry, . . N. C. militia
March 13, 1833; $93.33. Age 79.

Davis, Nathaniel, private, ... Virginia line
November 15, 1833; $40. Age 80.

Ford, William, private, ... Maryland militia
April 12, 1833; $36.66. Age 71.

Freer, Solomon, private of cavalry . . . . . South Carolina line
August 22, 1833; $100. Age 70.

Freeman, Michael, private of cavalry and infantry, . . N. C. line
August 22, 1833; $95.82. Age 70.

Guess, Joseph, private of cavalry, ... North Carolina militia
March 14, 1833; $32.50. Age 72.

Groom, Major, private, ... Virginia line
April 12, 1833; $29.30. Age 71.

Hart, John, private, ... North Carolina line
May 6, 1833; $40. Age 82.

Hamilton, John, private, ... Virginia militia
September 2, 1833; $21.56. Age 79.

Huey, John, private, ... Pennsylvania militia
January 8, 1834; $36.66. Age 80.

McNabb, John, private, ... South Carolina militia
March 2, 1833; $20. Age 86.

McVey, Hugh, private, ... Virginia militia
March 14, 1833; $50. Age 92.

Ogden, Benjamin, private, ... New Jersey line
October 6, 1832; $80. Age 70.

Scott, James, private, ... Virginia militia
March 14, 1833; $30. Age 78.

REVOLUTIONARY PENSIONER RESIDING IN THE COUNTY IN 1840.
(Collins, Vol. I, p. 6.)

Bowers, Reuben, age 74.

Total for the County, 34.

CALLOWAY COUNTY.

PENSIONER UNDER THE ACT OF MARCH 18, 1818.

Bridges, Benjamin, private, ... North Carolina line
June 30, 1818; May 25, 1818; $96. Age 80. Died Dec. 17, 1824.

PENSIONERS UNDER THE ACT OF JUNE 7, 1832.
(Began March 4, 1831.)

Barham, John, private, ... Virginia line
September 5, 1833; $32.33. Age 70.

Cooke, Robert, private of infantry and cavalry, . . Virginia line
December 14, 1833; $82.50. Age 78.

Greenwood, Joseph, private, ... Maryland line
January 26, 1833; $66.66. Age 80.

Glover, Joseph, private of infantry and cavalry, . . Virginia line
August 17, 1833; $84.54. Age 74.

Henson, sr., Jesse, private, ... Virginia line
January 26, 1833; $80. Age 75.

Hamlett, John, private, ... North Carolina militia
May 11, 1833; $40. Age 77.

Jones, John, private and sergeant, ... Virginia militia
May 13, 1833; $24.58. Age 74.

McGrew, Thomas, private, ... South Carolina line
January 26, 1833; $80. Age 102.

Melone, Andrew, private and captain, ... Maryland line
July 9, 1833; $87.88. Age 80.

Mullins, Charles, private of infantry and cavalry, N. Carolina line
August 17, 1833; $63.33. Age 85.

Owens, George, private, ... Maryland line
January 26, 1833; $20. Age 85.

Oglivie, Kimbrough, private, ... North Carolina militia
January 26, 1833; $20. Age 71.

Stone, Rowland, private, ... South Carolina militia
September 5, 1833; $23.33. Age 70.

Smith, Thomas, private, ... Virginia State troops
December 18, 1833; $30. Age 93.

Tayloe, Edmund, private, ... North Carolina militia
    October 21, 1833; $30. Age 78.
West, Leonard, private, ... North Carolina militia
    January 31, 1833; $43.33. Age 69.

REVOLUTIONARY PENSIONERS LIVING IN THE COUNTY IN 1840.
(Collins, Vol. I, p. 6.)

Dunn, Joseph, age 89.   Galloway, Charles, age 83.
Frizell, Nathan, age 82.   Wilkins, William, age 81.
    Total for the County, 22.

CAMPBELL COUNTY.
PENSIONER UNDER THE EARLY INVALID PENSION ACTS.

McGlasson, John, private, ... Revolutionary army
    January 11, 1830;. $30. Act of May 24, 1828.

PENSIONERS UNDER THE ACT OF MARCH 18, 1818.

Allphin, Ransom, private, ... Virginia line
    July 30, 1831; July 30, 1831; $96. Age 84. Dead.
Davis, Samuel, private, ... Virginia line
    September 16, 1819; April 27, 1818; $96. Age 98.
Keen, John, private, ... Virginia line
    December 19, 1823; October 27, 1823; $96. Age 74.
Maren, Benjamin, private, ... Virginia line
    March 14, 1820; June 15, 1818; $96. Age 74.
Marston, James, private, ... New Hampshire line
    September 16, 1819; May 1, 1818; $96. Age 83. Died Jan. 16, 1828
Massey (or Mercy), John, private, ... Armand's legion
    May 16, 1823; March 1, 1823; $96. Age 73.
Mefford, Jacob, private, ... Maryland line
    March 26, 1825; August 9, 1824; $96. Age 74.
Perkings, James, private, ... New York line
    June 19, 1826; June 7, 1826; $96. Age 75.
White, James, private, ... Virginia line
    March 12, 1830; March 10, 1830; $96. Age 89.

PENSIONERS UNDER THE ACT OF JUNE 7, 1832
(Began March 1, 1831.)

Byland, Samuel, private, ... Virginia line
    April 4, 1834; $40. Age 68.
Bellville, Samuel, private, ... Delaware militia
    April 14, 1834; $20. Age 72.
Baley, Samuel, private, ... North Carolina State troops
    November 25, 1833; $36.66. Age 77.

Collins, Stephens, private, ... Connecticut line
    January 19, 1833; $50. Age 80.
Casey, Joseph, private, ... Pennsylvania line
    April 11, 1834; $30. Age 71.
Ducker, John, private, ... Virginia line
    May 24, 1833; $60. Age 75.
Goodwin, Julius C., private, ... Virginia line
    October 18, 1833; $20. Age 70.
Hays, John, private, ... Pennsylvania line
    May 30, 1833; $40. Age 77.
Huling, Jonathan, private, ... Virginia militia
    October 18, 1833; $20. Age 73.
Herbert, sr., Josiah, private, ... Virginia militia
    December 14, 1833; $60. Age 79.
Long, Nicholas, sergeant, adjutant, and b. major, . Virginia line
    September 3, 1832; $193.33. Age 80.
Massey, Edmond, private, ... Virginia militia
    February 5, 1833; $20. Age 87.
Morin, Edward, private, ... Virginia line
    February 28, 1833; $80. Age 89.
Mason, Peter, private, ... Virginia line
    January 13, 1834; $40. Age 70.
Marshall, Robert, private, ... Maryland line
    May 27, 1834; $80. Age 71.
Parker, Abraham, private, ... Virginia line
    January 17, 1834; $40. Age 76.
Sutton, Benjamin, private, ... New Jersey militia
    June 6, 1834; $40. Age 78.
Todd, Samuel, private, ... Virginia militia
    August 23, 1833; $26.66. Age 73.

PENSIONERS UNDER THE ACT OF MAY 15, 1828.
(Began March 3, 1826.)

McKinney, John, lieutenant, 5th regiment, . Pennsylvania line
    July 23, 1828; $320. Died Nov. 25, 1833. Mary T. McKinney, widow.
Smith, Massa Ara, private, ... Virginia line
    March 29, 1830; $80. Hon. R. M. Johnson, agent.
Turner, George, captain, 1st regiment, . . . South Carolina line
    July 14, 1828; $480. Transferred from Hamilton County, Ohio.

REVOLUTIONARY PENSIONERS LIVING IN THE COUNTY IN 1840.
(Collins, Vol. I, p. 6.)

DeCourcey, William, age 85.   Harris, sr., Thomas, age 96.
Dickens, Joseph, age 75.   Orcutt, sr., William, age 81.
            Smith, Henry, age 90.
        Total for the County, 36.

CARROLL COUNTY.
(Formed after 1835.)

REVOLUTIONARY PENSIONERS LIVING IN COUNTY IN 1840.
(Collins, Vol. I, p. 6.)

Coghill, James, age 82.   Matthews, Amos V., age 79.
Deen, sr., John, age 84.   Scott, Robert, age 77.
Driskill, David, age 79.   Short, John, age 78.

Total for County, 6.

CARTER COUNTY.
(Formed after 1835.)

REVOLUTIONARY PENSIONER LIVING IN COUNTY IN 1840.
(Collins Vol. I, p. 6.)

Bates, William, age 77.

Total for County, 1.

CASEY COUNTY.
PENSIONERS UNDER THE ACT OF MARCH 18, 1818.

Clark, James, private, ... Virginia line
    July 21, 1819; February 23, 1819; $96. Age 73. Died July 12, 1832.
Coffman, Jacob, private, ... Maryland line
    January 11, 1822; November 26, 1821; $96. Age 73.
Havely, Jacob, private, ... Maryland line
    January 13, 1823; August 11, 1818; $96. Age 70. Dead.
Hogue, Andrew, private, ... North Carolina line
    March 2, 1831; February 19, 1831; $96. Age 83.
Jones, William, private, ... Virginia line
    July 7, 1825; June 7, 1825; $96. Age 84.
Morrow, Thomas, private, ... Pennsylvania line
    April 5, 1820; Sept. 1, 1818; $96. Age 79. Died August 30, 1830.
McConnell, Jonathan, lieutenant, ... New Hampshire line
    December 14, 1819; Nov. 28, 1818; $96. Age 81. Died May 10, 1829.
Minor, Jacob, private, ... Virginia line
    January 23, 1830; January 23, 1830; $96. Age 75.
Skeen, John, private, ... North Carolina line
    April 15, 1820; August 31, 1818; $96. Age 76.

PENSIONERS UNDER THE ACT OF JUNE 7, 1832.
(Began March 4, 1831.)

Canady, John, private, ... Virginia State troops
    May 6, 1833; $36.66. Age 71.
Coffey, Osbourne, private and sergeant, ... Virginia line
    May 11, 1833; $110. Age 75.

Carson, James, private and lieutenant, ... Virginia militia
October 18, 1833; $50. Age 73.

Glazebrook, Julius, private, ... Virginia militia
July 10, 1833; $26.66. Age 82.

Good, John, private, ... Virginia line
August 17, 1833; $30. Age 85.

McWhorter, John, private, ... North Carolina line
May 6, 1833; $80. Age 85.

Russell, Absalom, private, ... Virginia militia
May 6, 1833; $23.33. Age 74.

Royaltree, John, private, ... Virginia line
May 6, 1833; $26.66. Age 75.

Sutherland, William, private, ... Maryland line
September 25, 1833; $80. Age 87.

Total for the County, 18.

CHRISTIAN COUNTY.

PENSIONERS UNDER THE ACT OF MARCH 18, 1818.

Brewer, Henry, private, ... North Carolina line
March 31, 1820; July 5, 1819; $96. Age 74.

Carter, John, private, ... Pennsylvania line
May 18, 1819; August 25, 1818; $96. Age 70.

Conner, John, private, ... Colonel Armand's corps
December 4, 1818; October 13, 1818; $96. Age 70.

Nixon, Absalom, private, ... South Carolina line
January 26, 1833; January 10, 1833; $96. Age 82.

Woolsey, Thomas, private, ... Virginia line
May 18, 1820; July 9, 1819; $96. Age —.

Watener, Robert, private, ... Virginia line
Feb. 16, 1822; Sept. 1, 1819; $96. Age 68. Died Aug. 13, 1827.

PENSIONERS UNDER THE ACT OF JUNE 7, 1832.
(Began March 1, 1831.)

Anderson, John, private, ... North Carolina militia
May 13, 1833; $37. Age 87.

Barnes, George, private, ... Virginia line
February 13, 1833; $80. Age 78.

Clark, Jonathan, lieutenant, ... North Carolina line
September 26, 1833; $320. Age 75.

Dimkinson, Thomas, private, ... Virginia line
January 26, 1833; $40. Age 71.

Dupuy, William, private, ... Georgia militia
January 26, 1833; $21.66. Age 68.

Davis, Henry, private, ... North Carolina line
April 1, 1833; $80. Age 75.

Franklin, Absalom, private, ... Virginia militia
January 11, 1834. Age 70.

Gilmore, James, sergeant and private, ... Virginia line
August 17, 1833; $51.66. Age 89.

Gray, William, private, ... Virginia line
June 17, 1833; $60. Age 80.

Harlow, John, private, ... Virginia militia
January 26, 1833; $20. Age 83.

Johnson, Dalmath, private, ... Virginia militia
October 18, 1833; $20.55. Age 73.

Jones, Samuel, private, ... Virginia militia
June 7, 1832; $96. Age 78.

Knight, Night, private, ... South Carolina line
November 30, 1832; $80. Age 84.

Meacham, Joseph, private of cavalry, North Carolina State troops
November 10, 1832; $25. Age 73.

Philips, John, private, ... North Carolina line
October 29, 1832; $29.66. Age 100.

Patton, Matthew, private, ... Maryland militia
June 24, 1834; $25.60. Age 84.

Palmer, Isaac, private, ... Virginia militia
July 10, 1834; $25.77. Age 87.

Stroud, Isaac, private of infantry and cavalry and
orderly sergeant, ... North Carolina militia
January 26, 1833; $33.33. Age 73.

Stewart, James, private, ... South Carolina militia
November 9, 1833; $80. Age 72.

Thomas, Charles, private and sergeant, . . North Carolina line
January 4, 1834; $45.66. Age —.

Warren, William, private, ... Virginia line
January 6, 1833; $80. Age —.

Waggoner, Thomas, sergeant, ... Virginia line
January 8, 1834; $30. Age 72.

Younglove, Samuel, sergeant and private, ... Virginia line
April 16, 1833; $166.66. Age 71.

REVOLUTIONARY PENSIONERS LIVING IN THE COUNTY IN 1840.
(Collins, Vol. 1, p. 6.)

Cain, John, age 77.   Sullenger, James, age 77.

Total for the County, 31.

CLARK COUNTY.

Pensioners Under the Act of March 18, 1818.

Botts, Seth, private, ... Virginia line
January 26, 1819; June 27, 1818; $96. Age 81. Died Sept. 3, 1827.
Dunn, John, private, ... Virginia line
April 3, 1819; July 3, 1818; $96. Age 85.
Eastin, Elisha, private, ... Virginia line
July 21, 1819; June 26, 1818; $96. Age 82.
Fletcher, John, private, ... Virginia line
April 3, 1819; June 22, 1818; $96. Age 85.
Foster, William, private, ... Virginia line
February 11, 1819; June 22, 1818; $96. Age 73.
Hathpenny, alias Halfpenny, John, private, . Connecticut line
April 1, 1819; April 29, 1818; $96. Age 82.
Johnston, Martin, private, ... Virginia line
March 31, 1819; June 20, 1818; $96. Age 63. Dead.
Key, Price, corporal, ... Pennsylvania line
November 25, 1819; May 23, 1818; $96. Age 75. Died July 14, 1829.
Lockett, Benjamin, private, ... Virginia line
July 22, 1819; June 23, 1818; $96. Age 71.
Martin, John, private, ... Virginia line
June 19, 1820; October 4, 1818; $96. Age 74.
Martin, William, private, ... Virginia line
June 4, 1819; September 28, 1818; $96. Age 77.
Melton or Milton, Thomas, private, ... Virginia line
October 10, 1820; June 30, 1818; $96. Age 84.
Pool, John, private, ... New Jersey line
June 3, 1819; August 5, 1818; $96. Age 76. Died Feb. 20, 1826.
Sidebottom, John, private, ... Virginia line
July 8, 1819; **May 8,** 1819; $96. Age 70.
Scott, Drury, private, ... Virginia line
October 26, 1820; October 23, 1819; $96. Age 74.
Wilson, James, private, ... Maryland line
June 9, 1824; January 26, 1824; $96. Age 71.

Pensioners Under the Act of June 7, 1832.
(Began March 4, 1831.)

Anderson, James, private, ... Virginia line
April 2, 1833; $80. Age 74.
Alexander, sr., John, private, ... Pennsylvania militia
April 12, 1833; $23.23. Age 78.
Adkins, John, private, ... Virginia militia
September 24, 1833; $20. Age 88.

9

Arnold, John, private, ... Virginia State troops
  March 25, 1834; $80. Age 75.
Acton (Ecton), Smallwood, private, . . . Virginia State troops
  June 6, 1834; $30. Age 75.
Burbridge, Lincefield, private, ... Virginia line
  September 17, 1832; $80. Age 74.
Berry, Thomas, private, ... Virginia militia
  May 3, 1833; $50. Age 77.
Berkley, alias Bartlett, William, private, ... Virginia line
  May 11, 1833; $80. Age 79.
Bush, James, private, ... Virginia State troops
  September 25, 1833; $24.44. Age 75.
Dyke, John, private, ... Virginia line
  May 11, 1833; $30. Age 83.
Duke (Dyke), Matthew, private, ... Virginia militia
  September 24, 1833; $20. Age 76.
Davis, Septimus, lieutenant, ... Pennsylvania line
  November 29, 1833; $320. Age 78.
Dewitt, Peter, private, ... Virginia militia
  January 2, 1834; $20. Age 82.
Elkin, James, private, ... Virginia militia
  January 31, 1833; $63.33. Age 79.
Faudre, Vachel, private, ... Virginia militia
  January 31, 1833; $55. Age 72.
Franklin, Reuben, private, ... Virginia militia
  May 11, 1833; $60. Age 78.
Gordon, John, private, ... Virginia militia
  December 15, 1832; $26.66. Age 71.
Gravitt, John, ... Virginia militia
  April 10, 1833; $40. Age 77.
Greening, James, private, ... Virginia militia
  May 18, 1833; $24.44. Age 81.
Gay, sr., James, private, ... Virginia militia
  October 2, 1833; $80. Age 76.
Hickman, Joel, private, ... Virginia line
  May 7, 1833; $80. Age 73.
Halley, Benjamin, private, ... Virginia militia
  December 7, 1833; $23.33. Age 82.
Holliday, Stephen, private, ... Virginia line
  February 27, 1834; $36.66. Age 73.
Hall, Edward, private, ... Virginia line
  February 27, 1834; $80. Age 76.
Jones, Nicholas, private, ... Virginia line
  December 10, 1832; $36.66. Age 71.

Jones, Joshua, private, ... Maryland militia
April 12, 1833; $23.33. Age 75.
Jackson, Josiah, private, ... Virginia militia
November 9, 1833; $20. Age 72.
Lowry, Thomas, private, ... Virginia militia
October 2, 1833; $70. Age 74.
Miller, George, private, ... Virginia militia
January 31, 1833; $20. Age 72.
Merrill, Andrew, private, ... New Jersey line
May 20, 1833; $80. Age 77.
Martin, John, sergeant and captain, ... Virginia line
August 21, 1833; $127.83. Age 85.
Martin, William, private, ... Virginia militia
April 9, 1833; $80. Age 77.
Oliver, Richard, private, ... North Carolina line
January 11, 1834; $30, Age 82.
Palmer, Joseph, private, ... Virginia line
November 5, 1832; $53.33. Age 74.
Spillman, James, private, ... Virginia militia
February 22, 1833; $36.66. Age 78.
Smith, John, private, ... Maryland militia
May 31, 1833; $33.33. Age 85.
Snail, Christopher, sergeant and private, . North Carolina militia
$50. Age 82.
Stinson (Stevenson), John, ensign and private, Maryland militia
October 21, 1833; $33.33. Age 79.
Smith, Thomas, private and sergeant, ... Virginia militia
October 31, 1833; $40.83. Age 82.
Tracy, Charles, private, ... Maryland line
October 24, 1832; $76.66. Age 75. Died March 19, 1834.
Tuggle, William, private, ... Virginia line
August 17, 1833; $64.66. Age 75.
Thomas, James, private, ... North Carolina militia
May 10, 1834; $43.33. Age 69.
Wright, William, private, ... Virginia militia
December 15, 1832 ; $40. Age —.
Total for the County, 59.

CLAY COUNTY.

Pensioners Under the Act of March 18, 1818.

Jacobs, William, private, ... Virginia line
May 11, 1819; October 19, 1818; $96. Age 79.
Seaborn, Jacob, private, ... Virginia line
May 12, 1819; September 17, 1818; $96. Age 71.
Wood, Samuel, private, ... Maryland line
September 14, 1819; July 5, 1819; $96. Age 75.

PENSIONERS UNDER THE ACT OF JUNE 7, 1832.
(Began March 4, 1831.)

Burns, William, private, ... Virginia line
    January 30, 1833; $50. Age 78.
Baker, Bowling, private inf. and cavalry, . . North Carolina line
    January 26, 1833; $60.83. Age 71.
Bowling, Jesse, private, ... North Carolina militia
    January 26, 1833; $26.66. Age 76.
Benge, John, private, ... North Carolina militia
    June 18, 1834; $56.66. Age 74.
Chandler, John, private, ... Virginia militia
    December 2, 1833; $20. Age 69.
Lewis, Messenger, private, ... Connecticut line
    December 2, 1833; $46.66. Age 72.
Martin, Azariah, private, ... Virginia militia
    August 21, 1833; $36.66. Age 70.
Phillips, John, private, ... South Carolina militia
    October 2, 1833; $50. Age 73.
Ratcliffe, Harper, private, ... North Carolina militia
    January 9, 1834; $60. Age 72.
Stapleton, Thomas, private, ... North Carolina militia
    April 3, 1834; $24.66. Age 76.

REVOLUTIONARY PENSIONERS LIVING IN THE COUNTY IN 1840.
(Collins, Vol. I, p. 6.)

Burge, sr., David, age 80.   Garland, John, age 102.
    Total for the County, 15.

CLINTON COUNTY.
(Formed afrer 1835.)

REVOLUTIONARY PENSIONERS LIVING IN THE COUNTY IN 1840.
(Collins, Vol. I, p. 6.)

Barnes, Nicodemus, age 80.   Wade, Richard, age 88.
Davis, John, age 83.   Woody, James, age 79.
Miller, John, age 78.   Worsham, Charles, age 88.
            Pierce, Frances, age 81.
        Total for the County, 7.

CUMBERLAND COUNTY.

PENSIONERS UNDER THE ACT OF MARCH 18, 1818.

Conner, Lawrence, private, ... Virginia line
    July 7, 1820; Sep. 14, 1818; $96. Age 73. Died March 17, 1826.
Monroe, James, private, ... Virginia line
    October 22, 1819; June 9, 1818; $96. Age 79.

Maccoun, James, private, ... Virginia line
    January 24, 1824; September 8, 1828; $96. Age 90.
Rowe, William, private, ... Virginia line
    December 20, 1820; June 9, 1818; $96. Age 78. Died Feb. 26, 1825.

PENSIONERS UNDER THE ACT OF JUNE 7, 1832.
(Began March 4, 1831.)

Baker, John, sergeant, ... Virginia line
    April 1, 1833; $120. Age 83.
Baker, William, private, ... Virginia militia
    March 3, 1833; $21.66. Age 70.
Brummal, Benjamin, private, ... Virginia militia
    March 3, 1833; $40. Age 75.
Barrett, Francis, sergeant and private, ... Virginia line
    March 26, 1833; $99.16. Age 72.
Burchett, William, private, ... Virginia State troops
    September 24, 1833; $30. Age 79.
Burchett, John, private, ... Virginia State troops
    November 15, 1833; $20. Age 73.
Carter, Charles, private, ... Virginia line
    December 18, 1832; $80. Age 76.
Chetham, William, private, ... Virginia militia
    March 8, 1833; $38.34. Age 72.
Carry, William, private, ... Virginia militia
    March 8, 1833; $44.99. Age 78.
Chapman, John, private, ... Virginia militia
    May 18, 1833; $29.43. Age 72.
Claywell, Shadrach, private of cavalry and inf., . Virginia militia
    July 3, 1833; $70. Age 74.
Creasey, John, private, ... Virginia militia
    June 6, 1834; $20. Age 80.
Crockett, Robert, private, ... Virginia militia
    September 2, 1833; $45.43. Age —.
Elam, Godfrey, private, ... Virginia militia
    March 8, 1833; $40. Age 71.
Ferguson, William, private, ... Virginia line
    November 15, 1833; $60. Age 71.
Gryder, Martin, private, ... North Carolina line
    June 30, 1833; $66.66. Age 83.
Gryder, Valentine, private, ... North Carolina line
    August 17, 1833; $60. Age 72.
Gibson, John, private, ... North Carolina line
    July 10, 1834; $63.33. Age 84.
Goodman, William, ensign, ... Virginia militia
    November 7, 1833; $240. Age 75.

Jewell, Joseph, lieutenant, ... New York militia
 April 12, 1834; $320. Age 82.
King, George, private, ... Virginia militia
 May 13, 1833; $20. Age 85.
Morgan, Morgan, private, ... Virginia line
 May 13, 1833; $76.66. Age 73.
Miller, John, private, ... Maryland militia
 May 29, 1833; $20. Age 72.
Pierce, Francis, private, ... Virginia line
 March 18, 1833; $80. Age 74.
Prewitt, Solomon, private, ... Virginia line
 August 9, 1833; $80. Age 84.
Richardson, George, private, ... Virginia line
 May 6, 1833; $80. Age 77.
Radford, James, private, ... Virginia line
 October 31, 1833; $50. Age 72.
Smith, Samuel, private, ... North Carolina militia
 April 10, 1833; $30. Age 79.
Sewell, Joseph, private, ... South Carolina State troops
 June 17, 1833; $60. Age 80.
Scott, John, private, ... Virginia line
 August 9, 1833; $80. Age 73.
Self, John, private, ... Virginia militia
 August 9, 1833; $30. Age 72.
Thurman, Charles, private, ... Virginia line
 March 10, 1832; $80. Age 76.
Williams, 2d, James, private, ... Virginia militia
 August 29, 1833; $80. Age 72.
Wade, sr., Richard, private, ... North Carolina militia
 September 26, 1833; $80. Age 82.
Williams, Thomas, private, ... Virginia militia
 December 27, 1833; $80. Age 79.
Whittaker, William, private, ... Virginia militia
 July 10, 1834; $70. Age 74.

PENSIONER UNDER THE ACT OF MAY 15, 1828.
(Began March 3, 1826.)

Emerson, John, lieutenant, 13th regiment, ... Virginia line
 February 12, 1829; $320.

REVOLUTIONARY PENSIONERS LIVING IN THE COUNTY IN 1840.
(Collins, Vol. I, p. 6.)

Bledsoe, Elijah, age 68. Cash, sr., Thomas, age 65.
Brothers, Thomas, age 62. Gibson, John, age 95.
    Hurtt, John, age 71.
Total for the County, 46.

DAVEISS COUNTY.

Pensioners Under the Act of June 7, 1832.

(Began March 4, 1831.)

Briant, Zachariah, private, ... Virginia line
    June 24, 1833; $80. Age 68.
Calhoon, George, lieut., ensign, and q. m., . . Pennsylvania line
    June 11, 1833; $246.66. Age 80.
Field, Benjamin, private, ensign, and captain, . . . Virginia line
    August 17, 1833; $289.32. Age 77.
Hall, James, private, ... Virginia militia
    December 21, 1833; $30.44. Age 88.
Johnson, sr., Samuel, private, ... Virginia militia
    February 28, 1833; $36.66. Age 90.
Jones, James, private of inf. and cavalry,   North Carolina militia
    June 11, 1833; $49.16. Age 74.
Kelley, James, private, ... Virginia line
    March 1, 1833; $40. Age 76.
Thompson, Anthony, private and sergeant, ... Virginia line
    October 21, 1833; $33.33. Age 75.
Tannehill, James, private, ... Maryland line
    March 7, 1833; $26.66. Age 73.
Taylor, Benjamin, private, ... Pennsylvania line
    January 11, 1834; $54.66. Age 78.

Revolutionary Pensioner Living in the County in 1840.

(Collins, Vol. I, p. 6.)

Hansford, Charles, age 80.

Total for the County, 11.

ESTILL COUNTY.

Pensioners Under the Act of March 18, 1818.

Best, James, private, ... Virginia line
    February 12, 1819; February 23, 1818; $96. Age 73.
Hartman, Tandy, private, ... Virginia line
    May 12, 1819; September 2, 1818; $96. Age 84.
Harris, Thomas, private, ... Virginia line
    May 19, 1819; October 5, 1818; $96. Age 63. Died August 10, 1823.
Meadows, Israel, private, ... Virginia line
    May 12, 1819; September 2, 1818; $96. Age 78.
McChristy, James, private, ... Virginia line
    January 2, 1828; October 29, 1827; $96. Age 74.
Phillips, Zachariah, private, ... North Carolina line
    May 29, 1830; May 29, 1830; $96. Age 71.

Styvers, William, private, ... Virginia line
    February 12, 1819; October 6, 1818; $96. Age 78.
Ward, Lawrence, private, ... Virginia line
    July 10, 1819; April 20, 1819; $96. Age 84. Died Feb. 11, 1830.

PENSIONERS UNDER THE ACT OF JUNE 7, 1832.
(Began March 4, 1831.)

Brown, Thomas, private, ... Virginia militia
    April 20, 1833; $40. Age 92.
Horn Matthias, private, ... Virginia line
    December 11, 1832; $80. Age 72.
Harris, William, private, ... Virginia militia
    January 16, 1833; $23.33. Age 70.
Johnson, William, private, ... Virginia militia
    February 28, 1833; $40. Age 77.
Noland, James, private and captain, ... Virginia militia
    January 16, 1833; $280. Age 94.
Noland, Jesse, private, ... North Carolina militia
    January 16, 1833; $20. Age 73.
Oldham, Richard, private, ... North Carolina militia
    April 20, 1833; $30. Age 89.
Proctor, Joseph, private, ... Virginia line
    December 11, 1832; $80. Age 78.
Powell, Ambrose, private, ... Virginia militia
    March 25, 1833; $21.66. Age 73.
Robertson, Jesse, private, ... Virginia line
    January 16, 1833; $35. Age 76.
Stufflebean, John, private, ... Pennsylvania line
    March 29, 1833; $80. Age 82.
Snowden, David, private, ... Pennsylvania line
    March 29, 1833; $80. Age 75.
Sheffield, George, serg. and private, North Carolina State troops
    April 1, 1833; $68.33. Age 75.
Winkler, Henry, private, ... North Carolina State troops
    April 1, 1833; $46.66. Age 76.
Waters, John, private, ... Virginia militia
    April 20, 1833; $33.33. Age 82.
Witt, Elisha, private, ... Virginia militia
    January 16, 1833; $46.66. Age 83.

REVOLUTIONARY PENSIONERS LIVING IN THE COUNTY IN 1840.
(Collins, Vol. I, p. 6.)

Lackey, Andrew, age 78.
Eastis, Mary, age 81, widow of revolutionary soldier.
Ward, Elizabeth, age 107, widow of revolutionary soldier.
Total for the County, 27.

FAYETTE COUNTY.

PENSIONERS UNDER THE ACT OF MARCH 18, 1818.

Allen, David, private, ... New Hampshire line
   April 18, 1818; April 1, 1818; $96. Age 79.

Adams, 2d, William, fifer, ... New York line
   March 29, 1819; July 10, 1818; $96. Age 66.

Barker, William, private, ... Maryland line
   December 23, 1818; August 25, 1818; $96. Age 61.

Ball, James, private, ... Virginia line
   September 19, 1818; May 1, 1818; $96. Age 83.

Coons, Frederick, private, ... Virginia line
   April 26, 1819; May 29, 1818; $96. Age —.

Craig, Robert, lieutenant, ... Pennsylvania line
   September 19, 1818; April 29, 1818; $240. Age 78.

Carter, Obadiah, private, ... Virginia line
   July 7, 1819; June 16, 1818; $96. Age 65.

Cullin, Charles, private, ... Virginia line
   October 10, 1818; May 27, 1818; $96. Age 87.

Christian, William, private, ... Virginia line
   July 7, 1819; August 15, 1818; $96. Age 62.

Davenport, Adrain, private, ... Maryland line
   May 21, 1819; July 6, 1818; $96. Age 76.

Fletcher, James, private, ... Virginia line
   June 5, 1820; September 21, 1819; $96. Age 69. Died June 18, 1833.

Farrell, Isaac, private, ... Virginia line
   February 9, 1828; February 3, 1828; $96. Age 70.

Hicks, William, private, ... Virginia line
   March 5, 1819; June 15, 1818; $96. Age 82. Died Nov. 20, 1822.

Howell, Jonathan, private, ... New Jersey line
   Nov. 17, 1818; May 11, 1818; $96. Age 70. Died May 18, 1827.

Hickey, Daniel, private, ... Pennsylvania line
   October 22, 1819; August 25, 1818; $96. Age 84.

Jeter, Fielding, private, ... Virginia line
   June 9, 1820; June 20, 1818; $96. Age 72.

Jeter, Littleton, private, ... Virginia line
   December 11, 1828; December 10, 1828; $96. Age 80.

McGraw, Christopher, drummer, ... Maryland line
   October 18, 1819; May 13, 1818; $96. Age 74.

Mitchell, Hiram, private, ... U. S. navy
   December 7, 1818; June 24, 1818; $96. Age 63.

McVay, Daniel, private, ... Virginia line
   December 23, 1818; August 28, 1818; $96. Age 86.

Miles, William, private, ... Virginia line
    February 13, 1819; June 26, 1818; $96. Age 71.

Murray, James, private, ... New Jersey line
    October 26, 1822; September 20, 1819; $96. Age 73.

Nelson, John, ensign, ... Virginia line
    November 4, 1818; April 30, 1818; $240. Age 71.

Nailor, Isaac, private, ... Virginia line
    July 12, 1819; May 28, 1818; $96. Age 70. Dead.

Norwood, Charles, private, ... Virginia line
    January 7, 1831; January 7, 1831; $96. Age 78. Dead.

Prewitt, Byrd, private, ... Virginia line
    January 11, 1832; December 30, 1831; $96. Age 80.

Reilly, Christopher, private, ... Pennsylvania line
    September 19, 1818; May 1, 1818; $96. Age 74. Died Jan. 13, 1829.

Rankin, Hugh, private, ... Pennsylvania line
    February 11, 1819; June 22, 1818; $96. Age 66.

Shindlebowe, George, private, ...
    May 6, 1819; September 22, 1818; $96. Age 63.

Sharp, 2d, William, private, ... Virginia line
    April 15, 1819; August 15, 1818; $96. Age 73. Died Sept. 20, 1833.

Stephens, John, private, ... Virginia line
    April 15, 1819; August 24, 1818; $96. Age 62.

Stivers, Reuben, musician, ... Virginia line
    February 13, 1819; June 17, 1818; $96. Age 76.

Shannon, Andrew, private, ... Pennsylvania line
    October 21, 1818; May 18, 1818; $96. Age 71. Died Nov. 25, 1827.

Vaughan, James, private, ... Virginia line
    May 24, 1819; July 1, 1818; $96. Age 89. Died January 29, 1826.

White, Nathan, private, ... Virginia line
    July 7, 1819; June 15, 1818; $96. Age 82.

Wingate, John, private, ... Virginia line
    March 16, 1826; February 14, 1826; $96. Age 73.

York, John, private, ... Virginia line
    September 22, 1818; August 3, 1818; $96. Age 82.

Yount, John, private, ... Pennsylvania line
    November 10, 1821; February 22, 1819. Age —. Dead.

PENSIONERS UNDER THE ACT OF JUNE 7, 1832.
(Began March 4, 1831.)

Andrews, Thomas, private, ... Virginia militia
    January 15, 1833; $80. Age 76.

Armstrong, Ambrose, private, ... Virginia line
    March 15, 1833; $80. Age 74.

Adams, Peter B. F., private, ... North Carolina line
    December 18, 1833; $58.33. Age 76.

Blair, Samuel, private and sergeant, . . . Pennsylvania militia
  May 4, 1833; $23.33. Age 76.
Boyer, John G., private, ... Maryland line
  May 18, 1833; $30. Age 71.
Boone, Samuel, private, ... South Carolina line
  September 4, 1833; $40. Age 76.
Barton, John, private, ... New Jersey State troops
  October 18, 1833; $33.33. Age 79.
Christian, John, private, ... Virginia militia
  January 15, 1833; $76.66. Age 82.
Camper, Tilman, private, ... Virginia militia
  February 26, 1833; $79.23. Age 75.
Christian, Andrew, private, ... Virginia line
  August 13, 1833; $50. Age 73.
Davenport, James, private, ... Virginia militia
  January 15, 1833; $80. Age 92.
Darnaby, John, private, ... Virginia militia
  February 26, 1833; $40. Age 74.
Emerson, Reuben, private and sergeant, ... Virginia militia
  August 10, 1833; $23.10. Age 88.
Epperson, Francis, private, ... Virginia militia
  May 29, 1834; $20. Age 83.
Fowler, John, lieutenant, ... Virginia line
  October 30, 1832; $320. Age 78.
Ferguson, Abraham, private, ... Virginia line
  February 26, 1833; $80. Age 83.
Faulconer, Joseph, private, ... Virginia line
  August 22, 1833; $62.33. Age 76.
Graves, John, private, ... Virginia militia
  January 15, 1833; $20. Age 77.
Hunt, William, private, ... Virginia militia
  January 16, 1833; $40. Age 80.
Haley, Randall, private, ... Virginia line
  May 6, 1833; $30. Age 79.
Hamilton, James, private, ... Pennsylvania militia
  July 1, 1834; $58. Age 71.
Hunter, John, private, ... North Carolina line
  December 18, 1833; $63.33. Age 75.
Laffoon, James, private, ... Virginia line
  May 6, 1833; $56.66. Age 71.
McDowell, James, private and ensign, ... Virginia line
  January 19, 1833; $61.66. Age 75.
Masterson, James, private and ensign, . . North Carolina militia
  February 28, 1833; $88.33. Age 81.

McCalla, Andrew, sergeant, ... Pennsylvania line
    March 1, 1833; $50. Age 74. Died November 27, 1832.
McIsaacks, Isaac, private, ... Pennsylvania line
    September 5, 1833; $60. Age 83.
Mitchell, Richard, private, ... Virginia militia
    September 9, 1833; $20. Age 70.
Morrell, Benjamin, private, ... North Carolina militia
    October 18, 1833; $61.66. Age 74.
Mosby, Joseph, private, ... North Carolina militia
    March 3, 1834; $35. Age 76.
McCargo, Radford, private, ... North Carolina militia
    March 6, 1834; $46.66 Age 72.
Parker, John, private and wagon-master, . Pennsylvania militia
    January 15, 1833; $290. Age 80.
Proctor, George, private, ... Virginia line
    March 6, 1834; $30. Age 74.
Peck, John, mariner, ... Ship Queen of France
    April 12, 1834; $20. Age 65.
Palmateer, William, private, ... New York militia
    October 15, 1833; $26.66. Age 73.
Russell, Robert S., private and corporal, ... Virginia militia
    January 15, 1833; $53.33. Age 73.
Robinson, Benjamin, private, ... Virginia militia
    February 28, 1833; $60. Age 82.
Robertson, Benjamin, private, ... North Carolina line
    March 6, 1833; $60. Age 78.
Smith, James, private, ... Virginia line
    May 17, 1833; $80. Age 86.
Stewart, William, private, ... Virginia line
    August 17, 1833; $80. Age 72.
Sullivan, Cornelius, private, ... Virginia line
    September 5, 1833; $46.66. Age 78.
Stout, Elijah, private, ... New Jersey militia
    May 29, 1833; $80. Age 74.
True, James, private, ... Virginia line
    August 9, 1833; $30. Age 86.
Vallandigham, George, private, ... Virginia militia
    July 15, 1833; $20. Age 73.
Webb, Isaac, lieutenant, ... Virginia line
    May 31, 1833; $320. Age —.
Wickliffe, Charles, private of infantry and cavalry, Virginia militia
    May 31, 1833; $22.50. Age 68.
Young, John, private, ... North Carolina line
    February 28, 1833; $40. Age —.

PENSIONERS UNDER THE ACT OF MAY 15, 1828.
(Began March 3, 1826.)

Bowman, Abraham, colonel, ... Virginia line
    October 30, 1829; $600. George H. Bowman, agent.

McDowell, John, lieutenant, ... Wood's Virginia regiment
    May 26, 1831; $320. J. T. Johnson, agent.

Nelson, John, captain, fifth regiment, ... Virginia line
    September 17, 1828; $480. J. P. Robinson, agent.

Pindell, Richard, surgeon, first regiment, ... Maryland line
    August 2, 1828; $480. A. Ogden and J. R. Nourse, attorneys.

Schooler, William, sergeant, third regiment, . . . Virginia line
    February 7, 1829; $120. D. McC. Payne, agent.

REVOLUTIONARY PENSIONERS LIVING IN THE COUNTY IN 1840.
(Collins, Vol. I, p. 6.)

Clark, Thomas, age 85.   Scruggs, Elizabeth (widow),
Cowgill, Daniel, age 83.   age 74.

Total for County, 93.

FLEMING COUNTY.

PENSIONERS UNDER THE EARLY INVALID PENSION ACTS.

Moore, James, corporal, ... Revolutionary army
    March 4, 1795; $30; April 24, 1816, raised to $48.

Stocker, William, private, ... Revolutionary army
    January 1, 1803; $36; April 24, 1816, raised to $57.60.

PENSIONERS UNDER THE ACT OF MARCH 18, 1818.

Bayer, Edward, sergeant, ... New York line
    May 13, 1819; July 20, 1818; $96. Age 65. Died January 15, 1826.

Boyd, William, private, ... Washington's life guards
    October 13, 1821; Sept. 8, 1818; $96. Age 74. Died Dec. 30, 1828.

Combes, William, sergeant, ... Virginia line
    June 20, 1819; June 17, 1818; $96. Age 77.

Collins, John, private, ... Virginia line
    April 16, 1819; August 22, 1818; $96. Age 70. Died Jan. 21, 1828.

Davis, William, private, ... Virginia line
    May 17, 1819; September 8, 1818; $96. Age 60.

Estell, William, private, ... Pennsylvania line
    May 22, 1820; June 1, 1880; $96. Age 72.

Finley, John, brigade major, ... Pennsylvania line
    January 13, 1820; October 7, 1819; $96. Age 80. Transferred from
    Pennsylvania.

Hennis, Benjamin, private, ... Maryland line
 September 18, 1819; July 26, 1818; $96. Age 74.
Helphinstine, Philip, private, ... Virginia line
 July 24, 1821; October 2, 1819; $96. Age 77. Died Oct. 14, 1831.
Kendall, Peter, private, ... Virginia line
 May 17, 1819; September 12, 1818; $96. Age 58.
McAtinney, Thomas, private, ... Pennsylvania line
 June 5, 1820; December 6, 1819; $96. Age 72. Died Feb. 9, 1823
McKee, Guion, private, ... Pennsylvania line
 September 18, 1819; June 15, 1818; $96. Age 77. Died Dec. 9, 1827.
McCullough, William, private, ... Maryland line
 June 5, 1820; September 11, 1818; $96. Age 78.
Muse, George, private, ... Virginia line
 October 6, 1820; June 4, 1818; $96. Age 73. Died July 27, 1827.
McCoy, Alexander, ... Pennsylvania line
 January 6, 1826; December 9, 1825; $96. Age 82.
Stoker, William, private, ... Virginia line
 September 18, 1819; June 29, 1818; $96. Age 79.
Strahan, Samuel, private, ... Pennsylvania line
 June 20, 1822; September 7, 1818; $96. Age 73. Died June 2, 1825.
Wilson, Andrew, private, ... Pennsylvania line
 May 23, 1820; October 23, 1818; $96. Age 74.

PENSIONERS UNDER THE ACT OF JUNE 7, 1832.
(Began March 4, 1831.)

Crawford, James, private, ... Virginia militia
 October 18, 1833; $20. Age 75.
Davis, Joseph, private, ... Virginia line
 October 24, 1832; $20. Age 74.
Davis, Jesse, private, ... Virginia line
 March 18, 1833; $80. Age 72.
Davidson, Joshua, private of cavalry, ... Virginia line
 May 3, 1833; $100. Age 73.
Drennon, Hugh, private, ... Pennsylvania line
 May 16, 1834; $53.33. Age 74.
Fous, John, private, ... Virginia militia
 February 21, 1833; $20. Age 67.
Fraseur, John, private, ... Virginia militia
 April 12, 1833; $20. Age 69.
Ferguson, Thomas, private, ... Pennsylvania militia
 April 16, 1833; $37.77. Age 73.
Gorman, Archibald, private, ... Pennsylvania line
 September 24, 1833; $76.66. Age 80.
Goddard, Joseph, private, ... Virginia line
 March 25, 1833; $80. Age 73.

Hammond, John, private of artillery, ... Virginia line
    October 24, 1832; $100. Age 79.

Howe, David, private of infantry and cavalry, . . S. C. militia
    January 10, 1833; $83.33. Age 87.

Humphrees, Samuel, private, ... Virginia line
    March 18, 1833; $80. Age 85.

Hopkins, David, private, ... Pennsylvania line
    April 20, 1833; $80. Age 74.

Layton, William H., private, ... Pennsylvania line
    March 1, 1833; $80. Age 79.

London, George, private, ... Pennsylvania line
    March 16, 1833; $80. Age 76. Died November 14, 1832.

Miller, John, private, ... Pennsylvania volunteers
    September 10, 1832; $80. Age 69.

Miller, William, private, ... Pennsylvania line
    October 24, 1832; $80. Age 77.

McKee, John, private, ... Pennsylvania line
    January 10, 1833; $80. Age 70.

Manzy, Peter, private, ... Virginia militia
    March 20, 1833; $20. Age 83.

Madden, Joseph, lieutenant and private, ... Virginia militia
    January 20, 1834; $126.66. Age 77.

Proctor, William, private, ... Pennsylvania line
    January 25, 1833; $80. Age 75.

Ringo, Burtis, private of cavalry, ... Virginia line
    October 24, 1832; $100. Age 72.

Rigdon, James, private, ... Maryland militia
    December 28, 1832; $20. Age 72.

Robertson, William, private, ... North Carolina militia
    April 16, 1833; $25.66. Age 80.

Rhodan, Thomas, private, ... New Jersey militia
    May 6, 1833; $20. Age 83.

Ross, John, private, ... Virginia line
    December 24, 1833; $38.44. Age 79.

Summers, John, private, ... Virginia militia
    October 30, 1832; $20. Age 70.

Smith, Redmond, private, ... Virginia militia
    October 30, 1832; $63.33. Age 74.

Weaver, Philip, private, ... Virginia line
    May 20, 1833; $20. Age 70.

Williams, Lawrence, private and sergeant, . . . Maryland line
    March 27, 1833; $90. Age 76.

Williams, Gerard, private, ... Maryland line
    March 27, 1833; $91.66. Age 75. Died June 21, 1833.

PENSIONERS UNDER THE ACT OF MAY 15, 1828.
(Began March 3, 1826.)

Clack, Moses, dragoon, ... Virginia dragoons
November 20, 1833; $100.

Davis, William, dragoon, ... Virginia dragoons
October 22, 1828; $100.

Finley, John, captain, eighth regiment, . . . Pennsylvania line
August 22, 1828; $480.

REVOLUTIONARY PENSIONERS LIVING IN THE COUNTY IN 1840.
(Collins, Vol. I, p. 6.)

Blackburn, Samuel, age 80.   McCann, Patrick, age 80.
Clark, Moses, age 76.   Page, John, age 78.
Cord, Zacheus, age 64.   Terhune, Daniel, age 81.

Total for County, 61.

FLOYD COUNTY.

PENSIONERS UNDER THE ACT OF MARCH 18, 1818.

Bouney, Joseph, private, ... Virginia line
July 3, 1820; April 24, 1819; $96.   Age 74.   Died May 3, 1826.

Caines, Richard, private, ... Virginia line
June 22, 1819; November 20, 1818; $96.   Age 66.

Childres, Pleasant, private, ... North Carolina line
February 10, 1825; December 7, 1824; $96.   Age 71.

Ferguson, William, private, ... Pennsylvania line
May 23, 1820; May 20, 1818; $96.   Age 79.

Hopkins, Garner, private, ... New York line
September 22, 1819; July 12, 1819; $96.   Age 82.   Died June 4, 1832.

Haney, William, private, ... Virginia line
July 21, 1826; May 25, 1826; $96.   Age 76.

Jones, Gabriel, private, ... North Carolina line
September 28, 1819; October 18, 1818; $96.   Age 108.   (Born 1710.)

Jacobs, Roby, private, ... Virginia line
Sept. 6, 1820; Oct. 19, 1818; $96.   Age 72.   Died Feb. 19, 1825.

Jones, Ambrose, private, ... Virginia line
Dec. 12, 1825; Nov. 2, 1825; $96.   Age 73.   Died June 12, 1833.

Murray, Thomas, private, ... Pennsylvania line
May 23, 1820; May 20, 1818; $96.   Age 80.   Died April 26, 1824.

Mullins, John, private, ... Virginia line
September 10, 1823; May 26, 1823; $96.   Age 76.

Preston, Nathan, private, ... Virginia line
May 31, 1819; May 20, 1818; $96.   Age 71.   Died August 6, 1832.

Preston, Moses, private, ... Virginia line
May 29, 1820; June 16, 1818; $96.   Age 72.

Stone, Cudbeth, private, ... Maryland line
    June 10, 1819; October 21, 1818; $96. Age 62.

Smith, 3d, John, private, ... Virginia line
    June 10, 1824; March 23, 1823; $96. Age 88.

Sullivan, Peter, private, ... Virginia line
    June 20, 1825; June 1, 1825; $96. Age 82.

Young, Alexander, private, ... South Carolina line
    November 27, 1819; July 21, 1818; $96. Age 75.

PENSIONERS UNDER THE ACT OF JUNE 7, 1832.
(Began March 4, 1831.)

Brown, Thomas C., cornet, ... Virginia militia
    July 19, 1833; $320. Age 74.

Camron, James, private, ... Virginia line
    May 17, 1833; $80. Age 76.

Connelly, Henry, captain of cavalry, . . . North Carolina militia
    February 24, 1834; $150. Age 82.

Darten, Edward, private, ... Virginia line
    January 20, 1834; $80. Age 83.

Fairchild, Abina, private, ... North Carolina line
    March 27, 1834; $40. Age 72.

Harris, James, private, ... Virginia militia
    July 19, 1833; $70. Age 82.

Hitchcock, Joshua, private, ... North Carolina line
    January 20, 1834; $20. Age 92.

Justice, Simeon, drummer, ... North Carolina line
    February 20, 1833; $88. Age 69.

Moore, John, private, ... North Carolina line
    March 27, 1834; $33.33. Age 75.

Pytts, Jonathan, private, ... North Carolina line
    June 27, 1833; $80. Age 78.

Patrick, James, private, ... Virginia militia
    September 4, 1833; $80. Age —.

Porter, James, private, ... Virginia line
    February 7, 1834; $65.55. Age 75.

Watkins, Benedict, private, ... North Carolina line
    $80. Age 72.

Wells, Richard, private, ... North Carolina line
    March 29, 1834. Age 74.

REVOLUTIONARY PENSIONERS LIVING IN THE COUNTY IN 1840.
(Collins, Vol. I, p. 6.)

Hall, Anthony, age 78.   Thacker, Reuben, age 87.
Pitts, Mexico, age 75.   Williams, Philip, age 87.
    Henrel, Rebecca (widow), age 90.

Total for County, 36.

FRANKLIN COUNTY.

PENSIONERS UNDER THE EARLY INVALID PENSION ACTS.

White, Ambrose, private, ... Revolutionary army
    March 13, 1830.

PENSIONERS UNDER THE ACT OF MARCH 18, 1818.

Bond, William, private, ... Virginia line
    May 6, 1826; March 13, 1826; $96. Age 94. Died March 22, 1827.
Casey, John, private, ... Virginia line
    April 14, 1819; July 21, 1818; $96. Age 71.
Cavender, Joseph, private, ... Virginia line
    May 12, 1819; Aug. 31, 1818: $96. Age 67. Died Aug. 13, 1826.
Cummings, Matthew, private, ... Virginia line
    February 3, 1819; November 13, 1818; $96. Age 84.
Clemons, Bernard, private, ... Virginia line
    August 2, 1819; June 15, 1819; $96. Age 79.
Crutcher, John, private, ... Virginia line
    November 30, 1827; May 24, 1827; $96. Age 70.
Hollis, John, private, ... Pennsylvania line
    Dec. 31, 1823; July 14, 1823; $96. Age 90. Died Dec. 27, 1826.
Long, John, private, ... Virginia line
    Sept. 6, 1819; July 22, 1819; $96. Age 69. Died Feb. 7, 1820.
Pearson, Meshack, private, ... Virginia line
    July 19, 1819; March 1, 1819; $96. Age 80.
Poe, Virgil, private, ... Virginia line
    July 10, 1820; May 9, 1819; $96. Age 76. (Also invalid pensioner
    September 3, 1811.)
Richards, George, private, ... Virginia line
    Feb. 10, 1819; July 10, 1818; $96. Age 84. Died Aug. 15, 1827.
Roberts, Henry, private, ... Virginia line
    January 8, 1831; January 8, 1831; $96. Age 76.
Roberts, John, surgeon, ... Virginia line
    June 21, 1819; August 14, 1818; $96. Age 74.
Satterwhite, John S., private, ... Virginia line
    May 12, 1819; Aug. 22, 1818; $96. Age 79. Died March 7, 1829.
Shelton, Medley, private, ... Virginia line
    November 25, 1819; October 23, 1819; $96. Age 74.
Story, John (R.), private, ... Virginia line
    June 5, 1820; June 22, 1818; $96. Age 72.
Tyler, Charles, private, ... Virginia line
    August 9, 1819; July 20, 1818; $96. Age 76.

PENSIONERS UNDER THE ACT OF JUNE 7, 1832.

(Began March 4, 1831.)

Baley, Abraham, private, ... Virginia line
February 5, 1833; $80. Age —.

Biscoe, James, seaman, ... Virginia navy
December 12, 1832; $96. Age 74.

Bell, Thomas, private, ... Virginia line
May 21, 1833; $80. Age 74.

Crockett, Anthony, lieutenant, ... Virginia line
January 24, 1833; $320. Age 78.

Douthitt, Silas, private, ... Virginia militia
February 12, 1833; $20. Age 71.

Fenwich, William, private, ... Maryland militia
February 11, 1833; $73.33. Age 75. Died June 18, 1833.

Forsee, William, private and sergeant, ... Virginia line
December 27, 1833; $50. Age 76.

Fitzgerald, Daniel, private, ... Virginia line
January 20, 1834; $46.66. Age 77.

Gordon, Lawrence, private, ... North Carolina militia
July 21, 1834; $20. Age 72.

Hawkins, Elisha, private, ... Virginia line
October 29, 1832; $80. Age 79. Died November 24, 1833.

Hedges, Robert, private and sergeant of cavalry, . Virginia line
December 26, 1832; $98.33. Age 74.

Jackson, John C., private, ... Virginia militia
January 2, 1834; $30. Age 77.

Keeton, John, private, ... Virginia militia
February 23, 1833; $30. Age 72.

Marshall, Humphrey, captain-lieutenant, . Virginia State troops
July 25, 1832; $400. Age 72.

Magill, John, private, ... Virginia line
October 20, 1832; $23.33. Age 75.

McDonald, John, private, ... Vermont militia
May 28, 1833; $20. Age 69.

Oliver, John, private, ... Virginia line
December 12, 1832; $80. Age 78.

Reading, John, private, ... Pennsylvania line
November 29, 1832; $80. Age 74.

Stephens, sr., John, private, ... Virginia militia
October 19, 1832; $60. Age 71.

Sebree, Richard, private, ... Virginia line
December 6, 1832; $23.33. Age 82.

Scroggin, Thomas C., private, ... Maryland militia
February 11, 1833; $45.56. Age 70.

Triplett, Hedgman, lieutenant, ... Virginia line
    December 12, 1832; $320. Age —.
Taylor, James, private, ... Virginia line
    February 12, 1833; $60. Age —.
Yancy, Philemon, private, ... Virginia line
    September 17, 1833; $80. Age 78.

PENSIONERS UNDER THE ACT OF MAY 15, 1828.
(Began March 3, 1826.)

McQueen, Joshua, sergeant, ninth regiment, . . . Virginia line
    May 8, 1833; $120.
Reading, Ramnel, major, second regiment, . . New Jersey line
    July 29, 1828; $600.

REVOLUTIONARY PENSIONERS LIVING IN THE COUNTY IN 1840.
(Collins, Vol. I, p. 6.)

Swingle, George, age 83.
Brown, Frances, age 85, widow of revolutionary soldier.
Etherton, Mrs., age 90, widow of revolutionary soldier.
Total for County, 48.

GALLATIN COUNTY.
PENSIONERS UNDER THE ACT OF MARCH 18, 1818.

Carter, Henry, private, ... Virginia line
    December 26, 1818; November 5, 1818; $96. Age 83.
Coghill, James, private, ... Virginia line
    May 25, 1820; November 16, 1819; $96. Age 76.
Driskell, David, private, ... North Carolina line
    July 3, 1820; November 16, 1819; $96. Age 71.
Eaton, Henry, sergeant, ... Pennsylvania line
    Sept. 20, 1827; Sept. 4, 1827; $96. Age 95. Died June 27, 1829.
Garvey, Job, private, ... Virginia line
    September 17, 1819; October 26, 1818; $96. Age 60.
Hardin, Thomas, private, ... Virginia line
    April 10, 1821; August 26, 1819; $96. Age 74.
Lester, Thomas, private, ... Virginia line
    January 2, 1827; November 27, 1826; $96. Age 77.
McGannon, Darby, corporal and private, . . . Pennsylvania line
    December 13, 1819; August 27, 1818; $96. Age 69.
McDowell, Alexander, sergeant, ... Pennsylvania line
    February 12, 1819; August 24, 1818; $96. Age 79.
McIntire, William, private, ... Virginia line
    December 24, 1818; August 24, 1818; $96. Age 79.

Severn, David, private, ... Washington's life guards
    May 28, 1819; April 23, 1818; $96. Age 74. Died April 11, 1823.
Short, John, private, ... Virginia line
    January 7, 1828; December 8, 1827; $96. Age 74.
Tubbs, Cyrus, private, ... Connecticut line
    December 11, 1821; October 12, 1821; $96. Age 74.

PENSIONERS UNDER THE ACT OF JUNE 7, 1832.
(Began March 4, 1831.)

Barnes, Benjamin, private, ... Virginia militia
    May 6, 1833; $20. Age 69.
Barnes, Shadrach, private, ... Virginia line
    December 14, 1833; $80. Age 70.
Davis, Samuel C., private, ... Maryland militia
    May 28, 1833; $20. Age 74.
Dement, Jarret, private, ... Pennsylvania line
    December 10, 1833; $60. Age 74.
Dean, John, private, ... Pennsylvania line
    December 10, 1833; $40. Age 72.
Gowens, Charles, private, ... Virginia line
    December 16, 1833; $30. Age 71.
Hawes, Thomas, private, ... North Carolina line
    February 25, 1834; $30. Age 91.
Matthews, Amos V., private, ... Virginia line
    September 23, 1833; $80. Age 75.
McDowell, William, private, ... Virginia line
    October 30, 1833; $20. Age 73.
Noel, Thomas, private, ... Virginia militia
    December 2, 1833; $20. Age 72.
North, Abijah, private, ... Connecticut line
    January 6, 1834; $80. Age 75.
Scott, Reuben, private, ... Virginia line
    December 10, 1833; $30. Age 70.
Thompson, sr., William, private, ... New Jersey militia
    September 16, 1833; $80. Age 74.
Wells, John, private, ... North Carolina militia
    December 2, 1833; $20. Age 70.

PENSIONERS UNDER THE ACT OF MAY 15, 1828.

Thompson, William, dragoon, ... Armand's corps
    May 23, 1829; $100.

REVOLUTIONARY PENSIONERS LIVING IN THE COUNTY IN 1840.
(Collins, Vol. I, p. 6.)

Birks, John, age 67.   Haydon, sr., Jeremiah, age 78.
Furnish, James, age 74.   Slaughter, Mary (widow), age 89.
    Total for the County, 32.

GARRARD COUNTY.

PENSIONERS UNDER THE ACT OF MARCH 18, 1818.

Bryant, John, sergeant, ... Virginia line
August 11, 1819; August 26, 1818; $96. Age 83.

Bryant, John, private, ... Virginia line
January 13, 1824; December 15, 1823; $96. Age 72.

Brady, John, private, ... Virginia line
March 15, 1819; Nov. 21, 1818; $96. Age —. Died Sept. 18, 1828.

Clark, John, private, ... Virginia line
July 7, 1823; March 1, 1823; $96. Age 78.

Diddleston, Thomas, private, ... Virginia line
April 21, 1820; Sept. 25, 1818; $96. Age 84. Died May 9, 1828.

Goolsbury, Mark, private, ... Virginia line
December 7, 1820; August 2, 1819; $96. Age 83.

Hicks, William, corporal, ... Virginia line
Feb. 6, 1819; June 30, 1818; $96. Age 78. Died Dec. 19, 1822.

Hackney, Samuel, private, ... Virginia line
January 1, 1824; November 17, 1823; $96. Age 74.

Jackson, George, private, ... Virginia line
February 6, 1819; June 18, 1818; $96. Age 72. Died Feb. 19, 1831.

Johnson, 4th, John, private, ... Virginia line
May 6, 1820; December 31, 1819; $96. Age 79. Died Jan. 25, 1827.

McCoy, Daniel, private, ... Virginia line
October 17, 1818; April 28, 1818; $96. Age 71.

Powell, Richard, private, ... Virginia line
April 21, 1820; Sept. 20, 1818; $96. Age 67. Died July 29, 1825.

Ramsey, Thomas, private, ... Virginia line
February 6, 1819; June 30, 1818; $96. Age 77.

Small, George, private, ... New York line
March 5, 1819; Nov. 25, 1818; $96. Age 75. Died Feb. 11, 1831.

Sims, William, private, ... Virginia line
March 5, 1819; Nov. 25, 1818; $96. Age 71. Died July 19, 1830.

Somerville, John, private, ... Pennsylvania line
February 5, 1819; March 18, 1818; $96. Age 77. Died May 4, 1831.

Warmouth, Thaddeus H., private, ... Virginia line
February 5, 1819; September 21, 1818; $96. Age 74.

Webb, John, private, ... Virginia line
March 3, 1828; February 14, 1828; $96. Age 70.

PENSIONERS UNDER THE ACT OF JUNE 7, 1832.
(Began March 4, 1831.)

Brank, Robert, private, ... North Carolina line
September 3, 1832; $63.33. Age 87.

Baker, Joseph, private, ... North Carolina line
February 27, 1833; $60. Age 79.

Brown, Arabia, private, ... Virginia militia
  January 26, 1833; $26.66. Age 78.
Bryant, John, private, ... Virginia militia
  August 22, 1833; $50. Age 74.
Buford, John, private, ... Virginia line
  November 12, 1833; $30. Age 95.
Childers, Goolsberry, private, ... Virginia line
  October 18, 1832; $80. Age 78.
Crutchfield, John, private, ... North Carolina militia
  November 19, 1832; $20. Age 80.
Egerton, Benjamin, private, ... North Carolina line
  September 1, 1832; $30. Age 73.
Edmeston, Thomas, private, ... Pennsylvania militia
  $21.12. Age 73.
Floyd, John, private, ... Virginia militia
  January 22, 1833; $33.33. Age 74.
Floyd, George, private, ... Virginia militia
  January 26, 1833; $36.66. Age 78.
Fry, Joshua, private, ... Virginia militia
  May 6, 1834; $23.55. Age 74.
Haggard, William, private, ... North Carolina line
  May 16, 1833; $40. Age 78.
Jefferies, William, private, ... Virginia militia
  January 4, 1833; $25.10. Age 75.
Jones, John, private, ... Virginia militia
  July 18, 1834; $30. Age 70.
Kennedy, Thomas, private, ... North Carolina line
  September 3, 1832; $420. Age 78.
Kennedy, David, private, ... Virginia line
  October 12, 1833; $80. Age 67.
Logan, Timothy, private, ... Virginia line
  October 12, 1833; $80. Age 75.
Noel, Taylor, private, ... Virginia militia
  September 5, 1833; $20. Age 83.
Powe, William, private, ... Virginia militia
  January 4, 1833; $77.33. Age 76.
Parks, William, private, ... Virginia militia
  January 22, 1833; $45. Age 79.
Robertson, James, private, ... Virginia line
  March 30, 1833; $30. Age 79.
Robards, Jesse, private, ... Virginia militia
  January 22, 1833; $56.66. Age 72.
Reid, Alexander, private, ... Virginia militia
  September 2, 1832; $40. Age 82.

Sutton, Benjamin, private, ... Virginia State troops
    October 18, 1832; $80.   Age 78.

Slavins, John, private, ... North Carolina militia
    January 26, 1833; $20.   Age 77.

Street, Anthony, private, ... Virginia militia
    October 21, 1833; $26.66.   Age 77.

Williams, Elijah, private, ... Virginia militia
    November 9, 1832; $20.   Age 73.

Walden, John, private, ... Virginia militia
    January 26, 1833; $46.66.   Age —.

Wood, Joseph, private, ... New Jersey line
    February 27, 1833; $80.   Age 79.

PENSIONERS UNDER THE ACT OF MAY 15, 1828.
(Began March 3, 1826.)

Bailey, James, private, ... Virginia line
    January 5, 1833; $80.

Pollard, Absalom, private, ... Virginia line
    March 5, 1832; $80.

Salter, Michael, musician, ... Hazen's regiment
    August 19, 1828; $88.

REVOLUTIONARY PENSIONER LIVING IN THE COUNTY IN 1840.
(Collins, Vol. I, p. 6.)

Roberts, Naaman, age 75.

Total for the County, 52.

GRANT COUNTY.
PENSIONERS UNDER THE ACT OF MARCH 18, 1818.

Barker, private, ... New York line
    May 17, 1819; September 9, 1818; $96.   Age 75.

Spencer, Joseph, captain, ... Virginia line
    Feb. 13, 1819; May 28, 1818; $240.   Age 84.   Died Aug. 27, 1829.

PENSIONERS UNDER THE ACT OF JUNE 7, 1832.
(Began March 4, 1831.)

Bates, James. private of infantry and cavalry, . . Virginia line
    December 27, 1833 ; $85.   Age 69.

Childers, Henry, private, ... Virginia militia
    February 22, 1833; $20.   Age 69.

Crook, Jeremiah, private, ... Virginia militia
    February 22, 1833; $20.   Age 70.

Jones, Joshua, private, ... Virginia militia
    September 25, 1833; $60.   Age 74.

Jump, John, private, ... North Carolina State troops
December 18, 1833; $40. Age 86.
New, Jacob, private, ... Virginia militia
February 7, 1834; $20. Age 73.
Seward, Daniel, private, ... Pennsylvania militia
January 31, 1834; $30. Age 73.
Theobald, James, private, ... Virginia militia
January 9, 1833; $80. Age —.
Zinn, John, private, ... Virginia militia
June 11, 1834; $80. Age 71.

REVOLUTIONARY PENSIONERS LIVING IN THE COUNTY IN 1840.
(Collins, Vol. I, p. 7.)

Adams, Aaron, age 71.   Lawless, John, age 89.
Linn, John, age 79.

Total for the County, 14.

GRAVES COUNTY.

PENSIONERS UNDER THE ACT OF MARCH 18, 1818.

Ross, James, private, ... North Carolina line
July 1, 1829; February 7, 1829; $96. Age 78. Died Feb. 27, 1831.

PENSIONERS UNDER THE ACT OF JUNE 7, 1832.
(Began March 4, 1831.)

Adams, Walter, private, ... North Carolina militia
August 17, 1833; $43.33. Age 79.
Brimmage, John, private, ... Maryland militia
May 10, 1834; $20. Age 73.
Cook, William, private, ... North Carolina militia
January 26, 1833; $80. Age 71.
Gilbert, Charles, private, ... Maryland militia
January 11, 1834; $60. Age 78.
Hawthorn, John, private, ... South Carolina State troops
January 20, 1834; $63.33. Age 87.
Johnson, William, private, ... Virginia militia
August 21, 1833; $40. Age 74.
Lovelace, Vachel, private, ... North Carolina militia
August 17, 1833; $30. Age 76.
Odom, Willis, private of infantry and cavalry, S. Carolina militia
February 24, 1834; $28.16. Age 71.
Odill, John, private, ... South Carolina State troops
June 11, 1834; $67.50. Age 75.

Rhodes, Benjamin, private of cavalry, . . North Carolina militia
January 26, 1833; $29.16. Age 69. Died March 1, 1834.
Rowden, George, private of infantry and cavalry, Maryland militia
March 25, 1834; $84.54. Age 91.
Stokes, John, private, ... North Carolina militia
October 21, 1833; $66.66. Age 71.
Stafford, John, private, ... Maryland militia
May 13, 1834 ; $20. Age 67.

REVOLUTIONARY PENSIONERS LIVING IN THE COUNTY IN 1840.
(Collins, Vol. I, p. 7.)

Fox, Daniel, age 75.   Gamblin, Joshua, age 75.
Glover, Joseph, age 80.

Total for the County, 17.

GRAYSON COUNTY.

PENSIONERS UNDER THE ACT OF MARCH 18, 1818.

Beatty, Joseph, sergeant, ... Pennsylvania line
Dec. 13, 1823; Sept. 22, 1823; $96. Age 81. Died Sept. 8, 1827.
Bosworth, Jonathan, private, ... Pennsylvania line
Dec. 13, 1823; Sept. 22, 1823; $96. Age 80. Died Sept. 14, 1830.
Mimms or Minzes, Joseph, private, ... North Carolina line
August 28, 1830; August 28, 1830; $76. Age —.

PENSIONERS UNDER THE ACT OF JUNE 7, 1832.
(Began March 4, 1831.)

Ashcroft, Daniel, private, ... Virginia line
September 9, 1833; $30. Age 65.
Bowles, Matthew, private, ... Virginia militia
April 16, 1833; $36.66. Age 71.
Cleaver, William, private, ... Virginia militia
August 17, 1833; $33.33. Age 73.
Decker, William, private, ... Virginia militia
May 6, 1833; $22.33. Age 89.
Decker, John, private, ... Virginia militia
August 22, 1833; $33.33 Age 82.
Fulkerson, John, private, ... New Jersey line
March 16, 1833; $80. Age 79.
Gore, Isaac, private, ... Virginia militia
October 18, 1833; $40. Age 73.
Prior, Simon, private, ... New Jersey line
August 17, 1833; $80. Age 74.
Phelps, John, sergeant, ... Virginia line
June 6, 1834; $120. Age 75.

Skaggs, Henry, private, ... Virginia militia
  August 17, 1833; $30. Age 75.
Vanmeter, Isaac, private, ... Pennsylvania militia
  February 23, 1833; $35.96. Age 82.
Williams, Isaac, private, ... Virginia militia
  February 19, 1834; $30. Age 80.
Zerry, Josiah, private, ... Virginia line
  August 9, 1833; $70. Age 79.

REVOLUTIONARY PENSIONERS LIVING IN THE COUNTY IN 1840.
(Collins, Vol. I, p. 7.)

DeHaven, Edward, age 84.   Rowe, John, age 98.
Total for the County, 18.

GREEN COUNTY.

PENSIONERS UNDER THE ACT OF MARCH 18, 1818.

Berry, Thomas, private, ... Pennsylvania line
  October 1, 1819; April 28, 1818; $96. Age 82.
Emerson, John, lieutenant, ... Virginia line
  July 21, 1819; April 26, 1818; $240. Age 82.
Miles, 2d, John, private, ... Maryland line
  Sept. 22, 1819; May 2, 1818; $96. Age 94. Died March 17, 1827.
Minor, Larkin, private, ... Virginia line
  May 14, 1819; May 28, 1818; $96. Age 54.
Puryear, Jesse, private, ... Virginia line
  July 10, 1819; April 28, 1818; $96. Age 80.
Phipps, Joshua, private, ... Virginia line
  June 25, 1819; May 25, 1818; $96. Age 89.
Reily, 2d, John, private, ... Virginia line
  July 21, 1819; May 2, 1818; $96. Age 65.
Short, Joshua, private, ... Virginia line
  May 14, 1819; May 28, 1818; $96. Age 82.
Taylor, John S., private, ... Virginia line
  July 21, 1819; April 28, 1818; $96. Age 76.
Timberlake, Joseph, private, ... Virginia line
  December 12, 1822; November 18, 1822; $96. Age 82.
Wright, Thomas, private, ... Virginia militia
  October 2, 1819; May 28, 1818; $96. Age 80.

PENSIONERS UNDER THE ACT OF JUNE 7, 1832.
(Began March 4, 1831.)

Barbee, Elias, private, ... Virginia line
  March 29, 1833; $60. Age 71.
Bright, Wyndle, private, ... Virginia line
  April 9, 1833; $80. Age 78

Barnet, William, private, ... South Carolina militia
    May 30, 1833; $80.   Age 76.
Barnet, Andrew, private, ... South Carolina militia
    May 31, 1833; $80.   Age 73.
Cowherd, James, sergeant, ... Virginia line
    March 27, 1833; $120.   Age 76.
Chadoin, Andrew, private, ... Virginia State troops
    April 9, 1833; $60.   Age 73.
Campbell, Lawrence, private, ... Virginia militia
    April 12, 1833; $20.   Age 71.
Carlisle, James P., private, ... Virginia militia
    November 15, 1833; $60.   Age 73.
Cowherd, Jonathan, private and lieutenant, ... Virginia line
    December 7, 1833; $120.   Age 78.
De Spain, Peter, private, ... Virginia militia
    December 1, 1832; $60.   Age 71.
Dicken, John, private, ... Virginia militia
    August 22, 1833; $80.   Age 75.
Griffin, Sherrod, private, ... Virginia line
    May 29, 1833; $75.   Age 76.
Gaines, Thomas, bombardier, ... Virginia line
    August 17, 1833; $108.   Age 75.
Green, William, private and captain, ... Virginia line
    April 25, 1834; $76.66.   Age 80.
Hatcher, Henry, private, ... Virginia line
    November 7, 1832; $80.   Age 78.
Harding, Thomas, private, ... Pennsylvania line
    April 9, 1833; $80.   Age 76.
Lee, William, private and sergeant, ... Virginia militia
    November 7, 1832; $39.16.   Age 80.
Lee, Joshua, private, ... Georgia militia
    August 9, 1833; $24.88.   Age 76.
Meers, Moses, private, ... North Carolina militia
    August 21, 1833; $32.44.   Age 71.
McCockle, Samuel, private, ... Virginia militia
    August 9, 1833; $26.66.   Age —.
Morris, Jesse, private, ... South Carolina militia
    June 17, 1834; $21.13.   Age 77.
Parsons, Thomas, private, ... Virginia militia
    November 7, 1832; $65.54.   Age 86.
Pierceall, Richard, private, ... Virginia militia
    April 25, 1833; $20.   Age 90.
Price, William H., private, ... North Carolina militia
    September 26, 1833; $30.   Age 79.

Rice, Randolph, private, ... Virginia line
November 7, 1832; $80. Age 72. Died August 7, 1832.
Spoffner, Henry, private, ... North Carolina militia
November 7, 1832; $50. Age 79.
Smith, Thomas, private, ... Virginia line
November 7, 1832; $80. Age 72.
Smith, John, private, ... Virginia line
November 7, 1832; $80. Age 75.
Steerman, William W., ... Virginia line
November 8, 1832; $79. Age 79.
Sherrill, James, private, ... Virginia State troops
April 9, 1833; $63.33. Age 60.
Shown, John, private, ... Virginia militia
August 9, 1833; $25.48. Age 74.
Skaggs, William, private, ... Virginia militia
August 21, 1833; $36.66. Age 77.
Sympson, William, private, ... Virginia line
April 9, 1834; $20. Age 67.
Thurman, John, private, ... Georgia militia
October 21, 1833; $40. Age 67.
Tapscott, William, private, ... Virginia militia
June 11, 1834; $23.33. Age 70.
Woodard, George, private, ... Virginia militia
April 12, 1833; $36.66. Age 73.
Watson, David, private, ... : . . Virginia line
August 21, 1833; $80. Age 75.
Warren, Hugh, private, ... North Carolina militia
July 18, 1834; $40. Age 70.

REVOLUTIONARY PENSIONERS LIVING IN THE COUNTY IN 1840.
(Collins, Vol. i, p. 7.)

Bibb, James, age 87.   Ingram, Jeremiah, age 81.
Greenwell, John, age 80.   Purcell, Richard, age 99.
Tribble, Daniel, age 80.
Total for the County, 54.

GREENUP COUNTY.
PENSIONERS UNDER THE ACT OF MARCH 18, 1818.

Burns, Jeremiah, private, ... Virginia line
Dec. 9, 1818; July 28, 1818; $96. Age 72. Died Oct. 13, 1824.
Johnson, 2d, John, private, ... Connecticut line
July 21, 1819; July 29, 1818; $96. Age 89. Died Aug. 30, 1824.
Mayhew, Elisha, private, ... Congress regiment
July 21, 1819; Oct. 13, 1818; $96. Age —. Died Nov. 2, 1819.

Smith, Godfrey, private, ... Virginia line
　　May 11, 1820; October 24, 1819; $96. Age 59.
Zornes, Andrew, private, ... Pennsylvania line
　　January 15, 1823; April 24, 1820; $96. Age 77.

PENSIONERS UNDER THE ACT OF JUNE 7, 1832.
(Began March 4, 1831.)

Howe, John W., private, ... Virginia line
　　October 18, 1833; $33.33. Age 82.
Lawson, James, private, ... Virginia militia
　　August 21, 1833; $30. Age 74.
Patten, James, private, ... Pennsylvania line
　　November 12, 1833; $21.66. Age 83.
Riggs, Charles, private, ... Maryland line
　　June 8, 1833; $80. Age 78.
Sartin, Clayburn, private, ... Virginia line
　　August 9, 1833; $80. Age 79.

REVOLUTIONARY PENSIONERS LIVING IN THE COUNTY IN 1840.
(Collins, Vol. I, p. 7.)

Chadwick, John, age 75.　　　Norton, James, age 73.
　　　Hackworth, Thomas, age 77.
　　　Total for the County, 13.

HANCOCK COUNTY.
PENSIONERS UNDER THE ACT OF MARCH 18, 1818.

Leonard, Patrick, private, ... Pennsylvania line
　　June 23, 1819; June 27, 1818; $96. Age 82. Transferred from
　　Ohio March 4, 1820. Died August 11, 1822.

PENSIONER UNDER THE ACT OF JUNE 7, 1832.

Newman, Edward, sergeant, ... Virginia line
　　November 3, 1832; $90. Age 72.
　　　Total for the County, 2.

HARDIN COUNTY.
PENSIONERS UNDER THE ACT OF MARCH 18, 1818.

Belknap, James, private, ... Massachusetts line
　　June 25, 1819; May 27, 1818; $96. Age 76. Died February 16, 1824.
Carson John, private, ... South Carolina line
　　March 14, 1819; September 7, 1818; $96. Age 87.
Flanders, Jacob, private, ... New Hampshire line
　　April 28, 1820; June 30, 1818; $96. Age 74.

Howe, John, sergeant, ... Maryland line
    May 18, 1819; September 19, 1818; $96. Age 80.

Haycraft, sr., Samuel, private, ... Virginia line
    April 30, 1822; June 20, 1820; $96. Age 80.

McCandless, John, private, ... Pennsylvania line
    June 3, 1820; June 27, 1818; $96. Age 72. Died February 2, 1827.

Melton, Charles, private, ... Virginia line
    January 29, 1819; November 20, 1818; $96. Age 78.

Newton, John, private, ... Maryland line
    June 30, 1819; January 19, 1819; $96. Age 74. Died Feb. 9, 1830.

State, James, private, ... Virginia line
    May 14, 1819; September 9, 1818; $96. Age 77.

Turner, Solomon, private, ... Maryland line
    June 4, 1819; September 7, 1818; $96. Age 60.

Vertrees, Isaac, private, ... Pennsylvania line
    September 24, 1819; September 7, 1818; $96. Age 72.

Wilkins, Thomas, private, ... Virginia line
    May 14, 1819; September 7, 1818; $96. Age 77.

PENSIONERS UNDER THE ACT OF JUNE 7, 1832.
(Began March 4, 1831.)

Awby (Aubrey), Samuel, private, ... Virginia line
    April 12, 1833; $80. Age 75.

Anmet (Ament), Anthony, private, . . . Pennsylvania militia
    September 9, 1833; $20. Age 76.

Cash, Warren, private, ... Virginia line
    November 12, 1832; $80. Age 74.

Cundiff, John, private, ... Virginia militia
    September 2, 1833; $20. Age 78.

Davis, Forrest, private, ... Maryland militia
    September 2, 1833; $20. Age 72.

Green, John, private, ... New Hampshire militia
    March 26, 1833; $35.32. Age 70.

Goodin, Isaac, private, ... Pennsylvania line
    October 11, 1833; $43.33. Age 79.

Hargin, Michael, private, ... Maryland line
    March 24, 1833; $46.66. Age 80.

Murvin (Marvin), Patrick, private and sergeant, . . Virginia line
    September 5, 1833; $63.33. Age 75.

McWilliams, James, private, ... North Carolina militia
    September 24, 1833; $20. Age 72.

McCullum, James, private, ... Virginia militia
    November 9, 1832; $60. Age 73.

McDougal, Alexander, private, ... South Carolina line
    November 9, 1833; $66.66. Age 92.

Patton, Samuel, sergeant, ... Maryland line
    October 4, 1832; $75. Age 79.
Parker, Benjamin, private, ... Virginia militia
    March 26, 1833; $20. Age 75.
Rains, Henry, private, ... Virginia line
    April 12, 1833; $80. Age —.
Rider, Joseph, private, ... Massachusetts line
    February 2, 1833; $80. Age 75.
Scott, John, private, ... Virginia State troops
    April 2, 1833; $60. Age 91.
Smoot, John, private, ... Virginia militia
    September 2, 1833; $80. Age 79.
Smith, Joseph, private, ... Pennsylvania militia
    December 23, 1833; $20. Age 72.
Vanmeter, Jacob, ensign and captain, ... Virginia militia
    March 2, 1833; $105. Age 73.
Winchester, Richard, private, ... Rhode Island militia
    April 16, 1833; $36.66. Age 79.

REVOLUTIONARY PENSIONER LIVING IN THE COUNTY IN 1840.
(Collins, Vol. I, p. 7.)

Hoskins, Thenas, age 82.

Total for the County, 34.

HARLAN COUNTY.

PENSIONERS UNDER THE ACT OF JUNE 7, 1832.
(Began March 4, 1831.)

Ballard, Richard, priv. of infan. and cav., North Carolina militia
    February 14, 1834; $34.30. Age 71.
Brook, Jesse, private, ... North Carolina militia
    December 17, 1833; $30. Age 83.
Cawood, Berry, private, ... North Carolina militia
    May 23, 1824; $46.66. Age 76.
Green, Lewis, private, ... Virginia line
    December 10, 1833; $40. Age 83.
Hall, James, private, ... South Carolina line
    November 25, 1833; $46.66. Age 83.
Jones, Stephen, private, ... North Carolina militia
    May 23, 1834; $23.33. Age 83.
Shackleford, Henry, private, ... Virginia militia
    November 25, 1833; $20. Age 70.

REVOLUTIONARY PENSIONERS LIVING IN THE COUNTY IN 1840.
(Collins, Vol. I, p. 7.)

Cozad, Benjamin, age 80.   Jackson, sr., James, age 84.

Jones, Stephen L., age 99.

Total for the County, 10.

HARRISON COUNTY.

PENSIONERS UNDER THE ACT OF MARCH 18, 1818.

Abbott, Elijah, private, ... Virginia line
    October 17, 1825; October 3, 1825 ; $96. Age 73.

Barnes, John, private, ... Virginia line
    May 28, 1819; July 11, 1818; $96. Age 78.

Beggs, Moore, private, ... Pennsylvania line
    December 23, 1818; September 14, 1818; $96. Age 92.

Casey, Archibald, ... Delaware line
    Nov. 27, 1820; July 6, 1818; $96. Age 75. Died April 22, 1825.

Henry, Jacob, private, ... Pennsylvania line
    May 28, 1819; Oct. 15, 1818; $96. Age 71. Died August 10, 1823.

Jenkins, William, private, ... Virginia line
    July 21, 1819; March 18, 1818; $96. Age 64. Died July 17, 1830.

Rose, Jesse, private, ... Virginia line
    May 28, 1819; July 13, 1818; $96. Age 70.

Ravenscraft, Thomas, private, ... Virginia line
    December 24, 1818; August 12, 1818; $96. Age 68.

Robertson, Zachariah, private, ... Maryland line
    May 21, 1819; June 15, 1818; $96. Age 74.

Scott, John, private, ... Pennsylvania line
    Feb. 11, 1819; Oct. 14, 1818; $96. Age·76. Died March 3, 1827.

Sellers, Samuel, private . . . . Pennsylvania line
    Sept. 15, 1823; July 17, 1823; $96. Age 82. Died Feb. 2, 1830.

Tinney, John, private, ... Virginia line
    April 21, 1819; September 14, 1818; $96. Age 87.

Taylor, John, private, ... Maryland line
    May 21, 1819; September 15, 1818; $96. Age 68.

Whaley, William, sergeant, ... Virginia line
    May 17, 1819; Sept. 11, 1818; $96. Age 70. Died August 14, 1824.

PENSIONERS UNDER THE ACT OF JUNE 7, 1832.
(Began March 4, 1831.)

Chandler, Claiborne, private, ... Virginia militia
    February 11, 1833; $20. Age 73.

Chadd, Samuel, private, ... Maryland militia
    February 11, 1833; $20. Age 80.

Cleveland, John, private, ... Virginia line
    May 9, 1834; $80. Age 77. Died August 5, 1832.

Furnish, Thomas, ... Virginia militia
    January 15, 1833; $20. Age 74.

Furnish, James, private, ... Virginia militia
    February 1. 1833; $20. Age 70.

Foxworthy, John, private, ... Virginia militia
  May 18, 1833; $30. Age 81.
Gonsaul, James, private, ... New York line
  February 5, 1833; $60. Age 79.
Green, Gerard, private, ... Virginia militia
  June 23, 1833; $26.66. Age 72.
Johnson, sr., William, ... Virginia militia
  January 10, 1833; $36.66. Age 76.
Jenkins, John, private, ... Virginia militia
  February 11, 1833; $63.33. Age 74.
Kilander, Philip, private, ... New Jersey line
  August 25, 1833; $40. Age 71.
Laney, William, private, ... Virginia militia
  December 19, 1832; $30. Age 74.
Lanter, Jacob, private, ... Virginia militia
  February 5, 1833; $20. Age 73.
Moore, James, private, ... Virginia line
  January 17, 1833; $80. Age 84.
Morrow, Thomas, private, ... Pennsylvania line
  February 26, 1833; $30. Age 73.
Mann, Francis, private, ... Virginia militia
  February 28, 1833; $20. Age 76.
Miller, Jacob, private of infantry and cavalry, . . . Virginia line
  April 1, 1833; $22.50. Age 74.
Maffett, Jacob, private, ... Pennsylvania militia
  April 16, 1833; $50. Age 90.
Millner, Nicholas, private, ... Pennsylvania militia
  May 18, 1833; $30. &ge 71.
Millner, sr., Luke, private, ... Virginia line
  August 6, 1833; $70. Age 83.
McCauley, Thomas, private, ... Virginia militia
  April 16, 1833; $40. Age 76.
Oder, Joseph, private, ... Virginia militia
  February 11, 1833; $26.66. Age 83.
Pollard, Edmund, private, ... Virginia militia
  February 5, 1833; $50. Age 75.
Ralston, John, private, ... Virginia militia
  October 2, 1832; $40. Age 79.
Robinson, Francis, private, ... Virginia militia
  February 11, 1833; $26.66. Age 69.
Reno, Zela, private and sergeant, ... Virginia militia
  July 11, 1833; $83.33. Age 77.
Roberts, Philip, private, ... South Carolina line
  December 10, 1833; $80. Age 71.

Sutton, William, private, ... Virginia line
  December 19, 1832; $46.66. Age 69.
Smith, Michael, private, ... Massachusetts line
  January 25, 1833; $80. Age 82.
Trimble, John, private, ... Pennsylvania militia
  January 19, 1833; $46.66. Age —.
Venard, William, private, ... Virginia militia
  January 15, 1833; $23.33. Age —.
Watkins, John, private, ... Virginia militia
  May 13, 1833; $37.10. Age 78.
Woods, sr., William, private, ... Pennsylvania militia
  August 6, 1833; $43.33. Age 88.

REVOLUTIONARY SOLDIERS LIVING IN THE COUNTY IN 1840.
(Collins, Vol. I, p. 7.)

Bean, James, age 77.   Layton, William H., age 83.
Caswell, Samuel, age 77. McCalla, Thomas, age 87.
Eddleman, Leonard, age 79. Mears, Mrs., age 76, widow.
Jameson, Benoni, age 67. Whittaker, Ann, age 79, widow.
Wolf, sr., Lewis, age 89.

Total for the County, 56.

HART COUNTY.

PENSIONERS UNDER THE ACT OF MARCH 18, 1818.

Defever, John, private, ... Virginia line
  July 22, 1826; July 3, 1826; $96. Age 81.
Humphrey, John, private, ... Virginia line
  December 11, 1820; September 21, 1818; $96. Age 79.

PENSIONERS UNDER THE ACT OF JUNE 7, 1832.
(Began March 4, 1831.)

Boman, or Bomar, sr., Joseph, private, ... Virginia militia
  October 18, 1833; $25.16. Age 76.
Crump, Joshua, private, ... Virginia militia
  August 22, 1833; $23.33. Age 69.
Corder, Benjamin D., private, ... Virginia militia
  June 15, 1834; $20. Age 69.
Edgar, John, private, ... Pennsylvania line
  August 17, 1833; $80. Age 77.
Logsden, James V., private, ... North Carolina line
  August 21, 1833; $36.66. Age 68.
Morris, Daniel, private, ... North Carolina militia
  October 18, 1833; $26.66. Age 70.

Roundtree, Nathaniel, private and sergeant, . . Virginia militia
    May 30, 1833; $40.22. Age 74.
Rowe, John, private, ... Pennsylvania militia
    August 17, 1833; $40. Age 84.
Wright, John, private, ... North Carolina line
    December 2, 1833; $40. Age 73.
Whitman, Richard, private, ... Virginia militia
    June 6, 1834; $23.33. Age 78.

REVOLUTIONARY PENSIONERS LIVING IN THE COUNTY IN 1840.
(Collins, Vol. I, p. 7.)

Campbell, Lawrence, age 75.   Patterson, John, age 77.
Harber, Jeremiah, age 77.   Timberlake, Joseph, age 88.
Total for the County, 16.

HENDERSON COUNTY.

PENSIONERS UNDER THE ACT OF MARCH 18, 1818.

Gibson, Joel, private, ... North Carolina line
    May 19, 1825; April 25, 1825; $96. Age 87. Died Dec. 23, 1830.
Hughes, John, sergeant, ... North Carolina line
    April 23, 1819; June 23, 1818; $96.51. Age 87.

PENSIONERS UNDER THE ACT OF JUNE 7, 1832.
(Began March 4, 1831.)

Baker, Thomas, private, ... Virginia militia
    February 12, 1834; $80. Age —.
Carmon, Furna, private, ... North Carolina line
    November 10, 1832; $26.66. Age 74.
Moss, John, private, ... North Carolina militia
    November 10, 1832; $25. Age 72.
Ramsey, John, private, ... South Carolina militia
    May 30, 1833; $35. Age 75.
Rouse, Lewis, private, ... Virginia militia
    July 9, 1834; $30. Age 76.
Sellers, Isham, ... North Carolina State troops
    April 20, 1833; $68.22. Age 80.

PENSIONER UNDER THE ACT OF MAY 15, 1828.
(Began March 3, 1826.)

Dixon, Wynne, lieutenant, first regiment, . . North Carolina line
    August 22, 1828; $320. Died November 24, 1829. Archibald
    Dixon, administrator.

REVOLUTIONARY PENSIONER LIVING IN THE COUNTY IN 1840.

Baldwin, Edward, age 78.
Total for the County, 10.

HENRY COUNTY.

Pensioners Under the Act of March 18, 1818.

Adams, John, private, ... Pennsylvania line
August 12, 1818; January 6, 1819; $96. Age 65.

Bryan, Barich, private, ... Virginia line
May 29, 1824; September 5, 1823; $96. Age 83.

Downey, Thomas, private, ... Pennsylvania line
Nov. 12, 1818; May 16, 1818; $96. Age 70. Died Sept. 5, 1823.

Guthery, William, private, ... Pennsylvania line
Sept. 29, 1819; August 12, 1818; $96. Age 87. Died March 10, 1823.

Grimes, Leonard, private, ... Pennsylvania line
June 8, 1824; January 30, 1826; $96. Age 75.

Johnston, 3d, John, private, ... New Jersey line
September 17, 1819; January 21, 1819; $96. Age 88.

Johnston, Joseph, private, ... Virginia line
Nov. 27, 1819; May 13, 1819; $96. Age —. Died March 17, 1820.

Mead, John, private, ... Virginia line
December 24, 1818; November 6, 1818; $96. Age 80.

McCarty, Thomas, sergeant, ... Virginia line
December 1, 1818; July 17, 1818; $96. Age 97.

Miles, John, private, ... Virginia line
December 26, 1818; November 5, 1818; $96. Age 61.

Read, John, private, ... Virginia line
March 14, 1820; November 12, 1818; $96. Age 65.

Smith, sr., David, private, ... Virginia line
December 24, 1818; August 10, 1818; $96. Age 74.

Swift, Thomas, private, ... Virginia line
December 23, 1818; August 15, 1818; $96. Age 74.

Spillman, George, private, ... Virginia line
December 23, 1818; August 10, 1818; $96. Age 76.

Sidebottom, Joseph, private, ... Virginia line
December 23, 1818; August 17, 1818; $96. Age 79.

Waldren, John, private, ... Lee's legion
September 29, 1819; May 20, 1818; $96. Age 60.

Williams, John, private, ... Maryland line
July 11, 1825; June 18, 1825; $96. Age 86.

Williams, John, private, ... North Carolina line
May 30, 1832; August 17, 1818; $96. Age 79.

Pensioners Under the Act of June 7, 1832.
(Began March 4, 1831.)

Adams, William, private, ... Pennsylvania line
November 6, 1832; $40. Age 86.

Adams, David, private, ... Virginia militia
February 25, 1834; $20. Age 71.

Blackburn, John, lieutenant, ... Pennsylvania line
March 22, 1833; $320. Age 82.

Bush, Charles, private, ... Virginia militia
February 7, 1834; $23.33. Age 80.

Beetom, Adam, private, ... Pennsylvania line
October 30, 1833; $80. Age 75.

Bryant, Thomas, private, ... Virginia line
November 4, 1833; $66.66. Age 73.

Bice, Dennis, lieutenant, ... Pennsylvania line
December 14, 1833; $320. Age 89.

Bishop, Elisha, private, ... Pennsylvania line
January 4, 1834; $80. Age 74.

Brewer, William, private, ... Pennsylvania line
July 30, 1834; $26.66. Age 90.

Conine, Andrew, private, ... Virginia militia
May 11, 1833; $40. Age 73.

Cooper, Jonathan, private, ... Pennsylvania militia
September 23, 1833; $80. Age 76.

Criswell, David, private, ... Pennsylvania militia
January 3, 1834; $26.66. Age 73.

Collett, Isaac, private, ... Virginia militia
January 3, 1834, $20. Age 74.

Coon, William, private of cav. and inf., . Virginia State troops
February 7, 1834; $83.33. Age 74.

Dunaway, Samuel, private and sergeant, ... Virginia militia
October 1, 1833; $45. Age 70.

Downey, John, private, ... Pennsylvania militia
October 18, 1833; $40. Age 78.

Dogan, Jeremiah J., drummer, ... Virginia line
December 14, 1833; $88. Age 70.

Dunn, Alexander, private, ... Pennsylvania line
$80. Age 72. Died April 19, 1833.

Davis, 3d, Joseph, private, ... North Carolina militia
April 11, 1834; $30. Age —.

Davis, Samuel, private, ... Virginia militia
May 27, 1834; $80. Age 68.

Ellis, Leonard, private, ... Virginia line
December 10, 1833; $73.33. Age 80. Died August 22, 1833.

Force, Peter, private, ... North Carolina line
January 31, 1834; $80. Age 90.

Gevedann, John, private, ` ` . . . . Virginia line
October 1, 1833; $50. Age 78.

Hardin, Benjamin, private, ... Virginia line
September 25, 1832; $40. Age 81.

Haskins, James, private and sergeant, ... Virginia militia
June 3, 1833; $25. Age 77.

Hayden, Benjamin, private, ... Virginia militia
June 12, 1834; $33.33. Age 74.

Hugueley, Charles, private, ... Virginia militia
December 2, 1833; $20. Age 73.

Hisle, Samuel, private, ... Virginia militia
December 14, 1833; $20. Age 70.

Housworth, Henry, private, ... New York militia
March 4, 1834; $23.33. Age 70.

Haskins, Achilles, private, ... Virginia line
June 3, 1833; $68.33. Age 72.

Johnson, sr., John, private, ... Virginia line
October 19, 1832; $60. Age 75.

Johnston, James, private, ... Virginia militia
September 23, 1833; $30. Age 70.

Jones, George, private, ... Virginia militia
October 30, 1833; $50. Age 77.

Kidwell, Jonathan, private, ... North Carolina line
October 1, 1833; $50. Age 84.

Kiphart, Henry, private, ... Virginia militia
January 20, 1834; $20. Age 73.

Knight, William, private, ... North Carolina militia
June 15, 1834; $40. Age 75.

Lindsey, John, private, ... Pennsylvania militia
October 30, 1833; $60. Age 75.

Logan, James, private, ... Virginia line
December 2, 1833; $80. Age 75.

Logan, John, private, ... Virginia line
December 2, 1833; $80. Age 77.

List, Jacob, private, ... New York line
January 20, 1834; $30. Age 74.

Maynard, Richard, private, ... Virginia militia
March 29, 1833; $43.33. Age 84.

McGuire, Joseph, private, ... Virginia militia
March 29, 1833; $60. Age 82.

Mitchell, George, private, ... Virginia militia
March 29, 1833; $60. Age 71.

Minton, John, private, ... Virginia militia
March 4, 1834; $20. Age 73.

Meek, Basil, private, ... Virginia militia
April 17, 1834; $40. Age 93.

Neill, Lewis, private, ... Virginia militia
November 3, 1832; $20. Age 74.

Perry, Benjamin, ... Virginia line
    October 30, 1833; $63.33. Age 81.

Peake, William, private, ... Virginia militia
    March 14, 1834; $40. Age 69.

Prewitt, Joshua, private, ... Virginia militia
    June 11, 1834; $80. Age 69.

Ringo, Cornelius, private and sergeant, ... Virginia militia
    December 2, 1833; $28.33. Age 81.

Riddle, John, private, ... New Jersey militia
    April 11, 1834; $30. Age 73.

Shuck, Matthew, private, ... Virginia militia
    March 29, 1833; $20. Age 74.

Smith, Nicholas, private, ... Virginia militia
    March 29, 1833; $21.66. Age 75.

Scott, Thomas, private, ... North Carolina militia
    August 9, 1833; $40. Age 81.

Shelton, Wilson, private, ... Virginia militia
    June 6, 1834; $30. Age 87.

Simmons, William, private, ... Virginia militia
    November 25, 1833; $30. Age 82.

Sutherland, Traverse, private, ... Virginia militia
    February 4, 1834; $30. Age 89.

Sutherland, Walter E., private, ... Maryland militia
    February 4, 1834; $20. Age 85.

Vanhorne, Samuel, private, ... Virginia line
    December 10, 1833; $60. Age 81.

Wells, Littlebury, private, ... Virginia militia
    August 9, 1833; $46.66. Age 71.

Wooldridge, Thomas, private, ... Virginia militia
    January 4, 1834; $30. Age 78.

Waller, Joshua, private, ... South Carolina State troops
    January 20, 1834; $66.66. Age 73.

Younger, Kanard, private, ... Virginia militia
    November 25, 1833; $20. Age 74.

PENSIONERS UNDER THE ACT OF MAY 15, 1828.
(Began March 3, 1826.)

Jeffers, William, dragoon, ... Virginia dragoons
    December 22, 1829; $100.

REVOLUTIONARY PENSIONERS LIVING IN THE COUNTY IN 1840.
(Collins, Vol. I, p. 7.)

Bell, Thomas, age 81.   Wallace, Joshua, age 79.

Blakemore, John, age 78.   Dorcas, Anite, widow, age 77.

Johnston, Archibald, age 94. Goode, Rebecca, widow, age 85.

Martin, John, age 80.   Jourdan, Mary, widow, age 75.

Shuck, Matthias, age 84.   Powell, Sarah, widow, age 83.

Total for the County, 92.

HICKMAN COUNTY.

PENSIONER UNDER THE ACT OF MARCH 18, 1818.

Simpson, Jeremiah, private, ... Virginia line
  December 14, 1827; June 18, 1827; $96. Age 78.

PENSIONERS UNDER THE ACT OF JUNE 7, 1832.
(Began March 4, 1834.)

Bynam, Tapley, private of cavalry, . . . South Carolina militia
  May 11, 1833; $25. Age 74.
Bone, 2d, John, private, ... South Carolina line
  May 11, 1833; $80. Age 77.
Cunningham, Morrell, private, ... Virginia militia
  June 23, 1834; $30. Age 74.
Cockrum, William, drummer, ... Virginia militia
  January 11, 1834; $88. Age 71.
Gore, Notley, private, ... Virginia line
  January 13, 1834; $33.33. Age 81.
Huey, Lewis, private, ... North Carolina line
  January 13, 1834; $41.55. Age 72.
Jones, William, private, ... Virginia militia
  May 11, 1833; $40. Age 75.
Jones, Benjamin, private, ... South Carolina line
  January 11, 1834; $66.66. Age 71.
Messhew, Jesse, private, ... South Carolina line
  April 9, 1834; $80. Age 78.
Pickett, Henry, private, ... North Carolina militia
  January 13, 1834; $20. Age 76.
Tharp, Charles, private, ... Virginia State troops
  January 31, 1833; $44.66. Age —.

REVOLUTIONARY PENSIONERS LIVING IN THE COUNTY IN 1840.
(Collins, Vol. I, p. 6.)

Bane, sr., John, age 84.   Vicent, Thomas, age 81.
Depeyster, John, age 86.   Williams, Jacob, age 75.
        Total for the County, 16.

HOPKINS COUNTY.

PENSIONERS UNDER THE ACT OF MARCH 18, 1818.

Brown, Charles, private, ... Virginia line
  January 27, 1820; September 9, 1819; $96. Age 81.
Brown, Robert, private, ... Massachusetts line
  April 5, 1824; Feb. 28, 1824; $96. Age —. Died Aug. 20, 1826.

Davis, John, private, ... Virginia line
    Nov. 1, 1828; Oct. 17, 1828; $96. Age 82. Died Aug. 13, 1829.
Gray, Samuel, private, ... Virginia line
    May 13, 1819; September 14, 1818; $96. Age 72. Died May 29, 1832.
Littlepage, John, private, ... Virginia line
    February 15, 1820; July 8, 1818; $96. Age —. Died March 23, 1820.

PENSIONERS UNDER THE ACT OF JUNE 7, 1832.
(Began March 4, 1831.)

Ashley, Peter, private, ... Virginia militia
    November 16, 1832; $20. Age 84.
Asby, sr., Daniel, private, sergeant, and ensign, . Virginia militia
    November 11, 1852; $110. Age 75.
Bauldwin, Edward, private, ... North Carolina line
    July 15, 1833; $40. Age 67.
Castleberry, William M., private, ... Georgia militia
    February 6, 1833; $31.31. Age 79.
Carter, John, private, ... South Carolina militia
    February 6, 1833; $23.33. Age 86.
Clark, David, private of inf. and cav., . . North Carolina militia
    August 6, 1833; $53.33. Age 75.
Downey, Samuel, private, ... Virginia militia
    November 16, 1832; $22.20. Age 68.
Davis, William, private and sergeant, . . North Carolina militia
    February 6, 1833; $100.67. Age 73.
Dossett, Thomas, private, ... South Carolina line
    May 29, 1834; $20. Age 76.
Herrin, John, private, ... South Carolina line
    November 16, 1832; $54.44. Age 88.
Hill, John, private, ... North Carolina line
    November 16, 1832; $76.66. Age 75.
Hankins, John, private, ... Virginia line
    February 6, 1833; $80. Age 74.
Logan, James, private and wagon master, . . . New Jersey line
    November 16, 1832; $110. Age
Major, Alexander, private, ... Maryland militia
    May 13, 1833; $23.33. Age 79.
Matthews, Peter H., fifer and private, . . . Pennsylvania line
    April 25, 1834; $33.33. Age 77.
Newton, Robert, private, ... North Carolina line
    August 21, 1833; $38.88. Age 70.
Phipps, John, sergeant, ... Georgia line
    May 9, 1833; $120. Age 87.
Timmons, George, private, ... Virginia line
    November 16, 1832; $40. Age 70.

Weeks, David, private, ... North Carolina militia
    May 13, 1833; $28.55. Age 74.
Winstead, Mandley, private, ... North Carolina militia
    November 16, 1832; $30. Age —.
Wright, George, private, ... Virginia militia
    February 6, 1833; $47.97. Age —.
Wilson, Josiah, private, ... North Carolina militia
    November 16, 1832; $46.45. Age —.

REVOLUTIONARY SOLDIERS LIVING IN THE COUNTY IN 1840.
(Collins, Vol. I, p. 6.)

Curtis, James, age 84.   Herron, James, age 102.
Givens, William, age 78.   Montgomery, John, age 72.
Winstead, Manley, age 80.

Total for the County, 32.

JEFFERSON COUNTY.

PENSIONERS UNDER THE ACT OF MARCH 18, 1818.

Brock, Henry, private, ... Virginia line
    Jan. 30, 1822; Nov. 10, 1821; $96. Age 75. Died March 24, 1822.
Bartlett, John, private, ... Virginia line
    January 8, 1824; September 15, 1823; $96. Age 84.
Bateman, Thomas, private, ... Maryland line
    May 18, 1826; May 2, 1826; $96. Age 79.
Cooper, Leven, private, ... Virginia line
    June 8, 1819; May 12, 1818; $96. Age 79.
Gray, George, captain, ... Pennsylvania line
    February 10, 1819; April 30, 1818; $96. Age —.
Griffin, Reuben, private . . . . Virginia line
    May 6, 1820; November 20, 1819; $96. Age 73.
Griffin, William, private, ... Virginia line
    February 1, 1821; October 12, 1820; $96. Age 79. Dead.
Huston, William, private, ... Virginia line
    February 10, 1819; July 13, 1818; $96. Age 78.
Horseley, James, private, ... Virginia line
    November 27, 1821; July 24, 1821; $96. Age 63.
Kelly, 2d, Thomas, private, ... Virginia line
    May 23, 1822; February 15, 1821; $96. Age 73.
Leatherman, Michael, ... Pennsylvania line
    June 29, 1830; June 28, 1830; $96. Age 80. Died July 6, 1831.
Merritt, Archelaus, private, ... Virginia line
    Nov. 27, 1821; July 13, 1821; $96. Age 64. Died March 30, 1824.

McKinney, Thomas, private, ... Virginia line
Sept. 25, 1823; March 15, 1823; $96. Age 62. Died Dec. 10, 1832.
Penn, Benjamin, private, ... Maryland line
April 3, 1820; Aug. 23, 1819; $96. Age 81. Died May 10, 1827.
Pike, Robert, private, ... Virginia line
September 7, 1819; July 30, 1819; $96. Age 88.
Ross, Nathaniel, private, ... New York line
Feb. 10, 1819; July 14, 1818; $96. Age 75. Died Sept. 18, 1825.
Rooksbury, Jacob, private, ... Georgia line
February 11, 1820; June 8, 1818; $96. Age 60.
Stevenson, William, private, ... Pennsylvania line
June 8, 1819; June 9, 1818; $96. Age 78. Died September 16, 1821.
Taylor, William, major, ... Virginia line
November 6, 1818; May 1, 1818; $240. Age 81.
Wilkenson, Benjamin, private, ... Virginia line
May 23, 1822; May 16, 1818; $96. Age 80.
Wilson, Robert, captain, ... Pennsylvania line
June 8, 1819; May 9, 1818; $96. Age —.

PENSIONERS UNDER THE ACT OF JUNE 7, 1832.

(Began March 4, 1831.)

Briscoe, Henry, private, ... Maryland line
February 27, 1833; $20. Age 72.
Conn, Samuel, private, ... Virginia militia
April 17, 1834; $30. Age 74.
Goodwin, Amos, private, ... Virginia line
November 6, 1832; $80. Age 68.
Harding, Vachel, private, ... Maryland line
January 12, 1834; $30. Age 73.
Humfres, John, private, ... Virginia line
February 10, 1819; $96. Age 72. Reduced to $60 under act of
June 7, 1832.
Merewether, William, sergeant of cavalry, ... Virginia line
$177.25. Age 76.
Murphy, John, private of cavalry, ... Virginia line
May 6, 1833; $100. Age 71.
Miller, Frederick, private, ... North Carolina militia
May 29, 1833; $46.66. Age 78.
Maloney, Robert, private, ... Virginia militia
June 20, 1834; $24.16. Age 68.
Pounds, Hezekiah, private, ... New Jersey militia
April 16, 1833; $33.33. Age 72.
Pilkinton, Larkin, private, ... Virginia militia
August 21, 1833; $40. Age 72.

Parker, Thomas, **sergeant,** . . . . Virginia militia
    September 25, 1833; $120. Age 78.

Pennington, James, private, ... Virginia militia
    December 14, 1833; $47.77. Age 82.

Tyler, William, private, ... Virginia line
    April 16, 1833; $80. Age 78.

Urton, James, private, ... Virginia line
    April 17, 1834; $20. Age 82.

Wilson, Robert, captain, adjutant, and major, Pennsylvania line
    November 2, 1833, $480. Age 82.

Welsh, James, private, sergeant, and lieut., Pennsylvania militia
    November 22, 1832; $87.21. Age 82.

Weinnand, Philip, private, ... Maryland militia
    May 30, 1833; $26.66. Age 80.

White, David, private, ... Virginia line
    September 23, 1833; $42.44. Age 81.

Yeager, Elisha, private, ... Virginia militia
    February 2, 1833; $20. Age —.

PENSIONERS UNDER THE ACT OF MAY 15, 1828.
(Began March 3, 1826.)

Breckinridge, Robert, lieutenant, ... Virginia line
    August 2, 1823; $320. Died September 11, 1833. James D. Breckinridge, executor.

Hite, Abraham, captain, eighth regiment, ... Virginia line
    August 2, 1828; $480.

Nelson, John, musician, ... Lamb's artillery
    September 9, 1828; $104.

Taylor, Richard, major, eleventh regiment, ... Virginia line
    July 29, 1828; $600.

Total for the County, 45.

JESSAMINE COUNTY.
PENSIONERS UNDER THE ACT OF MARCH 18, 1818.

Adams, Benjamin, private, ... Virginia line
    September 12, 1820; June 4, 1818; $96. Age 85.

Biswell, John, private, ... Virginia line
    Feb. 13, 1819; May 18, 1818; $96. Age 64. Died Aug. 7, 1824.

Cox, John, private, ... North Carolina line
    June 14, 1822; February 18, 1822; $96. Age 71.

Ficklin, John, private, ... Virginia line
    April 22, 1820; June 17, 1818; $96. Age 64. Died June 6, 1819.

Green, Robert, private, ... Virginia line
April 21, 1818; April 6, 1818; $96. Age 70. Died May 17, 1831.

Grindstaff, Michael, corporal, ... North Carolina line
June 5, 1820; September 24, 1819; $96. Age 80.

Gilloch, John, private, ... Virginia line
February 1, 1830; January 23, 1830; $96. Age 81.

Irwin, James, private, ... Virginia line
January 6, 1819; May 25, 1818; $96. Age 84.

King, Jeremiah, corporal, ... Maryland line
December 13, 1824; December 16, 1823; $96. Age 75.

Lloyd, William, private, ... Virginia line
April 21, 1818; April 1, 1818; $96. Age 85.

Moore, David, private, ... Virginia line
June 2, 1820; August 24, 1818; $96. Age 82.

Richards, James, private, ... Pennsylvania line
March 5, 1819; June 16, 1818; $96. Age 78.

Ross, Daniel, private, ... Massachusetts line
June 20, 1818; June 8, 1818; $96. Age 79.

Sharp, William, private, ... Virginia line
February 11, 1819; Sep. 7, 1818; $96. Age 70. Died Feb. 23, 1822.

Wise, Samuel, private, ... Virginia line
March 5, 1819; June 16, 1818; $96. Age 78. Died July 1, 1821.

PENSIONERS UNDER THE ACT OF JUNE 7, 1832.
(Began March 4, 1831.)

Burk, Samuel, private, ... Virginia militia
August 6, 1833; $60. Age 75.

Campbell, Robert, private, ... Virginia militia
January 15, 1833; $36.66. Age 73.

Carothers, James, private, ... North Carolina militia
March 21, 1833; $80. Age 79.

Cassell, Abraham, private, ... Maryland militia
August 16, 1833; $60. Age 79.

Carroll, John, private, ... Maryland militia
May 24, 1833; $43.33. Age 80.

Crowder, Sterling, private, ... Virginia militia
February 11, 1819; $96. Age 77. Reduced to $80 by act of June
7, 1832. Died January 18, 1834.

Graves, James, private, ... Virginia militia
January 17, 1833; $23.33. Age 74.

Grindstaff, Jacob, private, ... North Carolina militia
May 29, 1833; $20. Age 68.

Hawkins, Giles, private, ... Virginia militia
September 24, 1833; $20.33. Age 78.

Martin, James, private, ... Virginia line
      May 18, 1833; $80. Age 75.

McGee, John, private, ... New Jersey militia
      September 2, 1833; $20. Age 74.

Miller, Francis, private, ... Virginia militia
      April 13, 1834; $20. Age 86.

Netherland, sr., Benjamin, lieutenant, ... Georgia line
      October 25, 1832; $320. Age 79.

O'Neal, George, private, ... Virginia militia
      September 3, 1832; $80. Age 79.

Overstreet, Henry, private, ... Virginia line
      April 25, 1833; $28.33. Age 71.

Rice, Samuel, private, ... Virginia militia
      February 28, 1833; $30. Age 73.

Simpson, Robert, private of inf. and cav., . . North Carolina line
      $81.04. Age 77.

Veatch, Jeremiah, private, ... Maryland line
      December 2, 1833; $33.33. Age 75.

Willoughby, Alexander, private, ... Virginia militia
      January 4, 1834; $40. Age 73.

PENSIONER UNDER THE ACT OF MAY 15, 1828.
(Began March 3, 1826.)

Crockett, Joseph, major, seventh regiment, ... Virginia line
      Feb. 7, 1829; $600. Died Nov. 7, 1829. Hon. Joel Yancey, agent.

REVOLUTIONARY PENSIONERS LIVING IN THE COUNTY IN 1840.
(Collins, Vol. I, p. 7.)

Bryan, Daniel, age 82.	Hicks, Mary, widow, age 80.
Jenkins, Kesiah, age 78.	Hunter, Ann, widow, age 75.
Walker, James, age 81.	Knight, Betsy, widow, age 77.

Total for the County, 42.

KENTON COUNTY.
(Formed after 1835.)

REVOLUTIONARY PENSIONERS LIVING IN THE COUNTY IN 1840.
(Collins, Vol. I, p. 7.)

Casey, Joseph, age 78.	Keen, John, age 81.
Collins, Stephen, age 85.	Massey, Edward, age 95.
Ducker, John, age 81.	Worthington, William, age 90.

McGlassen, Nancy, age 72.

Total for the County, 7.

KNOX COUNTY.

Pensioner Under the Act of March 18, 1818.

Edwards, Brown, private, ... North Carolina line
   September 29, 1819; July 14, 1819; $96. Age 82.
Garland, John, private, ... North Carolina line
   December 24, 1824; October 23, 1824; $96. Age 77.
Horn, Christopher, private, ... Virginia line
   January 13, 1824; December 8, 1823; $96. Age 82.
Henson, William, private, ... North Carolina line
   April 29, 1828; January 10, 1828; $96. Age 89.
Patterson, William, private, ... Virginia line
   January 23, 1829; January 18, 1829; $96. Age 84.

Pensioners Under the Act of June 7, 1832.
(Began March 4, 1831.)

Broughton, Job, private of infantry and cavalry, . Georgia militia
   September 9, 1833; $60. Age 79.
Chick, James, private, ... Virginia militia
   January 19, 1833; $25.96. Age 74.
Hamblin, Pierce Dant, private, ... North Carolina line
   September 26, 1833; $80. Age 79.
Hubbs, John, private, ... South Carolina militia
   April 11, 1834; $20. Age 70.
McHargue, William, private, ... North Carolina militia
   November 7, 1833; $40. Age 89.
Woodson, Wade M., private, ... North Carolina line
   September 27, 1833; $24.44. Age 71.
Hammon, Obadiah, private of inf. and cav., . North Carolina line
   October 12, 1833; $62.50. Age 78.
Horton, John Payton, private, ... Virginia line
   October 12, 1833; $80. Age 76.

Revolutionary Pensioners Living in the County in 1840.
(Collins, Vol. I, p. 7.)

Balleu, Richard, age 72.	Hammonds, Peter, age 78.
Browning, Edward, age 100.	Miller, James, age 93.
Cooper, Jacob, age 109.	Mullins, Joshua, age 82.

Total for the County, 19.

LAUREL COUNTY.

PENSIONERS UNDER THE ACT OF JUNE 7, 1832.
(Began March 4, 1831.)

Clark, Elijah, private, ... Maryland militia
April 25, 1824; $20. Age 81.

Evans, John, private, ... Virginia militia
June 20, 1834; $26.66. Age 79.

French, James, private, ... New York line
June 20, 1834; $80. Age 94.

Forbes, John, private and sergeant, ... North Carolina line
December 2, 1833. Age 75.

Freeman, John, private, ... Virginia militia
February 25, 1834; $20. Age 70.

Stansbury, Solomon, private, ... North Carolina line
February 19, 1833; $36.66. Age 79.

Simpson, John, private, ... North Carolina militia
June 1, 1833; $30. Age 72.

REVOLUTIONARY PENSIONERS LIVING IN THE COUNTY IN 1840.
(Collins, Vol. I, p. 7.)

Fanbush, John, age 81.   Nicks, John, age 84.
Mersham, Titus, age 91.   Pitman, Ambrose, age 92.
Total for the County, 11.

LAWRENCE COUNTY.

PENSIONERS UNDER THE ACT OF MARCH 18, 1818.

Atkinson, David, private, ... Virginia line
May 18, 1826; July 21, 1825; $96. Age 80.

Bates, William, private, ... Virginia line
February 18, 1819; July 7, 1818; $96. Age 69.

Burges, Edward, private, ... Virginia line
October 31, 1822; June 15, 1818; $96. Age —.

Wooton, Silas P., private, ... Virginia line
March 1, 1826; January 16, 1826; $96. Age 75.

PENSIONERS UNDER THE ACT OF JUNE 7, 1832.
(Began March 4, 1831.)

Brown, William, private, ... Virginia line
October 18, 1833; $80. Age 87.

Blumer, Gilbert, private, ... New York militia
February 14, 1834; $80. Age 82.

Cox, William, private, ... Virginia militia
June 26, 1834; $60. Age 73.

Castle, Basil, private, ... Virginia line
    February 28, 1834; $50. Age 73.

Crum, Adam, private, ... North Carolina line
    April 4, 1834. Age 77.

Davis, Joseph, private, ... Virginia line
    January 28, 1834; $40. Age 70.

Hardwick, George, private, ... Virginia line
    June 6, 1834; $80. Age 75.

Lyon, William, private, ... North Carolina line
    April 4, 1834; $40. Age 82.

Lee, Samuel, private, ... Virginia militia
    June 12, 1834; $30. Age 71.

Lastey, John, private, ... Virginia line
    November 9, 1833; $60. Age —.

Marcum, Josiah, private, ... Virginia militia
    February 14, 1834; Age 75.

Marshal, John, private, ... Virginia militia
    April 18, 1834; $80. Age 73.

Norton, James, private, ... Virginia militia
    June 6, 1834; $40. Age 74.

Pratt, James, private, ... Virginia line
    June 20, 1834; $26.66. Age 70.

Parkins, George, private, ... North Carolina militia
    June 17, 1834; $69.10. Age 80.

Sexton, John, private, ... South Carolina militia
    April 4, 1834; $50. Age 75.

Ward, James, private, ... Virginia line
    April 16, 1834; $80. Age 75.

REVOLUTIONARY SOLDIER LIVING IN THE COUNTY IN 1840.
(Collins, Vol. I, p. 7.)

Henny, Moses, age 83.

Total for the County, 22.

LEWIS COUNTY.

PENSIONERS UNDER THE ACT OF MARCH 18, 1818.

Campbell, John, private, ... Virginia line
    May 31, 1819; October 19, 1818; $96. Age 80. Died Aug. 14, 1829.

Criswell, Samuel, private, ... Virginia line
    April 16, 1819; April 16, 1818; $96. Age 73.

Dorch, William, private, ... Maryland line
    June 5, 1819; June 22, 1818; $96. Age 74.

Finch, Joseph, private, ... Maryland line
 June 7, 1819; July 25, 1818; $96. Age 94.
Hulet, James M., private, ...·. Virginia line
 June 11, 1824; September 19, 1823; $96. Age 70.
Whedon, Ichabod, private, ... Massachusetts line
 October 5, 1819; June 4, 1818; $96. Age 70. Died July 14, 1829.

PENSIONERS UNDER THE ACT OF JUNE 7, 1832.
(Began March 4, 1831.)

Bean, Richard, private, ... Virginia line
 May 6, 1833; $63.33. Age 82.
Bean, Richard, private, ... Virginia militia
 July 10, 1834; $63.33. Age 81.
Dyal, John, private, corp'l, and serg'nt, Pennsylvania State troops
 October 18, 1833; $41.66. Age 72.
Fink, David, private, Indian spy, ...
 January 8, 1834; $23.33. Age 78.
Grover, Jonathan M., private of inf. and cav., . . . Virginia line
 April 12, 1833; $86.54. Age 75.
Lucas, William, private, ... New York line
 April 2, 1833; $46.66. Age 70.
Swingle, sr., John, private, ... Maryland militia
 October 11, 1833; $28.33. Age 77.
Williams, Thomas, private, ... Virginia militia
 October 12, 1833; $20.56. Age 77.

REVOLUTIONARY PENSIONER LIVING IN THE COUNTY IN 1840.
(Collins, Vol. I, p. 7.)

Bane, Richard, age 88.
Total for the County, 15.

LINCOLN COUNTY.
PENSIONER UNDER THE EARLY INVALID PENSION ACTS.

Collier, John, private, ... Revolutionary army
 Sept. 4, 1791; $60. Died March 31, 1826.

PENSIONERS UNDER THE ACT OF MARCH 18, 1818.

Curtis, Peter, private, ... North Carolina line
 January 3, 1831; January 3, 1831; $96. Age 73.
Durham, James, private, ... Virginia line
 April 5, 1820; May 13, 1819; $96. Age 72.
Dinwiddie, John, private, ... Virginia line
 April 5, 1820; September 25, 1818; $96. Age 75.

Fleece, John, private, ... Virginia line and Lee's legion
    February 3, 1819; August 12, 1818; $96. Age 62.
Greenwood, Bartley, private, ... Virginia line
    January 19, 1832; January 19, 1832; $96. Age 80.
McPherson, Mark, lieutenant, ... Maryland line
    May 1, 1819; August 11, 1818; $90. Age 80.
McKinney, Dennis, private, ... Virginia line
    April 4, 1820; September 23, 1818; $96. Age 70.
Peak, Jesse, private, ... Virginia line
    December 10, 1822; September 4, 1819; $96. Age 70.
Salyas, Dunn, private, ... North Carolina line
    February 5, 1820; August 11, 1818; $96. Age 76.

PENSIONERS UNDER THE ACT OF JUNE 7, 1832.
(Began March 4, 1831.)

Alverson, John S., private, ... Virginia militia
    May 30, 1833; $40. Age 79.
Barnett, James P., private, ... North Carolina militia
    January 19, 1833; $40. Age 72. Died March 31, 1834.
Briggs, Benjamin, private, ... Virginia militia
    May 30, 1833; $80. Age 69.
Bruce, William, private, ... North Carolina militia
    August 22, 1833; $30. Age 74.
Duncan, Samuel, private, ... Virginia line
    January 19, 1833; $60. Age 74.
Divin, James, ensign, ... Virginia line
    January 30, 1833; $120. Age 86.
Dougherty, William, private, ... Virginia militia
    February 28, 1833; $20.55. Age 87.
Edwards, George, private, ... Virginia line
    January 22, 1833; $80. Age 74.
Elder, Robert, private, ... Virginia militia
    May 11, 1833; $20. Age 74.
Estes, Abraham, private, ... Virginia militia
    January 22, 1833; $26.66. Age 70.
Garven, Isaac, private, ... Virginia line
    January 16, 1833; $60. Age 73.
Givens, 1st, Robert, private, ... North Carolina line
    January 22, 1823; $20. Age 76. Died October 25, 1833.
Givens, 2d, Robert, private, ... Virginia line
    January 22, 1823; $80. Age 77.
Hall, Joseph, private, ... Virginia militia
    January 19, 1833; $46.66. Age 82.
Hazlewood, Luke, private, ... Virginia militia
    January 22, 1833; $40. Age 73.

Hughs, William, private, sergeant, and captain, . Virginia line
June 22, 1833; $405. Age 84.
Ham, Drury, private and sergeant, ... Virginia line
June 16, 1834; $200. Age 74.
Hunt, Richard, private of infantry and cavalry, . Virginia militia
February 18, 1834; $90. Age 76.
Lunsford, Rodham, private, ... Virginia line
January 26, 1833; $80. Age 72.
Morrison, Ezra, private, ... Georgia line
May 6, 1833; $80. Age 78.
Obanner, Benjamin, private, ... Virginia line
October 17, 1833; $80. Age 75.
Pemberton, John, private, ... Virginia militia
January 22, 1833; $46.66. Age 74.
Renich, James, private, ... South Carolina line
May 11, 1833; $80. Age 82.
Sublett, Abraham, private, ... Virginia militia
November 2, 1832; $20. Age 78.
Sampson, William, private, ... Virginia militia
February 16, 1833; $80. Age 69.
Skidmore, Joseph, private, ... North Carolina militia
April 9, 1834; $20. Age 73.
Taylor, John, private, ... Virginia line
November 2, 1832; $80. Age 70.
Woods, Caldwell, private, ... Virginia militia
November 3, 1832; $20. Age 80.

REVOLUTIONARY SOLDIERS LIVING IN THE COUNTY IN 1840.

Frost, Micajah, age 79.   Gale, Anthony, age 78.
Total for the County, 40.

LIVINGSTON COUNTY.

PENSIONER UNDER THE ACT OF MARCH 18, 1818.

Kirk, Robert, lieutenant, White's dragoons, . . . Virginia line
May 25, 1820; January 18, 1818; $240. Age 65. Raised to $400
under act of May 15, 1828. Died Sept. 1, 1828.

PENSIONERS UNDER THE ACT OF JUNE 7, 1832.
(Began March 4, 1831.)

Cox, Caleb, private, ... North Carolina militia
May 30, 1833; $20. Age 80.
Cain, Patrick, private, ... South Carolina militia
May 31, 1833; $63.33. Age 92.

Clark, William, sergeant and private, . . . South Carolina line
$65.33. Age 76. Died April 16, 1834.

Davis, Snead, private of inf. and cav., . . . North Carolina line
$92.50. Age 81.

Ford, Jesse, private, ... Virginia State troops
January 8, 1834; $26.66. Age 77.

Fiers, William, private, ... Virginia line
November 9, 1833; $20. Age 74.

Glass, James, private, ... Pennsylvania line
May 23, 1834; $20. Age 72.

Hicks, Solomon, private, ... South Carolina line
July 17, 1833; $80. Age 76.

Mattock, Nathaniel, private, ... Virginia line
July 15, 1833. $60. Age 91.

Pikins, William G., private, ... South Carolina militia
May 31, 1833; $80. Age 73.

Robertson, David, private, ... North Carolina line
January 17, 1834; $23.33. Age 82.

Stewart, William, private, ... North Carolina State troops
May 11, 1833; $30. Age 71.

Sullinger, James, private, ... North Carolina State troops
April 25, 1834; $50 Age 69.

Travis, Arthur, private, ... South Carolina militia
May 31, 1833; $26.66. Age 71.

Walker, James, private, ... North Carolina militia
May 30, 1833; $26.66. Age 71.

Wells, William, private, ... North Carolina line
June 17, 1833; $80. Age 74.

Wheeler, John, private, ... North Carolina line
September 24, 1833; $80. Age 77.

REVOLUTIONARY SOLDIER LIVING IN THE COUNTY IN 1840.
(Collins, Vol. I, p. 7.)

Clinton, James, age 80.

Total for the County, 19.

LOGAN COUNTY.

PENSIONERS UNDER THE ACT OF MARCH 18, 1818.

Berry, George, captain, ... Virginia line
Nov. 24, 1818; April 24, 1818; $240. Age 72. Died Oct. 29, 1823.

Curd, John, private, ... Virginia line
April 7, 1820; April 20, 1818; $96. Age 77.

Clark, John, sergeant, ... Maryland line
July 1, 1822; September 11, 1820; $96. Age 91.

Dunnington, William, private, ... Maryland line
May 21, 1819; July 24, 1818; $96. Age 84.

Grinter, John, private, ... Virginia line
August 28, 1829; Aug. 15, 1829; $96. Age 77. Died May 27, 1831.

Johnson, James, private, ... Georgia line
February 11, 1819; July 20, 1818; $96. Age —.

Jones, James, private, ... Virginia line
March 5, 1819; July 23, 1818; $96. Age 90.

Karr, James, lieutenant, ... North Carolina line
June 16, 1819; May 9, 1818; $96. Age —.

McCowan, James, private, ... Virginia line
February 17, 1819; July 21, 1818; $96. Age —.

McLardy, Alexander, sergeant, ... Virginia line
May 5, 1819; May 18, 1818; $96. Age —.

Rutherford, Archibald, private, ... Virginia line
July 3, 1821; October 24, 1818; $96. Age 79.

PENSIONERS UNDER THE ACT OF JUNE 7, 1832.
(Began March 4, 1831.)

Addison, William, private, ... South Carolina line
June 3, 1833; $80. Age 68.

Anderson, Leonard, private of cavalry, . . . North Carolina line
September 4, 1833; $100. Age 79.

Blakely, George, private, ... Virginia line
May 21, 1833; $80. Age 83.

Driggs, David, private, ... Virginia militia
June 13, 1833; $23.33. Age 75.

Danks, John, private, ... Virginia militia
May 13, 1833; $20. Age 73.

Ewing, John, private, ... Virginia militia
May 30, 1833; $30. Age 73.

Eads, Charles, private, ... Virginia line
November 9, 1833; $80. Age 80. Died July 27, 1833.

Gillian, John, private, ... Virginia militia
May 20, 1833; $43.33. Age 74.

Herndon, George, private, ... North Carolina line
December 10, 1832; $36.66. Age 72.

Hendricks, Moses, private, ... Virginia militia
March 21, 1833; $50. Age 68.

Ham, John, private, ... North Carolina militia
June 13, 1833; $80. Age 84.

Jones, Philip, private, ... Virginia line
January 28, 1833; $80. Age 72.

Kenner, Rodham, gunner, ... Virginia navy
May 30, 1833; $100. Age 71.

Murrah, Joshua, private, ... North Carolina militia
February 28, 1833; $63.33. Age 70.

McGoodwin, Daniel, private, ... North Carolina line
September 2, 1833; $80. Age 70.

Neal, Benjamin, private, ... Virginia line
January 9, 1834; $40; Age 74.

Page, Leonard, private, ... Virginia line
November 12, 1832; $80. Age 71.

Patillo, William, private, ... Virginia line
November 7, 1833; $60. Age 74.

Peake, John, private of infantry and cavalry, . . Virginia militia
January 28, 1834; $35. Age 78.

Powell, Nathaniel, private, ... North Carolina militia
March 21, 1834; $70. Age 77.

Stephenson, James, private, ... North Carolina militia
November 6, 1832; $36.66. Age 70.

Saunders, David, private, ... Virginia State troops
April 10, 1833; $40. Age 72.

Slaughter, James, private and lieutenant, ... Virginia militia
July 15, 1833; $180. Age 80.

Smith, Ambrose, private, ... Virginia line
August 9, 1833; $80. Age 78.

Taylor, Richardson, private, ... Virginia line
March 3, 1834; $30. Age 73.

Wilson, Samuel, private, ... Virginia militia
March 16, 1833; $22.41. Age 73.

PENSIONER UNDER THE ACT OF MAY 15, 1828.
(Began March 3, 1826.)

Morehead, Charles, private, ... Lee's legion
February 19, 1829; $180.

REVOLUTIONARY PENSIONERS LIVING IN THE COUNTY IN 1840.
(Collins, Vol. I, p. 7.)

Guffey, Alexander, age 77.   Wited, John, age 76.
Howke, Lawrence, age 80.   Williams, Judith (widow), age 75.

Total for the County, 42.

McCRACKEN COUNTY.

PENSIONERS UNDER THE ACT OF JUNE 7, 1832.
(Began March 4, 1831.)

Gamblin, Joshua, private, ... Virginia line
    October 18, 1833; $70. Age 72.
Lovelace, Elias, private, ... North Carolina line
    August 17, 1833; $43.33. Age 79.
Lynn, William T., private, ... North Carolina line
    October 18, 1833; $51.66. Age 72.

PENSIONERS UNDER THE ACT OF MAY 15, 1828.

Elwell, Charles, captain, ... Virginia line
    October 29, 1833; March 3, 1826; $480. Died April 1, 1830.
Lewis, Basil, private, ... Connecticut line
    November 28, 1833; March 3, 1826; $80. Died January 14, 1834.
        Total for the County, 5.

MADISON COUNTY.

PENSIONERS UNDER THE ACT OF MARCH 18, 1818.

Allenbaugh, Peter, private, ... Virginia line
    January 16, 1824; September 12, 1823; $96. Age 94.
Duke, Henry, private, ... Virginia line
    May 11, 1819; September 15, 1818; $96. Age 76.
Dooley, Jacob, private, ... Virginia line
    April 14, 1819; June 19, 1818; $96. Age 78.
Gunison, Samuel, private, ... Virginia line
    March 5, 1819; June 8, 1818; $96. Age 67.
Goine, Joseph, private, ... Virginia line
    May 4, 1819; Sept. 11, 1818; $96. Age 64. Died Aug. 29, 1822.
Galloway, John, lieutenant, ... Virginia line
    January 13, 1821; September 22, 1818; $240. Age 85.
Kinnard, Joseph, private, ... Pennsylvania line
    June 19, 1820; September 15, 1818; $96. Age 70.
Land, John, private, ... Virginia line
    October 25, 1819; March 12, 1819; $96. Age 78.
McQueen, Joshua, private, ... Virginia line
    October 2, 1819; May 19, 1819; $96. Age 64.
Parrish, William, private, ... Virginia line
    May 19, 1819; September 7, 1818; $96. Age 70. ·
Rawson, Enoch, private, ... Virginia line
    January 19, 1829; January 8, 1829; $96. Age 71.

Stevens, Jacob, private, ... Virginia line
 November 6, 1819; June 19, 1818; $96. Age 75.
Shanks, John, private, ... · · Virginia line
 April 23, 1824; Sept. 6, 1823; $96. Age 76. Died April 5, 1829.
Timberlake, John, private, ... Virginia line
 June 3, 1819; June 3, 1818; $96. Age 72.
Tutwiler, John, private, ... Virginia line
 June 3, 1818; June 3, 1818; $96. Age 78.
Tracy, Solomon, private, ... Virginia line
 November 25, 1819; October 27, 1819; $96. Age 75.

PENSIONERS UNDER THE ACT OF JUNE 7, 1832.
(Began March 4, 1831.)

Atkisson, Ellis, private, ... Virginia militia
 April 20, 1833; $20. Age 71.
Backnel, Thomas, private, ... North Carolina militia
 May 6, 1833; $23.33. Age 71.
Butler, Thomas, private, ... Virginia militia
 May 11, 1833; $20. Age 76.
Burk, Michael, private, ... Virginia line
 June 3, 1833; $60. Age 96.
Burnside, Robert, private, ... North Carolina line
 January 4, 1834; $50. Age 75.
Crook, John, private, ... Virginia militia
 November 5, 1832; $20. Age 68.
Corneilson, Conrad, private, ... North Carolina militia
 $24.63. Age 71.
Cooley, James, private, ... South Carolina State troops
 April 1, 1833; $49.20. Age 74.
Cradlebaugh, William, private, ... North Carolina line
 August 17, 1833; $80. Age 90.
Carver, James, private, ... Virginia line
 October 18, 1833; $23.33. Age 81.
Duncan, Gabriel, private, ... Virginia line
 December 26, 1832; $46.66. Age 76.
Dunbar, Thomas, private, ... Virginia line
 April 12, 1833; $20. Age 74.
Dowden, James, private, ... Virginia line
 June 8, 1833; $80. Age 77.
Estill, Samuel, private, ... Virginia line
 October 11, 1833; $80. Age 79.
Fullilove, Anthony, private, ... Virginia line
 June 17, 1833; $30. Age 74.
Faris, Thomas, private, ... Virginia line
 August, 17, 1833; $30. Age 77.

Flick, 2d, James, private, ... North Carolina line
    August 17, 1834; $50. Age 88.

Guthrie, Nathaniel, private, ... Virginia line
    May 27, 1833; $23.33. Age 71.

Gentry, Richard, private, ... Virginia line
    May 27, 1833; $26.66. Age 71.

Harris, Henry, private, ... North Carolina line
    March 1, 1833; $50. Age 92.

Howard, Benjamin, private of cavalry, ... Virginia line
    June 7, 1833; $100. Age 78.

Hodges, Jesse, private, ... Virginia line
    June 22, 1833; $80. Age 74.

Haines, Evan, private, ... Georgia militia
    December 23, 1833; $40. Age 78.

Hunter, John, private, ... Virginia line
    January 3, 1834; $80. Age 73.

Harrington, Anthony, private, ... Maryland line
    January 28, 1834; $80. Age 72.

Kennedy, Joseph, private, ... Virginia line
    December 28, 1832; $240. Age 74.

Kindred, William, private, ... Virginia line
    April 20, 1833; $80. Age 90.

Kidwell, John, private, ... North Carolina State troops
    May 11, 1833; $30. Age 81.

Lane, Isham, sergeant, ... Virginia line
    March 27, 1833; $120. Age 77.

Lanter, Thomas, private, ... Virginia militia
    August 6, 1833; $70. Age 70.

Lainhart, Isaac, private, ... Virginia militia
    August 21, 1833; $40. Age 79.

Lamb, Thomas, private, ... Virginia line
    August 21, 1833; $80. Age 83.

Lambert, Matthias, private, ... Virginia militia
    July 23, 1834; $30. Age 79.

McGee, Ralph, sergeant, ... Virginia line
    March 27, 1833; $45. Age 79.

Mullins, Matthew, private, ... Virginia line
    April 1, 1833; $40. Age 70.

Maupin, Daniel, sergeant, ... Virginia militia
    April 12, 1833; $60. Age —. Died August 29, 1832.

Maupin, Thomas, private, ... Virginia line
    April 16, 1833; $30. Age 70.

Morris, Thomas, private, ... South Carolina line
    December 17, 1833; $45. Age 74.

Morton, Samuel, private, ... Virginia militia
    June 19, 1834; $50. Age 88.
Oldham, Richard, private, ... North Carolina line
    January 26, 1833; $80. Age 72.
Oglesby, Jesse, private, ... Virginia militia
    October 18, 1833; $22.22. Age 72.
Parker, Wyatt, private, ... Virginia line
    November 10, 1832; $80. Age 77.
Perkins, Anthony, private, ... Virginia line
    November 12, 1832; $46.66. Age 77.
Perkins, Samuel, private, ... Virginia line
    November 12, 1832; $46.66. Age 72.
Parham, Thomas, private, ... South Carolina militia
    April 1, 1833; $26.66. Age 70.
Pace, John, private, ... Virginia militia
    May 6, 1833; $20. Age 70.
Pullins, Loftus, private, ... Virginia militia
    May 11, 1833; $20. Age 70.
Phelps, Josiah, private, ... Virginia State troops
    April 16, 1833; $45. Age 79.
Payton, Yelverton, private, ... Virginia line
    December 14, 1833; $80. Age 79.
Ross, John, private, ... South Carolina line
    April 1, 1833; $60. Age 73.
Roberts, Norman, private, ... Virginia militia
    June 18, 1834; $20. Age 69.
Tomlinson, George, private, ... Virginia line
    November 2, 1832; $80. Age 80.
Thompson, Lawrence, lieutenant and captain, North Carolina line
    November 2, 1832; $429.36. Age 81.
Todd, Peter, private, ... North Carolina militia
    November 5, 1832; $26.66. Age 79.
Tudor, John, private, ... North Carolina militia
    November 10, 1832; $30. Age 80.
Todd, Joseph, private, ... North Carolina militia
    November 13, 1832; $30. Age 76.
Todd, Thomas, private of inf. and cav., . . North Carolina militia
    March 9, 1833. Age 74.
Townsend, Oswald, private, ... Virginia militia
    May 30, 1833; $80. Age 76.
White, Galen, private, ... Virginia line
    November 2, 1832; $80. Age 75.
Watson, Joseph, private, ... Virginia line
    November 5, 1832; $26.66. Age 77.

Watson, William, lieutenant, ... Virginia line
    April 10, 1833; $160. Age 92.
Woods, Archibald, captain, ... Virginia militia
    January 26, 1833; $480. Age 76.
Walkup, Samuel, private, ... North Carolina line
    August 21, 1833; $80. Age 76.

PENSIONER UNDER THE ACT OF MAY 15, 1828.

Barnett, James, lieutenant, ... Virginia line
    December 18, 1828; March 3, 1826; $320. Daniel Breck, agent.

REVOLUTIONARY PENSIONERS LIVING IN THE COUNTY IN 1840.
(Collins, Vol. I, pp. 7, 8.)

Cask, John, age 81.   Kindred, William, age 80.
Covington, Robert, age 77.   Mason, Thomas, age 74.
Guttridge, Nathan, age 76.   Oliver, Richard, age 87.
             Tennal, George, age 89.
           Total for the County, 88.

MARION COUNTY.
PENSIONER UNDER THE ACT OF MARCH 18, 1818.

Cockerell, James, private, ... Virginia line
    Sept. 23, 1819; June 1, 1818; $96. Age 83.

PENSIONERS UNDER THE ACT OF JUNE 7, 1832.
(Began March 4, 1831.)

Dailey, Bennet, private of artillery, ... Pennsylvania line
    December 21, 1833; $100. Age 77.
Peck, William, private, ... Virginia militia
    April 16, 1833; $20. Age 70.
Ramsey, James, private, ... Armand's legion
    October 20, 1832; $50. Age 73.
Sparrow, Henry, private, ... Virginia militia
    January 4, 1834; $20. Age 69.
Sutton, Richard F., private, ... Virginia line
    January 4, 1834; $80. Age 78.
Walker, Philip, private, ... Pennsylvania line
    May 23, 1834; $80. Age 76.

PENSIONERS UNDER THE ACT OF MAY 15, 1828.
(Began March 3, 1826.)

Compton, Emund, lieutenant, first regiment, . . Maryland line
    August 19, 1828; $320.
Tharp, Perry, private, eighth regiment, . . Pennsylvania line
    October 6, 1828 $80.

118   *REVOLUTIONARY SOLDIERS IN KENTUCKY.*

Beams, Conrad, age 82.   Hendrick, William, age 95.
Corbett, James, age 81.   Whitecotton, James, age 91.
Spalding, sr., Geo., age 84.   Hardin, Mrs. (widow), age 80.

Smock, Margaret (widow), age 79.

Total for the County, 16.

MASON COUNTY.

PENSIONERS UNDER THE ACT OF MARCH 18, 1818.

Allen, Barnabas, marine, ... United States navy
    March 13, 1819; May 11, 1818; $96. Age —.
Bean, Leonard, private, ... Maryland line
    April 16, 1819; May 5, 1818; $96. Age 76.
Breeze, John, private, ... Pennsylvania line
    Sept. 18, 1819; May 28, 1818; $96. Age 79. Died Aug. 27, 1827.
Boucher, Richard, private, ... Virginia line
    May 13, 1822; May 31, 1819; $96. Age 70. Died June 14, 1822.
Cole, Benjamin, private, ... German regiment
    July 21, 1819; April 15, 1818; $96. Age 82. Died July 12, 1832.
Deaver, William, private, ... Maryland line
    May 14, 1819; May 26, 1818; $96. Age 78. (Transferred from Ohio.)
DeHart, Samuel, private, ... Pennsylvania line
    February 2, 1819; Aug. 29, 1818; $96. Age 80. Died May 21, 1824.
Fitzgerald, Benjamin, private, ... Maryland line
    June 8, 1819; June 12, 1818; $96. Age 81.
Howard, John, private, ... Maryland line
    June 4, 1819; May 22, 1818; $96. Age 74.
Hukins, John, private, ... Maryland line
    July 21, 1819; July 13, 1818; $96. Age 73. Died June 6, 1833.
Hukill or Hucans, Abiah, private, ... Lee's legion
    March 18, 1819; May 4, 1818; $96. Age 75.
Johnson, Hugh, private, ... Pennsylvania line
    October 6, 1820; March 28, 1820; $96. Age 74. Died April 4, 1823.
Pelham, Charles, major, ... Virginia line
    April 1, 1819; April 13, 1818; $600. Age 80.
Thomas, Nathan, private, ... Maryland line
    Sept. 7, 1819; May 18, 1818; $96. Age 61. Died July 24, 1822.
York, Joshua, private, ... Pennsylvania line
    September 23, 1819; May 18, 1818; $96. Age 78.

PENSIONERS UNDER THE ACT OF JUNE 7, 1832.
(Began March 4, 1831.)

Allen, William, private, ... Virginia line
March 14, 1834; $40.   Age 76.

Brierly, George, private, ... Maryland militia
April 12, 1833; $20.   Age 77.

Baldwin, John, private, ... North Carolina militia
May 1, 1834; $20.   Age 71.

Berry, Benjamin, private, ... Virginia militia
December 20, 1833; $40.   Age 78.

Bickley, William, private, ...
February 4, 1834; $80.   Age 78.

Devine, William, private, ... Maryland line
May 13, 1833; $80.   Age 68.

David, Michael, private, ... Virginia militia
May 13, 1833; $26.   Age 71.

Fritter, Moses, private, ... Virginia militia
September 24, 1833; $30.   Age 79.

Hargate, Peter, private, ... North Carolina militia
May 16, 1833; $30.   Age 79.

Kirk, Thomas, private, ... Maryland militia
May 16, 1833; $20.   Age 75.

Kercheval, John, private, ... Virginia line
April 29, 1834; $80.   Age 71.

Morris, Thomas, private, ... New Jersey militia
April 21, 1833; $40.   Age 84.

Rankin, William, private, ... Virginia line
December 10, 1833; $80.   Age 75.

Rust, John, private and ensign, ... North Carolina line
March 8, 1834; $154.44.   Age 79.

Salmon, John, private of cavalry, ... North Carolina line
August 21, 1833; $100.   Age 80.

Shepherd, George, private, ... Virginia line
November 13, 1832; $80.   Age 74.

Williams, Abraham, lieutenant, ... Maryland line
October 21, 1833; $120.   Age 87.

Williams, William, private, ... New Jersey militia
February 4, 1834; $35.   Age 75.

Young, Thomas, captain, ... Virginia line
December 26, 1832; $480.   Age —.

PENSIONERS UNDER THE ACT OF MAY 15, 1828.
(Began March 3, 1826.)

Burgess, Joshua, lieutenant, fourth regiment, . . Maryland line
July 29, 1828; $320.

Ward, John, dragoon, ... Virginia cavalry
August 13, 1829; $100.

Bell, Daniel, age 76.   Solomon, John, age 85.
Campbell, John, age 65.   Stitt, Samuel H., age —.
Owens, William, age 77.   Ward, John, age 78.
White, John, age 82.

Total for the County, 43.

MEADE COUNTY.

Hard, Zadock, private, ... Revolutionary army
    August 22, 1825; $32. Invalid pensioner. Transferred from New
    Hampshire.
Shanks, John, private, ... Maryland line
    May 29, 1827; February 6, 1827; $96. Age 75. Died March 23,
    1829. (Act of March 18, 1818.)
Spring, Levin, private, ... · · . . Virginia line
    December 28, 1832; $80. Age 77.
Stilth, Joseph, private, ... Virginia militia
    December 28, 1832; $20. Age 75.

Total for the County, 4.

MERCER COUNTY.

PENSIONERS UNDER THE ACT OF MARCH 18, 1818.

Alexander, William, private, ... Virginia line
    February 3, 1819; November 2, 1818; $96. Age 81.
Bradshaw, Larner, private, ... Virginia line
    June 19, 1820; October 4, 1819; $96. Age 77.
Brown, 2d, Charles, private, ... Virginia line
    June 5, 1830; January 1, 1830; $96. Age —.
Brittain, Samuel, private, ... Virginia line
    October 16, 1830; October 16, 1830; $96. Age 80.
Coovert, Isaac, private, ... New Jersey line
    January 27, 1820; October 4, 1819; $96. Age 65.
Decker, Samuel, private, ... Virginia line
    March 5, 1819; May 1, 1818; $96. Age 75. Died August 9, 1826.
Dean, Benjamin, private, ... New Jersey line
    February 16, 1819; June 3, 1818; $96. Age 79.
Ellis, Daniel, private, ... New Jersey line
    February 16, 1819; July 11, 1818; $96. Age 79. Died March 2, 1824.
Jones, Robert, private, ... Pennsylvania line
    February 3, 1819; September 9, 1818; $96. Age 66.

Jordan, Peter, private, ...Virginia line
 November 1, 1819; October 11, 1819; $96. Age 70.
Lafferty, John, private, ...New York line
 February 15, 1819; July 6, 1818; $96. Age 82.
Leonard, William, private, ... New Jersey line
 December 20, 1825; November 11, 1825, $96. Age 83.
McGohan, Mark, private, ... Pennsylvania line
 February 15, 1819; July 6, 1818; $96. Age 84.
McCormick, George, captain, ...Virginia line
 February 6, 1819; June 17, 1818; $96. Age —. Died Jan. 30, 1820.
Phillips (R.), Jacob, private, ...Virginia line
 January 27, 1820; Aug. 2, 1819; $96. Age —. Died Sept. 30, 1830.
Rains, James, private, ...Virginia line
 December 20, 1830; December 17, 1830; $96. Age 76.
Sandifer, James, private, ...Virginia line
 February 3, 1819; November 13, 1818; $96. Age 74.
Speak, George, private, ... Maryland line
 October 25, 1819; May 3, 1818; $96. Age 76.
Snead, John, private, ...Virginia line
 January 27, 1820; September 30, 1819; $96. Age 79.
Servants, William, private, ...Virginia line
 January 27, 1820; August 26, 1819; $96. Age 82.
Woods, Samuel, lieutenant, ...Virginia line
 January 7, 1824; Dec. 15, 1823; $96. Age 88. Died Feb. 3, 1826.

PENSIONERS UNDER THE ACT OF JUNE 7, 1832.
(Began March 4, 1831.)

Adair, John, major, ... South Carolina line
 July 14, 1832; $600. Age —.
Asher, Charles, private, ...Virginia line
 October 13, 1832; $80. Age 71.
Adams, Francis, trumpeter, ...Virginia line
 October 16, 1832; $120. Age 83.
Allin, Thomas, private and quartermaster, . North Carolina line
 January 15, 1833; $186.66. Age 77.
Alsop, James, private, ... Virginia militia
 February 28, 1833; $30. Age 71.
Alexander, Isaac, private, ... North Carolina line
 June 3, 1833; $20. Age 71.
Bradshaw, Claiborne, private, ...Virginia line
 July 27, 1832; $80. Age 75.
Brewer, Samuel, private, ... Pennsylvania line
 February 1, 1833; $46.66. Age 77.
Bereman, Thomas, private, ... New Jersey line
 February 1, 1833; $26.66. Age 73.

13

Barber, Joshua, sergeant and cornet, ... Virginia line
    December 5, 1832; $112. Age 73.

Board, Philip, private, ... New Jersey militia
    February 28, 1833; $80. Age 74.

Bohon, John, private, ... Virginia line
    March 26, 1833; $80. Age 78.

Burris, Nathaniel, private, ... Virginia militia
    March 30, 1833; $40. Age 73.

Burnes, Philip, private, ... North Carolina line
    July 15, 1833; $53.33. Age 75

Barbee, Daniel, sergeant, ... Virginia militia
    December 5, 1832; $120. Age 77.

Bridges, John, private, ... Virginia militia
    February 1, 1833; $80. Age 92.

Bruster, James, private of inf. and cav., ... Virginia militia
    May 23, 1834; $22.50. Age 71.

Carter, Martin, private, ... Virginia militia
    September 11, 1832; $23.33. Age 72.

Coovert, Daniel, private, ... New Jersey line
    November 10, 1832; $80. Age 77.

Crain, Thomas, private, ... Virginia State troops
    February 1, 1833; $70. Age 79.

Crawford, Thomas, private, ... Pennsylvania State troops
    March 30, 1833; $65. Age 79. Died June 20, 1833.

Carey, Ebenezer P., private, ... Vermont State troops
    March 30, 1833; $63.33. Age 73.

Coleman, Robert, private, ... Virginia line
    March 30, 1833; $40. Age 86. Died January 9, 1834.

Comingore, John, private, ... Pennsylvania militia
    June 3, 1833; $20. Age 85.

Comingore, Henry, private, ... Pennsylvania militia
    June 3, 1833; $40. Age 85.

Coulter, Matthew, private of inf. and cav., . South Carolina line
    November 15, 1833; $50.94. Age 75.

Clark, Patrick, private, ... Virginia militia
    December 2, 1833; $20. Age 77.

Clark, James, private, ... Virginia militia
    December 21, 1833; $20. Age 75.

Dickey, Robert, private, ... Pennsylvania militia
    September 11, 1832; $26.66 Age 84.

Demott, Peter, private, ... New Jersey line
    November 10, 1832; $80. Age 76.

Demaree, John, private, ... Virginia line
    November 10, 1832; $70. Age 73.

Deshazure, Henry, private, ... Virginia line
  February 1, 1833; $80. Age 74.
Fisher, Elias, sergeant and private, ... Virginia line
  December 2, 1833; $41.66. Age 74.
Gabbert, Michael, private, ... Virginia militia
  February 28, 1833; $20. Age 69.
Galloway, James, private, ... Pennsylvania line
  March 26, 1833; $80. Age 76.
Gritton, John, private, ... Pennsylvania line
  March 26, 1833; $73.33. Age 78.
Graham, Thomas, private and sergeant, ... Virginia militia
  May 30, 1833; $85.73. Age 75.
Grant, John, private, ... New Jersey militia
  August 3, 1833; $53.33. Age 78.
Gabbert, George, private, ... North Carolina militia
  January 4, 1834; $24.21. Age 73.
George, John, private and sergeant, ... New Jersey line
  June 7, 1832; $120. Age 76.
Holman, Richard, private, ... Virginia line
  October 3, 1832; $33.33. Age 78.
Huff, Peter, private, ... New Jersey line
  November, 10, 1832; $80. Age 78.
Harlan, George, private, ... Virginia line
  January 19, 1833; $80. Age 73.
Houchins (Hutchins?), Edward, private, ... Virginia militia
  February 1, 1833; $33.33. Age 75.
Hart, Charles, private, ... North Carolina line
  February 1, 1833; $80. Age 73.
Harris, Samuel, private, ... Pennsylvania line
  March 30, 1833; $63.33. Age 70.
Hutton, James, private and ensign, ... Virginia line
  March 30, 1833; $110. Age 72.
Hawkins, Nathan, private, ... Virginia militia
  November 15, 1833; $28.65. Age 71.
Hedger, Thomas, private, ... Virginia militia
  November 15, 1833; $20. Age 88.
Jenkins, Anthony, private, ... Virginia line
  February 1, 1833; $70. Age 70.
Kelly, William, private, ... Virginia militia
  February 28, 1833; $30. Age 72.
Kirkland, John, private of cavalry, ... Virginia line
  March 30, 1833; $100. Age 80.
Kyle, Thomas, private, ... Massachusetts line
  October 18, 1833; $40. Age 76.

Moore, Thomas, private and captain, ... Virginia militia
November 10, 1832; $130. Age 80.

Moore, John, private, ... Pennsylvania line
March 26, 1833; $80. Age 77.

May, Humphrey, sergeant, ... Virginia line
September 6, 1833; $120. Age 76.

Nourse, William, midshipman, frigates "Confederacy"
and " South Carolina," . . . .
September 27, 1833; $144. Age 71.

Newton, Benjamin, private, ... North Carolina militia
February 1, 1833; $30. Age 82.

Pearson, William, private, ... Maryland militia
February 1, 1833; $37.88. Age 96.

Poller, John, private, ... Virginia militia
March 26, 1833; $30. Age 73.

Philips, George, private of cavalry, ... Virginia militia
October 16, 1832; $100. Age 77.

Rosser, Richard, private, ... Virginia State troops
September 1, 1832; $23.33. Age 78.

Ray, James, captain and lieutenant, ... Virginia line
March 30, 1833; $340. Age 74.

Roberts, George, sergeant and lieutenant, ... Virginia line
October 20, 1832; $160. Age 68. Died July 13, 1835.

Rice, James, private, ... Virginia militia
February 1, 1833; $40. Age 74.

Randolph, Malachi, private, ... New Jersey militia
February 28, 1833; $80. Age 76.

Rule, Thomas, private, ... North Carolina line
December 2, 1833; $40. Age 73.

Richardson, David, private, ... Maryland line
January 28, 1834; $30. Age 78.

Rose, Benjamin B., private, ... North Carolina militia
April 23, 1834; $32.44. Age 74.

Smithey, Thomas, private, ... Virginia line
February 1, 1833; $60. Age 80.

Sky, Jesse, private, ... Virginia line
June 7, 1833; $60. Age 74.

Sleet, James, sergeant and private, ... Virginia line
September 25, 1833; $80. Age 82.

Shelton, Samuel, private, ... Virginia militia
July 10, 1834; $60. Age 75.

Taylor, William, private, ... Virginia line
September 11, 1832; $70. Age 72.

Trower, Solomon, private, ... Virginia militia
September 11, 1832; $40. Age 101.

Thompson, John, lieutenant, ... Virginia line
October 16, 1832; $98.21. Age 78.

Thomas, Elisha, private, ... Virginia line
March 30, 1833; $26.66. Age 71.

Thompson, George, major, ... Virginia militia
March 30, 1833; $436.66. Age 85. Died March 22, 1834.

Teumey, John, private, ... New Jersey militia
February 1, 1833; $80. Age —.

Tolley, William, private and sergeant, . . North Carolina militia
December 21, 1833; $35. Age 79.

Taylor, Leonard, private, ... Virginia militia
December 21, 1833; $73.33. Age 76.

Vanarsdall, Lawrence, private, ... New Jersey line
November 11, 1832; $50. Age —.

Vanarsdall, Cornelius C., private, ... New Jersey militia
June 17, 1834; $51.66. Age 86.

Vanarsdall, Cornelius, lieutenant, ... Virginia line
November 26, 1833; $320. Age 86.

Voris, John, private and sergeant, ... Pennsylvania line
March 30, 1833; $81.66. Age 75.

Wilhite, Tobias, private, ... Virginia State troops
March 30, 1833; $22.33. Age 84.

Whitecotton, James, private, ... Virginia militia
October 21, 1833; $70. Age 83.

PENSIONERS UNDER THE ACT OF MAY 15, 1828.
(Began March 6, 1826.)

Basey, William, sergeant, ... Washington's cavalry
December 9, 1828; $180. Died August 29, 1829.

Falls, Isaac, private, fifth regiment, ... Pennsylvania line
May 14, 1832; $80.

Williams, David, lieutenant, eighth regiment, . . . Virginia line
$320. Died November 8, 1831.

REVOLUTIONARY PENSIONERS LIVING IN THE COUNTY IN 1840.
(Collins, Vol. I, p. 8.)

Conn, Timothy, age 84.	Sparrow, Henry, age 79.
Fallis, Isaac, age 77.	Webb, Lewis, age 83.
Hackney, Samuel, age 79.	Pipes, Mary (widow), age 81.
Hamler, Henry, age 81.	Verbryck, Rebecca (widow),
Potter, sr., John, age 79.	age 83.
Rice, John, age 78.	Wilson, Mary (widow), age 76.

Total for the County, 122.

MONROE COUNTY.

PENSIONERS UNDER THE ACT OF MARCH 18, 1818.

Brown, Thomas, musician, ... Virginia line
    July 3, 1820; June 8, 1818; $96. Age 80.
Metheany, Luke, private, ... Virginia line
    May 6, 1819; September 14, 1818; $96. Age 81.
Rasner, John, private, ... Virginia line
    December 20, 1820; September 20, 1819; $96. Age 84.
Shipley, Samuel, private, ... Maryland line
    October 10, 1831; October 5, 1831; $96. Age 96.

PENSIONERS UNDER THE ACT OF JUNE 7, 1832.
(Began March 4, 1831.)

Curtis, Fielding U., private and sergeant, . South Carolina line
    August 17, 1833; $75. Age 77.
Campbell, James, private, ... North Carolina line
    September 2, 1833; $33. Age 81.
Dickerson, Salomon, private, ... Maryland line
    April 12, 1833; $20. Age 80.
Dicken, Ephraim, private, ... Virginia militia
    April 16, 1833; $20. Age 72.
Gist, John, private, ... Virginia line
    April 12, 1833; $80. Age 83.
Goodman, Jacob, private, ... North Carolina line
    September 5, 1833; $38.33. Age 72.
Giles, John, private, ... North Carolina line
    May 16, 1834; $80. Age 74.
Haley, Pleasant, private, ... Virginia militia
    May 13, 1833; $40. Age 74.
Kidwell, Matthew, private, ... Maryland militia
    August 7, 1833; $23.33. Age 72.
Morehead, John, private, ... Virginia militia
    August 21, 1833; $40. Age 84.
Smith, Fleming, private, ... South Carolina militia
    October 21, 1833; $25. Age 88.
White, Thomas, private, ... Maryland militia
    April 12, 1833; $40. Age 76.
Welch, James, private, ... North Carolina line
    January 11, 1834; $80. Age 72.

REVOLUTIONARY PENSIONERS LIVING IN THE COUNTY IN 1840.
(Collins, Vol. I, p. 8.)

Bartley, Thomas, age 77.   Denham, Hardin, age 78.
Veach, Elijah, age 89.
Total for the County, 20.

MONTGOMERY COUNTY.

PENSIONERS UNDER THE ACT OF MARCH 18, 1818.

Adams, 2d, John, private, ... Virginia line
February 12, 1819; December 3, 1818; $96. Age 67.

Brown, John, private, ... Delaware line
Feb. 13, 1819; July 17, 1818; $96. Age 70. Died Aug. 20, 1825.

Benningfield, Henry, private, ... Virginia line
January 26, 1819; July 17, 1818; $96. Age 79.

Caffen, Reuben, corporal, ... Virginia line
February 12, 1819; December 3, 1818; $96. Age 71.

Downs, Robert, private, ... Delaware line
February 12, 1819; July 13, 1818; $96. Age 64.

Dunlap, James, private, ... Pennsylvania line
February 12, 1819; July 8, 1818; $96. Age 94.

Goff, John, private, ... Virginia line
Feb. 12, 1819; Dec. 3, 1818; $96. Age 80. Died March 1, 1823.

Howard, James, private, ... Virginia line
February 11, 1819; December 3, 1818; $96. Age 80.

Hammon, Philip, private, ... Virginia line
April 1, 1820; November 13, 1819; $96. Age 69.

Johnson, 2d, James, private, ... Virginia line
June 15, 1819; July 7, 1818; $96. Age 80.

Moore, Nicholas, private, ... Virginia line
February 12, 1819; Dec. 3, 1818; $96. Age 85. Died June 15, 1821.

McCullough, James, private, ... Virginia line
February 10, 1819; July 7, 1818; $96. Age 62. Died Dec. 17, 1818.

McCulley, James, private, ... Virginia line
February 12, 1819; December 3, 1818; $96. Age —.

Piles, William, private, ... Virginia line
Feb. 13, 1819; Dec. 3, 1818; $96. Age —. Died prior to Dec. 17, 1818.

Roberts, Edward, private, ... Virginia line
November 6, 1819; October 7, 1819; $96. Age 66.

Smith, John, private, ... Pennsylvania line
February 12, 1819; July 8, 1818; $96. Age 62.

Steen, Edward, private, ... Pennsylvania line
February 13, 1819; July 8, 1818; $96. Age 68.

Sims, John, private, ... Virginia line
September 9, 1819; October 9, 1819; $96. Age 74.

Tolen, Eli, private, ... Virginia line
Feb. 12, 1819; December 3, 1818; $96. Age 69. Died July 14, 1824.

White, Aquilla, captain, ... Pennsylvania line
January 27, 1819; July 3, 1818; $240. Age 89.

PENSIONERS UNDER THE ACT OF JUNE 7, 1832.

(Began March 4, 1831.)

Anderson, William, private, ... Virginia line
April 2, 1833; $80. Age 69.
Beatty, Daniel, private, ... North Carolina line
December 28, 1833 ; $80. Age 76.
Bourne, James, private, ... Virginia militia
December 23, 1833; $20. Age 75.
Beatty, John, private, ... Virginia militia
November 6, 1819; $96. Age —.
Cave, William, private, ... North Carolina line
March 6, 1833; $30. Age 85.
Clement, Roger, private, ... North Carolina line
December 28, 1833; $50. Age 72.
Clark, Joseph, private, ... Virginia militia
December 28, 1833; $30. Age 76.
Conner, William, private, ... North Carolina militia
February 24, 1834; $80. Age 70.
Daniel, Beverly, private, ... Virginia militia
March 10 1834; $30. Age 74.
Foster, Nathaniel, private, ... Virginia militia
December 28, 1833 ; $21.55. Age 73.
Gray, William, private, ... Pennsylvania line
March 6, 1833; $33.33. Age 79.
Garrett, Robert, private, ... Virginia line
December 25, 1833; $55. Age 84.
Hiatt, Shadrach, private, ... Maryland line
March 6, 1833; $66.66. Age 85.
Hatcher, Samuel, private, ... Virginia line
March 6, 1833; $52.09. Age 74.
Hall, Thomas, private, ... Virginia line
March 20, 1833 ; $80. Age 74.
Hamlin, John, private, ... North Carolina militia
March 10, 1834; $20. Age 74.
Lockridge, John, private, ... Virginia militia
April 2, 1833 ; $20. Age 72.
Lee, John, private, ... Virginia militia
April 2, 1833; $30. Age 79.
Moss, John, private, ... Virginia militia
February 20, 1833; $20. Age 72.
McCulloch, James, private and lieutenant, . North Carolina line
August 21, 1833; $200. Age 74.
Montgomery, John, private, ... Virginia militia
November 15, 1833; $25.32. Age 72.

McCarty, Daniel, private, ... Virginia militia
 November 20, 1833; $66.66. Age 71.
Mosley, Thomas, private, ... Virginia militia
 March 27, 1834; $31.55. Age 75.
Orear, John, private and sergeant, ... Virginia line
 December 28, 1833; $46.66. Age 85.
Raney, James, private, ... Virginia militia
 December 28, 1833; $33.33. Age 72.
Stewart, Ezekiel, private, ... Virginia militia
 December 28, 1833; $20. Age 93.
Spencer, Hezekiah, private, ...
 ———. Age —.
Tipton, sr., William, private, ... Virginia State troops
 March 6, 1833; $54.98. Age —.
Terry, 2d, Thomas, private, ... Virginia line
 December 28, 1833; $60. Age —.
Wilkinson, Joseph, private, ... Virginia line
 June 7, 1832; $80. Age 77.
Willis, Henry, private, ... Virginia militia
 April 2, 1833; $60. Age 69.
Wilson, Henry, sergeant and private, ... Virginia line
 August 21, 1833; $93.33. Age 74.

REVOLUTIONARY PENSIONERS LIVING IN THE COUNTY IN 1840.

(Collins, Vol. I, p. 8.)

Fisher, John B., age 70. Ramsey, James, age 78.
Grigsby, Benjamin, age 91. Robinson, Benjamin, age 84.
McKee, Samuel, age 76. Steen, Edward, age 70.
   Stephens, John, age 79.

Total for the County, 59.

MORGAN COUNTY.

PENSIONERS UNDER THE ACT OF MARCH 18, 1818.

Montgomery, Alexander, private, ... Virginia line
 April 5, 1828; February 9, 1828; $96. Age 84.
Wages, Benjamin, private, ... Virginia line
 April 5, 1828; February 9, 1828; $96. Age 93.

PENSIONERS UNDER THE ACT OF JUNE 7, 1832.

(Began March 4, 1831.)

Butler, John, private, ... Virginia line
 August 22, 1833; $66.66. Age 73.
Blevin, James, private,. . . . . Virginia line
 March 22, 1834; $53.33. Age 83.

Barker, George, private, ... Virginia line
   May 12, 1834; $50. Age 76.
Cooper, John, private, ... Pennsylvania militia
   July 10, 1834; $55. Age 75.
Cooke, William, private, ... North Carolina line
   April 29, 1834; $30. Age 70.
Day, John, private, ... Virginia line
   December 2, 1833; $76.66. Age 74.
Ellington, David, private, ... Virginia militia
   April 29, 1834; $41.12. Age 71.
Hamilton, Thomas, private, ... Virginia line
   April 12, 1833; $80. Age 76.
Howerton, William, private, ... Virginia line
   February 7, 1834; $60. Age 75.
Hamilton, Benjamin, private, ... Virginia line
   February 25, 1834; $43.33. Age 73.
Johnson, Jacob, private, ... South Carolina line
   May 11, 1833; $80. Age 76.
Keeton, Isaac, private, ... North Carolina line
   April 29, 1834; $60. Age 70.
Kelly, Samuel, private, ... North Carolina militia
   May 1, 1834; $31.66. Age 78.
Lewis, Thomas, private, ... Virginia line
   September 25, 1833; $41.33. Age 76.
McKinzee, Isaac, private, ... Virginia militia
   October 31, 1833; $25. Age 71.
McGuire, John, private, ... Virginia line
   January 4, 1834; $20. Age 78.
Ratliff, Reuben, private, ... Virginia militia
   July 10, 1834; $43.33. Age 72.
Smethers, John, private, ... Virginia line
   March 20, 1833; $80. Age 71.
Stevens, Gilbert, private, ... Virginia militia
   May 1, 1834; $60.79. Age 74.
Swanson, Levi, private, ... Virginia militia
   May 2, 1834; $25. Age 77.
Williams, Philip, private, ... Virginia line
   September 24, 1833; $80. Age 77.
Walsh, William, private, ... North Carolina militia
   September 25, 1833; $20. Age 74.

REVOLUTIONARY PENSIONERS LIVING IN THE COUNTY IN 1840.
(Collins, Vol. I, p. 8.)

Hamilton, B., age 76.	Smothers, John, age 79.
Kulby, John, age 87.	Stevenson, Levi, age 85.
Kuton, Isaac, age 79.	Hopkins, Mary, widow, age 84.
Prewitt, John, age 85.	Jones, Martha, widow, age 80.

Total for the County, 32.

MUHLENBERG COUNTY.

PENSIONERS UNDER THE ACT OF MARCH 18, 1818.

Hines, Hardy, private, ... North Carolina line
  March 31, 1820; December 8, 1818; $96. Age 62.

Harper, John, private, ... Pennsylvania line
  October 24, 1821; June 2, 1818; $96. Age 79.

McMahon, John, private, ... South Carolina line
  April 24, 1820; June 2, 1818; $96. Age 70.

PENSIONERS UNDER THE ACT OF JUNE 7, 1832.
(Began March 4, 1831.)

Atkinson, Elisha, private, ... North Carolina militia
  December 21, 1833; $30. Age 89.

Bone, 1st, John, private and sergeant, . . . North Carolina line
  March 27, 1833; $68.33 Age 71.

Elkin, Joshua, private, ... South Carolina militia
  March 14, 1833; $20. Age 72.

Edwards, David, private, ... Virginia line
  September 3, 1833; $80. Age 76.

Glenn, Andrew, private, ... Pennsylvania line
  August 21, 1833; $80. Age 80.

Garris, Sikes, private, ... North Carolina line
  February 27, 1833; $80. Age 85.

Harper, Nathan, private, ... North Carolina line
  June 7, 1833; $40. Age 70.

Hancock, Isaiah, private, ... North Carolina line
  August 21, 1833; $20. Age 67.

Hill, Michael, private, ... North Carolina line
  August 21, 1833; $60. Age 80.

Hunt, John, private, ... North Carolina militia
  May 1, 1834; $20. Age 84.

Jarvis, Edward, private, ... North Carolina line
  October 18, 1833; $70. Age 71.

Pitt, Joseph, private, ... North Carolina militia
  February 19, 1834; $66.66. Age 70.

Reynolds, Richard D., private, ... Virginia militia
  February 27, 1833; $40. Age 77.

Roll, Michael, private, ... Pennsylvania line
  June 6, 1834; $50. Age 71.

Worthington, William, private, ... Pennsylvania line
  September 25, 1833; $56.21. Age 73.

Willis, Britton, private, ... South Carolina line
  October 21, 1833; $80. Age 76.

Young, William, sergeant, ... Virginia militia
  February 27, 1833; $120. Age —.

Hopkins, William, age 73.   Neal, Benjamin, age 80.

Total for the County, 22.

NELSON COUNTY.

PENSIONERS UNDER THE ACT OF MARCH 18, 1818.

Bird, Joshua, private, ...Virginia line
April 25, 1820; October 4, 1819; $96. Age 90.

Brooks, James, private, ...Virginia line
Nov. 6, 1819; Aug. 10, 1819; $96. Age 91. Died April 10, 1827.

Carter, Barnabas, private, ...Virginia line
December 16, 1828; December 1, 1828; $96. Age 77.

Hagan, James, private, ...Maryland line
March 22, 1819; March 20, 1818; $96. Age 80. Died Dec. 30, 1829.

Keech, John J. S., private, ...Maryland line
June 10, 1819; August 19, 1818; $96. Age —. Died May 15, 1825.

Lamb, George, private, ...Massachusetts line
January 22, 1819; May 18, 1818; $96. Age 106.

Moxley, George, private, ...Virginia line
January 29, 1819; August 3, 1818; $96. Age 61.

Murphy, James, drummer, ... Pennsylvania line
June 9, 1819; May 19, 1818; $96. Age 72.

Murphy, Gabriel, private, ...Virginia line
July 30, 1823; March 1, 1823; $96. Age 75.

Murphy, Gabriel, private, ...Virginia line
November 17, 1819; September 3, 1819; $96. Age 62.

O'Connor, Thomas, private, ...Maryland line
June 5, 1819; October 5, 1818; $96. Age 83.

Tennell, George, private, ...Virginia line
April 21, 1819; July 29, 1818; $96. Age 78.

Townsend, Samuel, private, ...New York line
January 22, 1819; August 4, 1818; $96. Age 67. Died Oct. 20, 1820.

Winsett, Raphael, private, ...Maryland line
March 22, 1819; May 27, 1818; $96. Age 75. Died May 25, 1818.

Wilson, David, private, ...Virginia line
January 27, 1820; September 3, 1819; $96. Age 80.

PENSIONER UNDER THE ACT OF JUNE 7, 1832.
(Began March 4, 1831.)

Ashlock, William, private, ...Virginia militia
September 20, 1833; $20. Age 72.

Bishop, Solomon, private, ... Virginia line
    November 2, 1832; $80. Age 79.
Blandford, Richard, private, ... Maryland militia
    November 8, 1832; $20. Age 78.
Bell, John, ensign, ... Pennsylvania militia
    November 1, 1832; $340. Age 84.
Dodson, William, private, ... Virginia militia
    December 21, 1833; $80. Age 75.
Hansford, Charles, private, ... Virginia militia
    March 2, 1833; $43.33. Age 75.
Johnson, Abraham, private, ... Virginia line
    March 3, 1834; $80. Age 77.
Johnson, Robert, private, ... South Carolina line
    April 18, 1834; $30. Age 84.
Dent, William, private, ... Virginia line
    November 14, 1832; $80. Age 76.
McConn, Alexander, private, ... Pennsylvania militia
    December 28, 1832; $36.66. Age 79.
Martenson, John, private, ... Pennsylvania militia
    February 23, 1833; $20. Age 75.
Milligan, Joseph, private, ... Pennsylvania line
    March 2, 1833; $26.66. Age 79.
Montgomery, Thomas, private, ... Pennsylvania line
    April 2, 1833; $80. Age 84.
McAtee, Walter, private, ... Pennsylvania militia
    April 16, 1833; $23.33. Age 77.
Thompson, William, private, ... Maryland line
    November 12, 1833; $30. Age 86.
Vittilon (Vittitoe?), Samuel, ... Pennsylvania militia
    February 23, 1833; $20. Age —.
Wood, Jonathan, private, ... Maryland militia
    December 18, 1832; $40. Age —.

PENSIONERS UNDER THE ACT OF MAY 15, 1828.
(Began March 3, 1826.)

Carter, Nicholas, private, . . Putnam's Massachusetts regiment
    December 16, 1830; $80.
Smith, Benjamin, private, sixth regiment, . . . Maryland line
    January 15, 1829; $80.

REVOLUTIONARY PENSIONERS LIVING IN THE COUNTY IN 1840.
(Collins, Vol. I, p. 8.)

Bell, John, age 91.   Smith, Benjamin, age 79.
Lawson, John, age 83.   McCown, Susan, widow, age 74.

Total for the County, 38.

NICHOLAS COUNTY.

PENSIONERS UNDER THE ACT OF MARCH 18, 1818.

Ballanger, William, private, ... Virginia line
December 24, 1818; October 2, 1818; $96. Age —.

Bishop, Richard, private, ... Virginia line
April 3, 1819; June 10, 1818; $96. Age 70. Died June 19, 1824.

Burns, John, private, ... Pennsylvania line
April 18, 1820; June 23, 1818; $96. Age 85.

Blackburn, Samuel, private, ... Pennsylvania line
October 25, 1819; June 17, 1818; $96. Age 79.

Caughey, John, private, ... Pennsylvania line
April 18, 1820; June 29, 1819; $96. Age 87.

Caldwell, Robert, private, ... Pennsylvania line
January 29, 1822; June 23, 1818; $96. Age 77.

Fitzpatrick, James, private, ... Virginia line
April 13, 1820; June 22, 1818; $96. Age 74.

Geoghan, John, ensign, ... Maryland line
January 6, 1819; Dec. 2, 1818; $240. Age 78. Died Feb. 20, 1826.

Grosvenor, Richard, drummer, ... Pennsylvania line
April 13, 1819; June 25, 1818; $96. Age —. Died Nov. 10, 1819.

Hopkins, Robert, private, ... Connecticut line
April 10, 1819; June 16, 1818; $96. Age 60.

Hanna, John, private, ... Pennsylvania line
July 6, 1819; September 10, 1818; $96. Age 80.

Hargis, John, ensign, ... Virginia line
November 12, 1822; July 30, 1818; $240. Age 85.

Ishmael, Benjamin, private, ... Pennsylvania line
January 15, 1823; Oct. 1, 1818; $96. Age 83. Died July 10, 1822.

Morris, Thomas, fifer, ... Virginia line
April 13, 1820; June 22, 1818; $96. Age 81.

Miller, Nicholas, private, ... Congressional regiment
June 25, 1819; July 27, 1818; $96. Age 86.

Neves, Daniel, private, ... Virginia line
January 8, 1819; September 30, 1818; $96. Age 81.

Robertson, Stephen, private, ... Virginia line
August 1, 1820; July 3, 1820; $96. Age 92.

Smith, 2d, John, private, ... Pennsylvania line
May 23, 1822; July 6, 1818; $96. Age —.

Walls, Reuben, private, ... Virginia line
September 6, 1830; September 4, 1830; $96. Age 77.

PENSIONERS UNDER THE ACT OF JUNE 7, 1832.
(Began March 4, 1831.)

Allison, John, private, ... North Carolina militia
March 6, 1833; $26.66. Age 75.

Bryant, George, private, ... North Carolina militia
March 21, 1834; $30. Age 85.

Barnett, Ambrose, private, ... Virginia militia
February 28, 1833; $80. Age 85. Died December 18, 1832.

Conway, John, private, ... Virginia line
May 12, 1834; $80. Age 75.

Fifer, Jacob, private, ... Maryland militia
August 17, 1833; $30. Age 80.

Foster, Henry, private, ... Virginia line
December 20, 1833; $80. Age 72.

Henry, John, private, ... Virginia line
December 26, 1832; $50. Age 75.

Kersey, John, private, ... Virginia militia
May 30, 1833; $80. Age 70.

Logan, William, private, ... Virginia line
April 16, 1833; $80. Age 75.

McClintock, Hugh, private, ... Pennsylvania militia
February 26, 1833; $20. Age 76.

Utterback, Hammon, private, ... North Carolina line
December 7, 1833; $23.33. Age 79.

Wilson, James, private, ... Virginia line
November 12, 1833; $80. Age 78.

REVOLUTIONARY PENSIONERS LIVING IN THE COUNTY IN 1840.
(Collins, Vol. I, p. 8.)

Atkins, Edward, age 85.	Ritchey, Esau, age 63.
Collier, Coleman A., age 61.	Stoker, Edward, age 77.
Layton, William H., age 86.	Walls, Reuben, age 86.

Total for the County, 37.

OHIO COUNTY.

PENSIONERS UNDER THE ACT OF MARCH 18, 1818.

Brandon, Peter, ... Virginia line
July 6, 1822; August 24, 1819; $96. Age 84.

Cooper, William, private, ... Maryland line
May 21, 1819; July 13, 1818; $96. Age 84.

Campbell, William, private, ... Lee's legion
May 6, 1819; July 13, 1818; $96. Age 81.

Howell, John, captain, ... New Jersey line
April 24, 1820; August 20, 1818; $240. Age 73.

Johnson, Moses, private, ... Virginia line
February 15, 1820; July 13, 1818; $96. Age 85.

Mosely, Robert, lieutenant, ... Pennsylvania line
  February 15, 1819; November 11, 1818; $240. Age 69.
Pender, Thomas, private, ... Maryland line
  May 21, 1819; July 13, 1818; $96. Age 76. Died Jan. 14, 1833.
Parks, Peter, private, ... North Carolina line
  March 1, 1825; January 31, 1825; $96. Age 70.

PENSIONERS UNDER THE ACT OF JUNE 7, 1832.
(Began March 4, 1831.)

Barnard, William L., private, ... Maryland militia
  February 28, 1833; $20. Age 75.
Burton, Seley, private, ... North Carolina militia
  January 19, 1833; $40. Age 78.
Calloway, Chesley, private, ... Massachusetts line
  June 11, 1833; $80. Age 74.
Carter, William, private, ... Virginia militia
  May 23, 1824; $33.33. Age 74.
Monroe, John, private, sergeant, and lieutenant, . Virginia militia
  January 10, 1834; $68.33. Age 84.
Sorrels, John, private and sergeant, ... North Carolina line
  October 11, 1833; $92.33. Age 78.
Shults, Matthias, private, ... Virginia militia
  November 7, 1833; $29.76. Age 76. Died May 19, 1834.

PENSIONER UNDER THE ACT OF MAY 15, 1828.

(Began March 3, 1826.)

Burch, Benjamin, sergeant, third regiment, . . . Maryland line
  May 8, 1829; $120. Died December 17, 1830.

REVOLUTIONARY PENSIONERS LIVING IN THE COUNTY IN 1840.
(Collins, Vol. I, p. 8.)

Arnold, Zebra, age 83.   Maddox, sr., John, age 78.
Total for the County, 18.

OLDHAM COUNTY.

PENSIONERS UNDER THE ACT OF JUNE 7, 1832.
(Began March 4, 1831.)

Austin, John, private, ... Virginia line
  November 6, 1832; $80. Age 98.
Archer, Edmund, private, ... Virginia militia
  March 16, 1833; Age 75.
Ashby, Fielding, private, ... Virginia line
  November 7, 1833; $28.33; Age 71.

Force, Jesse, private, ... Virginia militia
April 12, 1833; $26.66. Age 72.

George, Thomas, private, ... Virginia militia
April 9, 1833; $36.66. Age 74.

Hindley, John, private, ... North Carolina line
January 13, 1834; $60. Age 71.

Humphrey, Merritt, private, ... North Carolina line
January 25, 1834; $30. Age 74.

Lingenfelter, Michael, private, ... Maryland line
October 10, 1833; $40. Age 72.

Law, Jesse, private, ... Virginia line
November 7, 1833; $73.33. Age 77.

Morgan, John, private, ... Maryland militia
September 9, 1833; $30. Age 73.

Morgan Thomas, private, ... Maryland line
October 18, 1833; $46.66. Age 73.

Netherton, John, captain and major, ... Virginia militia
May 30, 1833; $135. Age 87.

Reed, John, private, ... Virginia line
December 18, 1832; $80. Age 77.

Singer, George, private, ... Virginia militia
February 27, 1833; $20. Age 72.

True, John, private, ... Virginia militia
October 21, 1833; $30. Age 81.

Wright, George, private, ... Virginia militia
February 4, 1834; $30. Age 71.

PENSIONERS UNDER THE ACT OF MAY 15, 1828.
(Began March 3, 1826.)

Love, David, sergeant, first regiment, ... Maryland line
August 13, 1828; $120. Died December 6, 1830.

Outhouse, Peter, private, first regiment, . . . Maryland line
August 12, 1828; $80. Transferred to Clinton County, Illinois.

Taylor, William, major, ninth regiment, ... Virginia line
July 29, 1828; $600. Died April 14, 1830.

Wirble, Henry, private, ... Hazen's regiment
August 13, 1828; $80.

REVOLUTIONARY PENSIONERS LIVING IN THE COUNTY IN 1840.
(Collins, Vol. I, p. 8.)

Coons, Benjamin, age 66.　　　Hoskins, James, age 83.

Total for the County, 22.

14

OWEN COUNTY.

Jennings, Solomon, private, ... New York line
    May 3, 1820; Jan. 26, 1820; $96. Age 69. Died Nov. 30, 1820.
Mason, James, private, ... New York line
    Dec. 20, 1822; Nov. 11, 1822; $96. Age 106. Died July 15, 1833.

(Began March 4, 1831.)

Berry, John, private, ... Virginia militia
    February 11, 1833; $23.33. Age 84.
Burke, Robert, private and sergeant, ... Virginia militia
    June 26, 1833; $70. Age 73.
Bonds, John, private, ... Virginia militia
    February 12, 1833; $80. Age 71.
Chandler, James, sergeant and private, . . . North Carolina line
    April 16, 1833; $115. Age 78.
Conway, Hugh, private, ... Pennsylvania militia
    June 26, 1833; $73.33. Age 71.
Ellis, Isaac, priv., serg't, lieut., and captain, Pennsylvania militia
    June 26, 1833; $256.66. Age 81.
Garnett, John, private, ... Virginia line
    February 25, 1834; $30. Age 84.
Hoover, Lawrence, private, ... Virginia militia
    April 25, 1833; $80. Age 74.
Holliday, Benjamin, private and sergeant, South Carolina militia
    $65. Age 83.
Hunter, Jacob, private, ... Virginia line
    September 23, 1833; $80. Age 71.
Jones, Joseph, private, ... Virginia line
    February 5, 1833; $80. Age 83.
Jamison, John, private, ... New Jersey line
    April 16, 1833; $80. Age 83.
Kugel, John, private, ... Connecticut line
    April 25, 1833; $40. Age 76.
Ligon, William, private, ... Virginia line
    December 3, 1832; $42.50. Age 72.
Lorrance, William, private, ... North Carolina militia
    June 26, 1833; $73.33. Age 71.
Maddox, Sherwood, private, ... Virginia line
    February 12, 1833; $26.66. Age 73.
Minor, Joseph, private, ... Virginia line
    April 25, 1833; $68.33. Age 73.

Radcliff, Minus, private, ... Delaware line
December 2, 1833; $88. Age 71.
Stamper, Jacob, private, ... North Carolina line
February 5, 1833; $60. Age 71.
Sanders, John, private, ... Virginia militia
February 11, 1833; $23.33. Age 83.
Sparks, Henry, private, ... Virginia militia
April 25, 1833; $30. Age 80.
Stewart, Robert, capt., lieut., sergt., and private, . Virginia line
September 23, 1833; $283.33. Age 79.
Searcy, John, private, ... North Carolina line
January 6, 1834; $38.43. Age 72.
Toon, Henry, private, ... Maryland militia
May 7, 1833; $30. Age 78.
Thomas, John, private, ... Virginia line
February 25, 1834; $60. Age 71. Died June 27, 1833.
Vallandingham, Lewis, private, ... Virginia State troops
February 12, 1833; $80. Age —.
Wade, John, private, ... Virginia line
April 16, 1833; $80. Age 80.
Wilhite, John, private, ... Virginia militia
January 15, 1833; $36.66. Age —.

REVOLUTIONARY PENSIONERS LIVING IN THE COUNTY IN 1840.
(Collins, Vol. I, p. 8.)

Bond, John, age 78.
Boone, Samuel, age 83
Carter, Henry, age 91.
Grill, John, age 82.
Kenny, Edward D., age 78.

Lawrence, William, age 77.
Parsley, Thomas, age 78.
McCormack, Rebecca (widow),
age 88.

Total for the County, 38.

PENDLETON COUNTY.

PENSIONERS UNDER THE ACT OF MARCH 18, 1818.

Belew, Solomon, private, ... Virginia line
December 28, 1818; May 26, 1818; $96. Age —.
Lawless, John, private, ... Virginia line
February 16, 1819; May 29, 1818; $96. Age 84.
Love, Charles, private, ... Virginia line
September 16, 1819; June 15, 1818; $96. Age 67.
Mountjoy, John, captain, ... Virginia line
November 6, 1819; June 15, 1818; $240. Age 77.

Mountjoy, Alvin, lieutenant, ... Virginia line
  March 14, 1820; June 15, 1818; $240. Age 73.
Mann, Benjamin, private, ... Virginia line
  March 14, 1820; June 15, 1818; $96. Age 77.
Wharton, William, private, ... Pennsylvania line
  April 21, 1819; September 3, 1818; $96. Age 87.
Wyatt, Henry, private, ... Virginia line
  November 25, 1819; October 19, 1819; $96. Age 67.
Williams, Benjamin, private, ... Virginia line
  May 13, 1819; June 16, 1818; $96. Age 70.

PENSIONERS UNDER THE ACT OF JUNE 7, 1832.
(Began March 4, 1831.)

Berry, Joel, private, ... Virginia militia
  August 26, 1833; $80. Age 81.
Colvin, Henry, private, ... Virginia line
  November 21, 1832; $80. Age 72.
Conner, Isaac, private, ... North Carolina militia
  January 9, 1833; $80. Age 77.
Cleaveland, William, private, ... Virginia militia
  August 22, 1833; $40. Age 77.
Cookendorfer, Michael, fifer, ... Maryland militia
  August 22, 1833; $88. Age 84.
Demoss, Peter, private, ... Virginia line
  October 14, 1832; $80. Age 82.
Glinn, John, private, ... Virginia line
  January 17, 1833; $40. Age 75.
Gibson, Alexander, private, ... Virginia line
  March 20, 1834; $80. Age 78.
Hammerly, James, private, ... Pennsylvania line
  December 28, 1833; $23.33. Age 73.
Hand, John, sergeant, ... Virginia line
  January 13, 1834; $120. Age 83. Died March 8, 1833.
Latimer, William, private, ... Virginia militia
  January 10, 1833; $36.66. Age 72.
Mullins, Gabriel, private, ... Virginia line
  August 26, 1833; $88. Age 76.
Pollard, Braxton, corporal of artillery, ... Virginia line
  March 29, 1833; $108; Age 76.
Pribble, James, private and sergeant, . . . Pennsylvania militia
  May 7, 1833; $80.33. Age 72.
Reardon, John, private, ... Virginia line
  October 10, 1833; $80. Age 82.
Ridinhour, John, private, ... North Carolina line
  April 25, 1834; $80. Age 77.

Taylor, Adam, private, ... Pennsylvania line
    March 7, 1834; $80. Age 70.
Taylor, Robert, private, ... Virginia militia
    June 16, 1834; $36.66. Age 76.
Yelton, James, private, ... Virginia militia
    August 26, 1833; $80. Age 86.

REVOLUTIONARY PENSIONERS LIVING IN THE COUNTY IN 1840.
(Collins, Vol. I, p. 8.)

Cordy, James, age 87.   Hammerty, John, age 70.
              Tilton, James, age 94.
              Total for the County, 31.

PERRY COUNTY.

PENSIONERS UNDER THE ACT OF MARCH 18, 1818.

Combs, John, private, ... Virginia line
    January 13, 1826; November 19, 1825; $96. Age 73.
Ellis, Charles, private, ... Massachusetts line
    July 1, 1829; May 14, 1829; $96. Age 72.
Hall, Anthony, private, ... Virginia line
    December 14, 1825; November 17, 1825; $96. Age 82.
Kelly, John, private, ... North Carolina line
    September 10, 1827; July 11, 1827; $96. Age 79.
McDaniel, George, private, ... North Carolina line
    December 19, 1823; October 23, 1823; $96. Age 86.
Mullins, Joshua, private, ... Virginia line
    January 20, 1832; January 20, 1832; $96. Age 76.
Polly, Edward, private, ... Virginia line
    February 15, 1828; February 10, 1828; $96. Age 76.

PENSIONERS UNDER THE ACT OF JUNE 7, 1832.
(Began March 4, 1831.)

Burns, Andrew, private, ... Virginia State troops
    November 15, 1833; $25.88. Age 76.
Bush, Drury, private of cavalry, ... Virginia line
    July 10, 1834; $100. Age 76.
Cordill, Stephen, private, ... North Carolina line
    November 7, 1833; $30. Age 71.
Cornett, William, private, ... Virginia line
    November 7, 1833; $40. Age 72.
Cordill, James, private, ... North Carolina line
    November 7, 1833; $20. Age 81.
Craft, Achilles, private, ... North Carolina line
    November 15, 1833; $46.66. Age 76.

Hammond, Peter, private, ... North Carolina line
    November 15, 1833; $36.66. Age 75.
Hagins, William, private, ... North Carolina line
    November 15, 1833; $50. Age 75.
Hurst, Henry, private, ... Virginia militia
    November 25, 1833; $36.66. Age 72.
Howard, James, private, ... Virginia line
    January 20, 1834; $80. Age 82.
Howard, Thomas, private, ... Virginia line
    January 20, 1834; $80. Age 84.
Harwell, Andrew, private, ... Virginia line
    January 20, 1834; $33.33. Age —.
Stidham, Samuel, private, ... North Carolina militia
    January 19, 1833; $30. Age 87.
Turner, Roger, private, ... North Carolina militia
    January 19, 1833; $53.33. Age —.
Watkins, Thomas, private, ... North Carolina line
    May 29, 1834; $60. Age 83.

REVOLUTIONARY PENSIONERS LIVING IN THE COUNTY IN 1840.
(Collins, Vol. I, p. 8.)

Candill, James, age 90.   Justice, Simon, age 87.
Croft, Archelaus, age 81.   Polly, Edmund, age 84.
Total for the County, 26.

PIKE COUNTY.

PENSIONER UNDER THE ACT OF MARCH 18, 1818.

Dailey, Dennis, private, ... Virginia line
    April 22, 1819; August 11, 1818; $96. Age 73.

PENSIONERS UNDER THE ACT OF JUNE 7, 1832.

Adkinson, James, private, ... Virginia line
    March 21, 1834; $40. Age 86.
Ford, Joseph, private, ... North Carolina line
    March 27, 1834; $79.63. Age 77.
Jackson, James, private, ... North Carolina line
    May 21, 1834; $80. Age 77.
Stipp, Moses, private, ... South Carolina line
    March 6, 1834; $63.10. Age 77.

REVOLUTIONARY PENSIONER LIVING IN THE COUNTY IN 1840.
(Collins, Vol. I, p. 8.)

Trant, Christian, age 87.
Total for the County, 6.

PULASKI COUNTY.

Newell, Samuel, lieutenant, ... Campbell's regiment
January 6, 1817; March 2, 1811; $96. Invalid pensioner. Trans-
ferred from Tennessee.

PENSIONERS UNDER THE ACT OF MARCH 18, 1818.

Aldridge, Francis, private, ... North Carolina line
February 25, 1832; December 24, 1831; $96. Age 71.
Beakman, Michael, private, ... South Carolina line
Dec. 14, 1819; Oct. 21, 1818; $96. Age 82. Died Sept. 9, 1831.
Blackledge, Ichabod, private, ... New Jersey line
Jan. 12, 1821; April 27, 1818; $96. Age 90. Died June 15, 1829.
Edwards, John, drummer, ... Pennsylvania line
August 22, 1820; April 30, 1818; $96. Age 60.
Girdler, James, private, ... Pennsylvania line
February 2, 1819; April 30, 1818; $96. Age 78.
Hansford, William, private, ... Virginia line
December 14, 1819; October 30, 1818; $96. Age 80.
Heath, William, private, ... North Carolina line
March 15, 1824; March 1, 1823; $96. Age 65. Died July 16, 1829.
Lee, John, private, ... Virginia line
December 14, 1819; October 30, 1818; $96. Age 73.
Perry, John, private, ... Virginia line
April 5, 1820; August 31, 1818; $96. Age 83.
Rainey, James, private, ... North Carolina line
February 2, 1819; October 29, 1818; $96. Age 68.
Reagan, Michael, private, ... Pennsylvania line
April 17, 1820; October 29, 1818; $96. Age 74.
Seaton, Thomas, private, ... Virginia line
February 1, 1819; July 27, 1818; $96. Age 82. Died Feb. 11, 1831.
Sayers, Robert, private, ... Virginia line
March 15, 1824; September 1, 1823; $96. Age 82.
Young, Michael, private, ... North Carolina line
Sept. 16, 1831; Aug. 26, 1831; $96. Age 78. Died Aug. 24, 1833.

PENSIONERS UNDER THE ACT OF JUNE 7, 1832.
(Began March 4, 1831.)

Anderson, Robert, private, ... Virginia line
September 5, 1833; $49.76. Age 71.
Allen, sr., Samuel, private, ... Virginia militia
September 24, 1833; $50. Age 78.
Burter, Michael, private of inf. and cav., . Virginia State troops
September 24, 1833; $83.57. Age 76.

Barron, William, private, ... North Carolina State troops
     October 11, 1833; $33.33. Age 72.

Baugh, Henry, private, ... North Carolina militia
     October 18, 1833; $21.55. Age 72.

Barker, John, private, ... Virginia line
     October 18, 1833; $80. Age 72.

Barron, John, private, ... Virginia militia
     July 18, 1834; $26.66. Age 84.

Dogan, Lovel H., private, ... Virginia State troops
     October 18, 1833; $20. Age 70.

Evans, John, sergeant, ... New Jersey line
     May 13, 1833; $120. Age 77.

Earp, Joseph, private, ... Virginia militia
     December 21, 1833; $20. Age 73.

Goggin, Richard, private, ... Virginia militia
     December 3, 1832; $40. Age 72.

Hamilton, James, private, ... Virginia line
     September 5, 1833; $40. Age 77.

Hays, William, private, ... Virginia militia
     September 24, 1833; $31.66. Age 79.

Horrell, James, private, ... Virginia militia
     October 11, 1833; $37.66 Age 75.

Martin, Moses, drummer, ... North Carolina militia
     August 17, 1833; $31.77. Age 79.

Murray, Barnabas, private, ... North Carolina militia
     August 17, 1833; $40. Age 77.

McAlister, Joseph, private, ... Pennsylvania militia
     July 18, 1834 ; $80. Age 79. Died July 22, 1833.

Newell, sr., Samuel, sergeant and lieutenant, . . Virginia militia
     September 11, 1833; $231.93. Age 79.

Newby, John, private, ... Virginia line
     December 2, 1833; December 2, 1833; $100. Age 75.

Owens, William, private and sergeant, ... Virginia militia
     February 14, 1834; $100. Age 83.

Roper, David, private, ... Virginia line
     October 31, 1833; $40. Age 78.

Swinney, William, private, ... North Carolina militia
     $26.66. Age 73.

Turpin, Martin, private, ... Virginia militia
     October 21, 1833; $30. Age 74.

Trimble, William, private of infantry and cavalry, . Virginia line
     December 2, 1833; $32.77. Age 72.

Tomlinson, Nathaniel, private, ... Virginia militia
     December 21, 1833; $20. Age 86.

Tarter, Peter, private, ... North Carolina line
    May 6, 1834 ; $20. Age 76.
Wilson, John, private, ... Virginia line
    September 5, 1833 ; $33.15. Age 78.

REVOLUTIONARY PENSIONER LIVING IN THE COUNTY IN 1840.
(Collins, Vol. I, p. 8.)

Decker, George, age 80.
Total for the County, 43.

ROCKCASTLE COUNTY.

PENSIONER UNDER THE EARLY INVALID PENSION ACTS.

Dysart, James, captain, ... Revolutionary army
    December 18, 1806 ; $120.

PENSIONERS UNDER THE ACT OF MARCH 18, 1818.

Abney, William, private, ... Virginia line
    October 25, 1818 ; September 7, 1818 ; $96. Age 77.
Chasteen, James, private, ... Virginia line
    October 25, 1819 ; September 7, 1818 ; $96. Age 73.
Hamm, John, private, ... Virginia line
    February 23, 1826 ; February 23, 1826 ; $96. Age 76.
Moore, William, private, ... Virginia line
    December 22, 1833 ; July 2, 1823 ; $96. Age 78.
Owsley, sr., Thomas, private, ... Virginia line
    March 5, 1819 ; Nov. 25, 1818 ; $96. Age 74. Died Nov. 3, 1825.
Pruett, John, private, ... Virginia line
    September 6, 1830 ; September 4, 1830 ; $96. Age 80.
Stevens, James, private, ... Virginia line
    November 6, 1819 ; June 17, 1819 ; $96. Age 81.

PENSIONERS UNDER THE ACT OF JUNE 7, 1832.
(Began March 4, 1831.)

Anderson, James, private, ... Virginia line
    March 1, 1833 ; $80. Age 72.
Bates, Humphrey, private, ... North Carolina militia
    August 6, 1833 ; $20. Age 69.
Craig, William, private, ... Virginia militia
    August 6, 1833 ; $20. Age 72.
Cash, William, private, ... Virginia militia
    May 23, 1824 ; $40. Age 81.
Denny, Elijah, private, ... North Carolina line
    August 22, 1833 ; $60. Age 72.

Frost, Micajah, private, ... North Carolina militia.
 August 6, 1833; $33.33. Age 72.
Faris, Moses, private, ... Virginia militia
 July 16, 1834; $40. Age 75.
Gentry, Richard, private, ... South Carolina line
 January 19, 1833; $43.33. Age 79.
Gadd, Thomas, private, ... Maryland militia
 May 30, 1833; $20. Age 74.
Haggard, Henry, private, ... Virginia militia
 May 11, 1833; $40. Age 76.
Houk, Nicholas, private, ... North Carolina militia
 November 12, 1833; $20. Age 70.
Harlew, George, private, ... Virginia line
 December 31, 1833; $50. Age 78.
Johnson, Thomas, private, ... Virginia militia
 July 10, 1834; $20. Age 70.
Lawrence, William, private, ... Virginia militia
 June 11, 1834; $58.76. Age 70.
Proctor, George, private, ... Virginia militia
 October 31, 1833; $20. Age 92.
Pew, Reuben, private, ... New Jersey line
 December 31, 1833; $80. Age 77.
Pumphrey, Peter, private, ... Virginia State troops
 January 8, 1834; $80. Age 80.
Roberts, Mourning, private, ... Virginia militia
 August 9, 1833; $33.33. Age 76.
Scott, Jessie, private, ... North Carolina militia
 May 30, 1833; $40. Age 72.
Taylor, William, private, ... Virginia militia
 January 16, 1833; $20. Age —
Woodall, Charles, private, ... Virginia militia
 January 5, 1833; $40. Age —.
Woodall, Jesse, sergeant and private, ... Maryland line
 August 17, 1833; $21.26. Age 84.

PENSIONER UNDER THE ACT OF MAY 15, 1828.

Ramsey, Francis, dragoon, ... Lee's legion
 December 24, 1830; March 3, 1826; $100.

REVOLUTIONARY PENSIONERS LIVING IN THE COUNTY IN 1840.
(Collins, Vol. I, p. 8.)

Harlow, George, age 89. Stevens, Jacob, age 84.
Sigmon, George, age 83. Sweeney, William, age 80.
Total for the County, 35.

RUSSELL COUNTY.

PENSIONER UNDER THE ACT OF MARCH 18, 1818.

Miller, John, private, ... Pennsylvania line
  Sept. 18, 1819; Sept. 15, 1818; $96. Age —. Died August 23, 1825.

PENSIONERS UNDER THE ACT OF JUNE 7, 1832.
(Began March 4, 1832.)

Cape, John, lieutenant, ... Virginia line
  June 8, 1834; $320. Age 89.

Conn, James, private, ... North Carolina line
  March 14, 1834; $80. Age 83.

Goodman, Ansel, private, ... Virginia line
  January 5, 1833; $70. Age 82.

Graves, Thomas, private, ... Virginia militia
  August 17, 1833; $30. Age 71.

George, Jordan, private, ... Virginia militia
  October 18, 1833; $69.33. Age 70.

Hall, John, private, ... North Carolina line
  September 24, 1833; $33.33. Age 75.

Haynes, sr., James, ... Virginia line
  October 18, 1833; $80. Age 82.

Law, Henry, private, ... Virginia militia
  December 2, 1833; $23.33. Age 75.

Perryman, William, private, ... Virginia militia
  April 12, 1833; $22.50. Age 75.

Payne, Ledford, private, ... Virginia line
  September 9, 1833; $80. Age 72.

Polly, John, private, ... Virginia militia
  January 23, 1834; $30. Age 73.

Robertson, Matthew, private, ... North Carolina line
  June 5, 1833; $80. Age 73.

Smith, William, private, ... Virginia militia
  October 21, 1833; $30. Age 78.

Sharp, Isham, private, ... North Carolina militia
  June 17, 1834; $40. Age 79.

Underdoun, Stephen, private, ... North Carolina line
  October 21, 1833; $33.33. Age 78.

Total for the County, 16.

SCOTT COUNTY.

PENSIONER UNDER THE ACT OF MAY 15, 1828.

Mothershead, Nathaniel, private, ... Revolutionary army
  January 23, 1830.

PENSIONERS UNDER THE ACT OF MARCH 18, 1818.

Atkins, Alexander, private, ... Virginia line
    January 6, 1819; April 24, 1818; $96. Age 67.
Brown, Henry, private, ... Virginia Continental line
    Nov. 17, 1818; April 13, 1818; $96. Age 83. Died Dec. 15, 1830.
Bennett, Richard, private, ... Virginia line
    Nov. 27, 1819; June 1, 1818; $96. Age 71. Died May 24, 1829.
Chism, George, private, ... Continental line
    Nov. 17, 1818; April 15, 1818; $96. Age 74. Died Dec. 13, 1830.
Carothers, Thomas, private, ... North Carolina line
    January 12, 1819; September 2, 1818; $96. Age 67.
Driver, Francis, private, ... Virginia line
    February 9, 1820; June 3, 1818; $96. Age 58.
Erwin, Charles, private, ... Virginia line
    Nov. 17, 1818; May 11, 1818; $96. Age 67. Died March 9, 1820.
Ewing, Will, private, ... Pennsylvania line
    December 7, 1822; March 8, 1821; $96. Age 80. Died Jan. 23, 1823.
Fargeson, Larkin, private, ... Virginia line
    January 6, 1819; April 24, 1818; $96. Age 60.
Garrett, John, private, ... Virginia line
    September 23, 1818; August 3, 1818; $96. Age 78.
Green, Charles, dragoon, ... Virginia line
    September 5, 1818; May 5, 1818; $96. Age —.
Green, John, private, ... Pennsylvania line
    November 17, 1818; May 9, 1818; $96. Age 66. Died Feb. 12, 1830.
Guill, John, private, ... Virginia line
    December 23, 1818; October 19, 1818; $96. Age 76.
Hubbell, William, lieutenant, ... New York line
    May 28, 1819; April 27, 1818; $240. Age 63.
Haley, Morris, private, ... Pennsylvania line
    February 13, 1819; June 17, 1818; $96. Age 76. Died May 19, 1822.
James, Joseph, private, ... Virginia line
    December 23, 1818; September 7, 1818; $96. Age 68.
Johnson, Charles, ... Maryland line
    January 6, 1819; April 27, 1818; $96. Age 84.
Johnson, John, ensign, ... South Carolina line
    February 13, 1819; April 6, 1818; $240. Age 76. Died May 27, 1825.
Kirley, John, private, ... Virginia line
    July 15, 1819; May 9, 1819; $96. Age 75.
Kenney, John (Edward D.), private, ... Pennsylvania line
    August 26, 1828; July 24, 1828; $96. Age 81.
Landrum, Thomas, private, ...
    January 27, 1819; May 1, 1818; $96. Age 61.

McClain (McLean), Daniel, private, ... Pennsylvania line
February 9, 1820; Sept. 8, 1819; $96. Age 72. Died June 6, 1821.

McCormick, Hugh, private, ... Pennsylvania line
February 13, 1819; April 24, 1818; $96. Age 65. Died May 22, 1822.

March, Samuel, private, ... New Jersey line
January 6, 1819; May 18, 1818; $96. Age 96.

Milligan, John, private, ... Virginia line
February 12, 1819; July 16, 1818; $96. Age 86. Died Aug. 25, 1824.

McHatton, John, captain, ... Pennsylvania line
February 4, 1828; Jan. 12, 1828; $240. Age 100. Died Feb. 21, 1831.

Neal, Charles, private, ... Virginia line
February 13, 1819; April 22, 1818; $96. Age 69. Died Aug. 27, 1831.

Patterson, John, private, ... New Hampshire line
June 2, 1819; May 20, 1818; $96. Age 67.

Paslay, Thomas, private, ... Virginia line
February 27, 1830; February 27, 1830; $96. Age 73.

Price, William, private, ... Virginia line
January 4, 1831; Jan. 3, 1831; $96. Age 83. Died Sept. 3, 1831.

Smith, Gerard, private, ... Maryland line
June 6, 1818; January 16, 1819; $96. Age 64.

Tucker, John, private, ... North Carolina line
November 17, 1818; April 17, 1818; $96. Age 81.

Thompson, Robert, musician, ... Delaware line
June 28, 1820; April 25, 1818; $96. Age 78. Died July 9, 1826.

Vance, Joseph, private, ... Virginia line
September 23, 1818; August 1, 1818; $96. Age 79.

West, Thomas, private, ... Virginia line
June 2, 1819; July 17, 1818; $96. Age 65. Died Jan. 9, 1820.

Wright, James, private, ... Virginia line
October 8, 1818; April 18, 1818; $96. Age —.

Wells, Samuel, private, ... Virginia line
March 2, 1829; Feb. 19, 1829; $96. Age 79. Died Nov. 20, 1830.

Young, Nathan, private, ... Virginia line
February 13, 1819; May 21, 1818; $96. Age 108.

PENSIONERS UNDER THE ACT OF JUNE 7, 1832.
(Began March 4, 1831.)

Burbridge, George, private, ... Virginia militia
September 18, 1832; $20. Age 72.

Burch, Joseph, private, ... Virginia militia
October 5, 1832; $26.66. Age 71.

Brown, Thomas, private and lieutenant, . Virginia State troops
November 2, 1832; $54.98. Age 89.

Berkley, John, private, ... Virginia militia
January 25, 1833; $20. Age 72.

Barnhill, Samuel, private, ... Pennsylvania militia
 January 9, 1833; $43.33. Age 74.
Beatty, William, private, ... Virginia militia
 December 19, 1832; $30. Age 72.
Bryan, Daniel, private, ... North Carolina militia
 September 25, 1833; $59.76. Age 76.
Chisham, James, private, ... Virginia militia
 October 5, 1832; $23.33. Age 66.
Campbell, John, private, ... Maryland line
 June 10, 1833; $23.33. Age 73.
Downing, Francis, ... Maryland militia
 September 17, 1832; $20. Age 88.
Dabney, John O., private, ... Virginia militia
 January 9, 1833; $30. Age 71.
Fugate, Randall F., private, ... Virginia militia
 January 9, 1833; $80. Age 72.
Gibson, John, private, ... Virginia volunteers
 September 17, 1832; $20. Age 73.
Gibbs, Julius, private, ... Virginia line
 October 5, 1832; $60. Age 81.
Garth, John, private, ... Virginia militia
 October 5, 1832; $33.33. Age 72.
Gatewood, John, private, ... Virginia militia
 January 9, 1833; $20. Age 69.
Greenwell, Bennett, private, ... Maryland militia
 February 28, 1833; $40. Age 72.
Gano, Daniel, captain and lieutenant, ... New York line
 July 25, 1832; $400. Age 76.
Hiles, John, private, ... Virginia militia
 October 5, 1832; $20. Age 72.
Hurst, Henry, private, ... Virginia line
 June 5, 1833; $30. Age 79.
Jacobs, John, private, ... Virginia line
 June 10, 1833; $100. Age 71.
Jones, James, private, ... Pennsylvania line
 December 10, 1833; $40. Age 68.
Kerr, David, private, ... South Carolina line
 October 5, 1832; $80. Age 77.
Landrum, Thomas, private, ... Virginia line
 September 29, 1832; $80. Age 82.
Lackland, John, private, ... Virginia militia
 January 9, 1833; $20. Age 79.
Leathers, Paul, sergeant, ... Virginia line
 February 11, 1833; $120. Age 88.

McCrosky, James, private, ... Virginia militia
    January 9, 1833; $60. Age 74.

Miller, John, private, ... Pennsylvania line
    May 16, 1833; $80. Age —.

Minor, Jeremiah, private, ... Pennsylvania militia
    October 14, 1833; $30. Age 88.

Officer, James, private, ... Pennsylvania militia
    October 5, 1832; $26.66. Age 75.

Osborn, Bennett, private and lieutenant, . . South Carolina line
    $62.66. Age 70.

Powers, Jeremiah, private, ... Virginia militia
    January 9, 1833; $80. Age 80.

Price, Isaac, private, ... New Jersey line
    April 9, 1833; $80. Age 74.

Robinson, Jonathan, captain, ... Pennsylvania line
    December 5, 1832; $480. Age 82.

Slap, Achilles, private, ... Virginia line
    October 5, 1832; $80. Age 79.

Scruggs, William, private, ... Virginia line
    October 5, 1832; $40. Age —.

Suggett, John, private, ... Virginia militia
    December 3, 1832; $40. Age 83.

Sharp, John, private, ... Virginia militia
    November 25, 1833; $20. Age 71.

Stewart, Charles, sergeant, ... Virginia militia
    March 13, 1834; $120. Age 81.

Twyman, James, private, ... Virginia militia
    January 9, 1833; $23.33. Age —.

Vinzant, John, private, ... Pennsylvania line
    January 25, 1833; $70. Age 80.

PENSIONER UNDER THE ACT OF MAY 15, 1828.

Buford, Abraham, colonel, ... Virginia line
    September 8, 1828; March 3, 1826; $600. Died June 29, 1833.

REVOLUTIONARY PENSIONERS LIVING IN THE COUNTY IN 1840.
(Collins, Vol. I, pp. 8, 9.)

Bamhill, Samuel, age 82.   Gresham, Kindness (widow)
Dooley, James, age 106.   age 97.
Hill, Herman, age 87.   Tarlton, Eleanor (wid.), age 78.

Total for the County, 86.

SHELBY COUNTY.

PENSIONERS UNDER THE ACT OF MARCH 18, 1818.

Alvis, Jesse, private, ... Virginia line
September 16, 1819; June 24, 1819; $96. Age 77.

Ballew, Charles, private, ... Virginia line
Sept. 29, 1819; May 28, 1818; $96. Age 67. Died Sept. 13, 1818.

Callett, John, private, ... Virginia line
June 2, 1819; Sept. 23, 1818; $96. Age 73. Died Sept. 21, 1830.

Chapman, Amos, sergeant, ... Pennsylvania line
April 20, 1820; May 18, 1818; $96. Age 75. Died Feb. 17, 1820.

Dougherty or Doherty, John, private, ... Virginia line
September 6, 1820; June 30, 1820; $96. Age 78.

Fitzsimmons, Thomas, private, ... Virginia line
September 24, 1819; May 23, 1818; $96. Age 61.

Hartley, Daniel, private, ... Morgan's rifle regiment
December 24, 1819; June 25, 1818; $96. Age 80.

Johnson, 1st, James, private, ... Virginia line
January 6, 1819; May 20, 1818; $96. Age 80.

Johnson, 2d, James, private, ... Virginia line
October 18, 1821; January 13, 1820; $96. Age 77.

Morgan, William, private, ... Virginia line
April 20, 1820; November 1, 1819; $96. Age 63.

Mullikin, John, private, ... Virginia line
June 26, 1822; May 18, 1818; $96. Age 84.

Petit, Thomas, private, ... Maryland line
November 29, 1821; April 17, 1820; $60. Age 70.

Randolph, Henry, private, ... Pennsylvania line
September 7, 1820; September 28, 1819; $96. Age 83.

Stratton, Seth, private, ... Virginia line
February 5, 1819; June 20, 1818; $96. Age 61.

Sampson, Isaac, private, ... North Carolina line
April 8, 1825; July 20, 1824; $96. Age 69. Died April 21, 1829.

Sacrey, James, private, ... Virginia line
December 8, 1830; December 7, 1830; $96. Age 79.

Wentworth, Levi, private, ... Connecticut line
October 13, 1818; May 11, 1818; $96. Age 72.

Wayland, Joshua, private, ... Virginia line
December 3, 1819; April 5, 1819; $96. Age 60.

Yager, Samuel, private, ... Virginia line
April 20, 1820; July 1, 1819; $96. Age 82.

PENSIONERS UNDER THE ACT OF JUNE 7, 1832.
(Began March 4, 1831.)

Blomkenbaker, Nicholas, private, ... Virginia line
October 24, 1832; $63.33. Age 75.

Blackmore, John, private, ... Virginia militia
    November 3, 1832; $23.33. Age 72.

Brown, William, private, ... Virginia line
    December 26, 1832; $31.66. Age 75.

Baskett, Martin, private, ... Virginia militia
    September 23, 1832; $23.33. Age 73.

Brevard, Benjamin, private, ... North Carolina militia
    November 29, 1833; $20. Age 73.

Blackwell, John, private, ... Virginia militia
    January 16, 1834; $46.66. Age 76.

Bryant, Peter, private, ... Virginia line
    November 29, 1833; $60. Age 73. Died December 9, 1833.

Brumback, Peter, private, ... Virginia line
    June 10, 1832; $100. Age 80.

Christie, James, private, ... Virginia militia
    February 11, 1833; $56. Age 76.

Carnine, Peter, sergeant, ... New Jersey line
    September 24, 1833; $120. Age 82.

Casey, Charles, private, ... Virginia militia
    February 7, 1834; $20. Age 85.

Conyers, Benjamin, private, ... Virginia militia
    May 23, 1834; $40. Age 74.

Clark, Obadiah, private and corporal, . . North Carolina militia
    May 27, 1834; $40. Age 78.

Farra, Samuel, private, ... Pennsylvania militia
    May 16, 1833; $20. Age 85.

Ford, Elisha, private, ... South Carolina line
    September 23, 1833; $80. Age 76.

French, William, private, ... Virginia militia
    June 6, 1834; $40. Age 73.

Franklin, James M., private, ... North Carolina line
    January 9, 1834; $80. Age 71.

Force (Foree?), Joseph, private, ... Virginia militia
    May 23, 1834; $28.33. Age 92.

Gale, Robert F., private, ... Virginia militia
    August 3, 1833; $60. Age 68.

Grigsby, Benjamin, private, ... Pennsylvania militia
    September 23, 1833; $23.33. Age 85.

Gibson, Elisha, private, ... Virginia militia
    July 10, 1834; $20. Age 86.

Graves, Edmund, private, ... North Carolina line
    May 27, 1834; $40. Age 72.

Hawkins, George, private, ... Virginia line
    October 26, 1832; $80. Age 84.

Holland, James M., sergeant, ... Virginia militia
$38.33. Age 78.
Higgason, Thomas, sergeant, ... Virginia militia
$55.33. Age 73.
Heppard, William, private, ... New Jersey militia
$40. Age 73.
Herring, George, private, ... Virginia militia
$20. Age 76.
Hickman, James, private, ... Virginia militia
$20. Age 73.
Johnson, Archibald, private, ... Virginia militia
$20. Age 83.
Kelso, Thomas, private, ... Maryland militia
$30. Age 70.
Kendricks, William, sergeant, ... Virginia militia
$35. Age 87.
Knox, John, private, ... Delaware militia
February 11, 1832; $100. Age 75.
Lemaster, Hugh, private, ... Virginia line
February 7, 1834; $30. Age 83.
Maddox, Wilson, private, ... Virginia militia
February 11, 1833; $80. Age 79.
McCalister, Daniel, private, ... Virginia militia
May 29, 1833; $36.66. Age 74.
McCleland, Daniel, captain, ... North Carolina line
July 15, 1833; $480. Age 82.
Moore, Abraham, private, ... Virginia militia
September 28, 1833; $51.33. Age 77.
Mitchell, Charles, private, ... Virginia militia
January 20, 1834; $23.33. Age 75.
Morse, Alexander, private, ... Virginia militia
April 25, 1834; $30.22. Age —.
Neal, Micajah, private, ... Virginia line
January 21, 1834; $80. Age 81.
Paris, Robert, private, ... Virginia line
January 4, 1834; $80. Age 84.
Rowe, James, private of artillery, ... Virginia line
October 21, 1832; $100. Age 75.
Riley, John, private, lieutenant, and ensign, . . . Virginia line
October 26, 1832; $26.66. Age 78.
Roberts, Benjamin, captain, ... Virginia line
November 3, 1832; $480. Age 84.
Ragsdale, Godfrey, sergeant of cavalry, ... Virginia line
January 22, 1833; $180. Age 72.

Richards, Joshua, private, ... Virginia militia
December 2, 1833; $25. Age 71.
Rayzor, Paul, private, ... Virginia State troops
$20. Age 83.
Stout, Reuben, private, ... Virginia line
March 18, 1833; $60. Age 73.
Sanders, Reuben, private, ... Virginia militia
September 23, 1833; $30. Age 75.
Smith, Henry, private, ... Maryland militia
July 21, 1834; $20. Age 75.
Thompson, Evan, sergeant, ... South Carolina line
April 25, 1833; $45. Age 71.
Tinsley, William, private, ... Virginia militia
October 21, 1833; $20. Age 71.
Thompson, Joseph, private, ... Virginia militia
January 4, 1834; $20. Age 71.
Thompson, John, private, ... North Carolina militia
January 7, 1834; $52.50. Age 79.
Travis, James, private, ... Virginia militia
June 18, 1834; $80. Age —.
Van Swearingen, ——, lieutenant, ... Pennsylvania line
October 26, 1832; $80. Age 80.
Watts, Peter, private, ... North Carolina line
August 21, 1833; $40. Age 78.
Washburn, Benjamin, private, ... Virginia line
January 21, 1833; $80. Age —.
Woolfolk, Robert, private, ... Virginia line
January 19, 1833; $60. Age —.
Wilcoxen, Daniel, lieutenant, ... North Carolina line
March 2, 1833; $120. Age —.
Wiley, Henry, private, ... North Carolina militia
May 26, 1834; $40. Age 80.

PENSIONERS UNDER THE ACT OF MAY 15, 1828.
(Began March 3, 1826.)

Holley, Samuel, private, second regiment, . . . New York line
September 1, 1828; $80.
Jones, Thomas, dragoon, ... White's dragoons
September 5, 1828; $100.
Knight, John, surgeon, second regiment, ... Virginia line
December 18, 1828; $480.
Long, William, corporal, tenth regiment, . . North Carolina line
$88.
Rucker, Elliott, lieutenant, ... Gibson's Virginia regiment
December 11, 1830; $320.
Winlock, Joseph, lieutenant, ... Gibson's Virginia regiment
July 25, 1828; $320.

REVOLUTIONARY PENSIONERS LIVING IN THE COUNTY IN 1840.
(Collins, Vol. I, p. 9.)

Ballard, Bland W., age 81.   Fearson, Meshack, age 86.

Blankenbaker, Nicholas,   Reeves, Joseph, age 73.

age 82.   Reily, John, age 79.

Burke, Samuel, age 84.   Davis, Nancy (widow), age 81.

Total for the County, 93.

SIMPSON COUNTY.

PENSIONERS UNDER THE ACT OF JUNE 7, 1832.
(Began March 4, 1831.)

Breedlove, William, private, ... Virginia line
    September 26, 1833; $70. Age 72.

Cox, Solomon, private, ... North Carolina militia
    February 14, 1834; $40. Age 82.

Dickey, Ebenezer, private, ... North Carolina State troops
    January 28, 1833; $20. Age 72.

Hall, Robert, private, ... South Carolina line
    October 1, 1833; $46.66. Age 71.

Hay, Thomas, private, ... Virginia militia
    July 18, 1834; $20. Age 71.

Hickman, John, private, ... North Carolina line
    December 30, 1833; $40. Age 72.

Kelly, John, private, ... Virginia line
    August 30, 1832; $80. Age 72.

Lowe, William, ... North Carolina militia
    March 27, 1833; $26.66. Age 79.

McClanahan, Thomas, private, ... Virginia line
    April 25, 1833; $80. Age 80.

Roper, James, private, ... North Carolina line
    May 29, 1833; $66.66. Age 89.

Williams, James, private, ... Virginia militia
    July 10, 1833; $26.66. Age 78.

Williams, John, private, ... North Carolina line
    January 28, 1834; $80. Age 75.

REVOLUTIONARY PENSIONERS LIVING IN THE COUNTY IN 1840.
(Collins, Vol. I, p. 9.)

Cooper, Layton, age 82.   Pearce, George, age 85.

Moore, James, age 84.   West, William, age 87.

Total for the County, 16.

SPENCER COUNTY.

PENSIONERS UNDER THE ACT OF MARCH 18, 1818.

Maffitt, William, private, ... Virginia line
    January 29, 1819; August 14, 1818; $96. Age 79.

McMasters, Michael, private, ... Virginia line
    December 30, 1828; December 9, 1828; $96. Age 84.

PENSIONERS UNDER THE ACT OF JUNE 7, 1832.
(Began March 4, 1831.)

Anderson, John, private, ... Virginia militia
    March 2, 1833; $30. Age 77.

Bridwell, Simon, private, ... Virginia line
    January 26, 1833; $40. Age 78.

Barr, John, private, ... Pennsylvania line
    September 26, 1833; $80. Age 78.

Brown, Joseph, private, ... Pennsylvania State troops
    January 8, 1834; $23.33. Age 79.

Crafton, Anthony, private, ... Virginia militia
    February 16, 1833; $20. Age 87.

Davis, John, private, ... Pennsylvania militia
    March 2, 1833; $53.33. Age 81.

Gregory, Spittsby, sergeant, ... Virginia line
    December 8, 1832; $120. Age 77.

Gray, Joseph, sergeant, ... Virginia militia
    February 11, 1833; $30. Age 80.

Heady, Jacob, private, ... North Carolina line
    October 18, 1833; $30. Age 84.

Hugh, Moses, private, ... New Jersey militia
    February 19, 1834; $20. Age 75.

Murphy, Leander, private, ... Virginia line
    December 19, 1832; $80. Age 72.

Miller, Edward, private, ... Virginia militia
    February 22, 1833; $40. Age 83.

Pittinger, Abraham, private, ... Virginia line
    December 19, 1832; $40. Age 83.

Roberts, Abner, private, ... Virginia militia
    January 15, 1833; $23.33. Age 92.

Ringo, John, private, ... Virginia line
    January 26, 1833; $80. Age 73.

Reasor, Michael, private, ... Virginia militia
    March 2, 1833; $60. Age 74.

Stone, Bryant, private, ... Virginia line
    December 19, 1832; $80. Age —.

Strange, John, private, ... Virginia militia
  March 1, 1833; $30. Age 75.
Stout, Elijah, private, ... Virginia militia
  February 7, 1834; $26.66. Age 91.
Taylor, Philip W., private, ... Virginia State troops
  February 23, 1833; $20. Age —.
Walden, James, private, ... Virginia line
  July 15, 1833; $80. Age 72.
Watson, Joseph, private, ... Virginia line
  January 26, 1833; $73.33. Age —.
Womack, Massanello, sergeant, ... Virginia State troops
  February 21, 1833; $120. Age 83.
Weeks, James, private, ... Virginia militia
  December 7, 1833; $20. Age 85.
Young, Joseph, private, ... Pennsylvania line
  $62.78. Age 72.

PENSIONERS UNDER THE ACT OF MAY 15, 1828.
(Began March 3, 1826.)

Brittain, Jeremiah, sergeant, first regiment, . . . New Jersey line
  December 10, 1828; $120. Died May 20, 1833.
Carter, Benjamin, sergeant, third regiment, . . New Jersey line
  December 30, 1830; $120.
Kerrick, Benjamin H., musician, sixth regiment, Maryland line
  November 29, 1828; $88.
Triplett, George, lieutenant, ... Gibson's Virginia regiment
  September 20, 1831; $320.

Total for the County, 31.

TODD COUNTY.

Acock or Aycock, Robert, private, ... North Carolina line
  June 3, 1819; May 21, 1818; $96. Age 80.
McAlister, John, private, ... North Carolina line
  May 5, 1819; July 21, 1818; $96. Age 71. Died Nov. 17, 1827.

PENSIONERS UNDER THE ACT OF JUNE 7, 1832.
(Began March 4, 1831.)

Boyd, Henry, private, ... Virginia militia
  January 13, 1834; $80. Age 75.
Flack, 1st, James, private, ... North Carolina State troops
  August 22, 1833; $36.66. Age 72.
Gillispie, John, private, ... South Carolina line
  April 10, 1833; $66.96. Age 71.
Gibson, George, private, ... Virginia line
  August 21, 1833; $26.66. Age 69.

Gordon, Samuel, sergeant, ... South Carolina line
 November 15, 1833; $115. Age 72.
Harris, Overton, private, ... Virginia militia
 December 20, 1833; $26.66. Age 73.
Lear, Conrad, private and trumpeter, ... Virginia line
 January 31, 1834; $100. Age 95.
Madison, Ambrose, private, ... Virginia line
 October 22, 1833; $75. Age 77.
Mahen, Henry, private, ... South Carolina line
 May 6, 1833; $80. Age 77.
Petree, sr., Peter, private, ... North Carolina militia
 December 10, 1832; $40. Age 70.
Parmel, Benjamin, private, ... Virginia militia
 October 18, 1833; $51.88. Age 79.
Porter, Ephraim, private, ... Maryland State troops
 February 7, 1834; $33.33. Age 73.
Shuffield or Sheffield, Ephraim, private, North Carolina militia
 October 31, 1833; $30. Age 79.
Sherrod, Robert, private, ... North Carolina militia
 December 2, 1833; $20. Age 74.
Thompson, Gideon, private, ... North Carolina line
 January 31, 1833; $33.55. Age —.
Woolridge, Josiah, private, ... Virginia line
 August 21, 1833; $40. Age 79.

PENSIONER UNDER THE ACT OF MAY 15, 1828.

Terry, Nathaniel, captain, tenth regiment, ... Virginia line
 December 13, 1828; March 3, 1826; $480.

REVOLUTIONARY PENSIONERS LIVING IN THE COUNTY IN 1840.
(Collins Vol. I, p. 9.)

Pannel, Benjamin, age 83.   Turner, William, age 85.
Smith, Jonathan, age 83.   Boone, Anna (widow), age 67.
Quarles, Elizabeth (widow), age 75.
Total for the County, 24.

TRIGG COUNTY.

PENSIONERS UNDER THE ACT OF MARCH 18, 1818.

Anderson, William, private, ... Virginia line
 July 11, 1821; January 28, 1820; $96. Age 78.
Betts, Peter, private, ... Lee's legion
 Sept. 5, 1820; Oct. 7, 1818; $96. Age 75. Died December 4, 1833.
Gow, Eleazor, private, ... South Carolina line
 Feb. 3, 1825; July 24, 1824; $96. Age 68. Died Feb. 14, 1830.

PENSIONERS UNDER THE ACT OF JUNE 7, 1832.

(Began March 4, 1831.)

Curtis, Russell, corporal, ... North Carolina militia
  May 11, 1833; $45. Age 77.
Cohoon, Joel, private, ... North Carolina militia
  December 24, 1833; $20. Age 71.
Ezell, Balaam, private, ... Virginia militia
  April 2, 1833; $23.33. Age 78.
Grasty, John, private, ... North Carolina line
  May 6, 1833; $80. Age 72. Died November 17, 1833.
Hallowell, Miles, private, ... North Carolina line
  October 18, 1833; $30. Age 73.
Humphreys, Absalom, private, ... South Carolina line
  October 18, 1833; $60. Age 74.
Johnson, William, private, ... North Carolina militia
  May 13, 1833; $22.50. Age 79.
Kennedy, Charles, private, ... New Jersey line
  January 26, 1833; $30. Age 71.
Mabry, John, private, ... North Carolina line
  December 11, 1832; $80. Age 70.
Smith, Philip, private, ... New Jersey militia
  December 9, 1833; $43.33. Age 74.

REVOLUTIONARY PENSIONER LIVING IN THE COUNTY IN 1840.

(Collins, Vol. I, p. 9.)

Barham, James, age 78.   Mayberry, sr., John, age 76.
  Total for the County, 15.

TRIMBLE COUNTY.

(Formed after 1835.)

REVOLUTIONARY PENSIONERS LIVING IN THE COUNTY IN 1840.

(Collins, Vol. I, p. 9.)

Gray, Isaac, age 66.   Morgan, Thomas, age 79.
Hardin, Thomas, age 81.   Prewitt, Joshua, age 77.
Logan, John, age 82.   Vanhorn, Samuel, age 86.
McIntosh, Thomas, age 83.   Wright, George, age 76.
          Younger, Kennard, age 85.
          Total for the County, 9.

UNION COUNTY.

PENSIONERS UNDER THE ACT OF MARCH 18, 1818.

Blackwell, Thomas, captain, ... Virginia line
  February 16, 1820; April 22, 1818; $240. Age 77.
Bayliss, William, lieutenant, ... Virginia line
  March 29, 1819; April 2, 1818; $240. Age 77.

PENSIONERS UNDER THE ACT OF JUNE 7, 1832.
(Began March 4, 1831.)

Anderson, Armstead, private, ... Virginia line
May 16, 1833; $30. Age 78.

Binger, Nicholas, private, ... Virginia line
October 30, 1832; $80. Age 73.

Curry, Edward, private, ... South Carolina line
March 27, 1834; $50. Age 84.

Floyd, Henry, private, ... Virginia militia
July 21, 1834; $20. Age 73.

Givens, William, private, ... North Carolina line
January 11, 1834; $20. Age 72.

Hammock, William, private, ... North Carolina line
April 14, 1834; $30. Age 74.

Morrison, James, sergeant and private, ... Virginia line
May 21, 1833; $51.66. Age 79.

Neil, James, private, ... North Carolina militia
April 21, 1834; $20. Age 80.

Pierson, John, private, ... Connecticut militia
December 9, 1833; $50. Age 71.

Richards, Lewis, sergeant, ... Virginia line
October 30, 1832; $120. Age 70.

Ray, John, private, ... Maryland militia
April 20, 1833; $43.33. Age 77.

Woodyard, Richard, private, ... Virginia line
December 9, 1833; $30. Age 80.

REVOLUTIONARY PENSIONER LIVING IN THE COUNTY IN 1840.
(Collins, Vol. I, p. 9.)

Davenport, A., age 81.

Total for the County, 15.

WARREN COUNTY.

PENSIONERS UNDER THE ACT OF MARCH 18, 1818.

Allen, Charles, private, ... Virginia line
October 11, 1819; May 30, 1818; $96. Age 83.

Bettersworth, Richard, sergeant, ... Virginia line
Dec. 19, 1820; Sept. 15, 1818; $96. Age 74. Died Nov. 9, 1824.

Brown, William, private, ... Virginia line
December 11, 1832; October 7, 1822; $96. Age 79.

Franklin, John, private, ... Virginia line
Dec. 18, 1821; June 1, 1818; $96. Age —. Died March 4, 1823.

Nabois, Nathan, private, ... Virginia line
    January 15, 1824; May 5, 1823; $96. Age 90.

Ragland, John, private, ... Maryland line
    January 8, 1828; February 5, 1827; $96. Age 78.

PENSIONERS UNDER THE ACT OF JUNE 7, 1832.

(Began March 4, 1831.)

Alley, Isaiah, private, ... Virginia militia
    March 27, 1833; $40. Age 84.

Bryant, Benjamin, private, ... Virginia militia
    October 22, 1832; $20. Age 85.

Byron, John, private, ... South Carolina militia
    January 28, 1834; $20. Age 67.

Billingsly, John, private, ... North Carolina militia
    January 28, 1834; $40. Age 81.

Clayton, Augustine, private of cav. and inf., Virginia State troops
    April 20, 1833; $90. Age 79.

Clasby, John, private, ... Virginia line
    August 9, 1833; August 9, 1833; $40. Age 74.

Carson, William, private, ... South Carolina militia
    August 17, 1833; $20. Age 73.

Cox, Phineas, private, ... Virginia State troops
    January 28, 1834; $53.33. Age 70.

Clark, Micajah, captain, ... North Carolina militia
    January 28, 1834; $313.33. Age 84.

Garrison, Samuel, private, ... North Carolina line
    November 6, 1832; $30. Age 71.

Grider, Henry, sergeant, ... Virginia line
    October 19, 1832; $51.16. Age 79.

Hays, William, private, ... North Carolina militia
    June 20, 1834; $40. Age 74.

Heavener, Christopher, private, ... Pennsylvania militia
    January 28, 1834; $20. Age 83.

Hillen, George, private, ... North Carolina line
    May 6, 1834; $80. Age 72.

Isbell, James, private, ... North Carolina militia
    August 21, 1833; $40. Age 74.

Kirby, Leonard T., private, ... Virginia line
    October 22, 1832; $36.66. Age 74.

Kirby, Jesse, private, ... Virginia line
    October 22, 1832; $32.22. Age 77.

Kelly, Beall, private, ... Virginia line
    October 22, 1832; $20. Age 76.

Martin, Gideon, private, ... Virginia militia
    October 22, 1832; $20. Age 102.

Millican, James, private, ... North Carolina line
April 12, 1833; $23.33. Age 74.

Moore, Hugh, lieutenant, ... Virginia line
March 25, 1833 ; $320. Age 84. Died October 24, 1833.

Pendleton, Benjamin, private, ... Virginia militia
May 6, 1833 ; $40. Age 83.

Sweeney, Moses, private, ... Virginia line
October 22, 1832 ; $26.66. Age 81.

Simpson, Hugh, private, ... Virginia line
April 12, 1833 ; $80. Age 73.

Stepnens, James, private, ... Virginia militia
November 23, 1833; $80. Age 75. Died September 3, 1832.

Talbott, Thomas, private, ... Virginia line
June 28, 1834 ; $20. Age 72.

Watson, Evan T., private, ... Virginia line
October 31, 1833; $23.33. Age 75.

Young, Ralph, private, ... Virginia militia
January 28, 1834; $20. Age 74.

PENSIONERS UNDER THE ACT OF MAY 15, 1828.
(Began March 3, 1826.)

Craddock, Robert, lieutenant, fourth regiment, . . Virginia line
February 7, 1829; $320.

Meredith, William, captain, ... Virginia artillery
April 19, 1828; $600. Died February 20, 1833.

REVOLUTIONARY PENSIONER LIVING IN THE COUNTY IN 1840.
(Collins, Vol. I, p. 9.)

Bellowes, Miles, age 80. Haven, Christopher, age 88.

Total for the County, 38.

WASHINGTON COUNTY.

PENSIONERS UNDER THE ACT OF MARCH 18, 1818.

Bever, Charles, lieutenant, ... Maryland line
June 30, 1819; March 10, 1819; $240. Age 80.

Corbert, James, private, ... Maryland line
December 6, 1826; October 23, 1826; $96. Age 76.

Darnell, jr., Adam, private, ... Virginia line
March 14, 1820; August 9, 1819; $96. Age 94.

Fagan, Michael, private, ... Pennsylvania line
March 14, 1820; August 9, 1819; $96. Age 90. Died Oct. 18, 1820.

Fielder, George, private, ... Virginia line
March 14, 1820; May 18, 1819; $96. Age 73. Died Dec 5, 1825.

Fields, Joseph, private, ... Maryland line
March 19, 1823; March 1, 1823; $96. Age 78.
Hill, William, private, ... Virginia line
March 14, 1820; Oct. 13, 1818; $96. Age 83. Died July 25, 1831.
Hoskins, Randall, private, ... Maryland line
January 26, 1825; January 10, 1825; $96. Age 76.
Hill, Frederick, private, ... Pennsylvania line
December 27, 1830; December 24, 1830; $96. Age 75.
Lewis, James, private, ... Virginia line
March 14, 1820; July 9, 1818; $96. Age 75.
Rogers, Andrew, lieutenant, ... Virginia line
June 10, 1819; May 16, 1818; $240. Age 81.
Spalding, Aaron, private, ... Maryland line
March 14, 1820; Aug. 10, 1819; $96. Age 81. Died June 29, 1825.
Spalding, George, private, ... Maryland line
January 29, 1825; January 10, 1825; $96. Age 76.
Thurman, William, private, ... Virginia line
March 14, 1820; May 19, 1818; $96. Age 65. Died Aug. 29, 1824.
Thorp, Perry, private, ... Pennsylvania line
March 14, 1820; November 1, 1819; $96. Age 84.
Thomas, Lewis, lieutenant, ... Virginia line
March 14, 1820; November 4, 1819; $96. Age 68.
Yates, Robert, sergeant, ... Maryland line
January 27, 1819; November 10, 1818; $96. Age 80.

PENSIONERS UNDER THE ACT OF JUNE 7, 1832.
(Began March 4, 1831.)

Adams, John, private, ... Maryland militia
July 23, 1834; $20. Age 74.
Bunch, Richard, private, ... Virginia line
February 1, 1833; $20. Age 75.
Bean, Conrad, private, ... Maryland militia
December 21, 1833; $80. Age 81.
Carter, Joseph, private, ... Virginia militia
November 25, 1833; $80. Age 74.
Ceasy, Joseph, private, ... Virginia line
December 21, 1833; $80. Age 74.
Crump, Thomas, private of cavalry, ... Virginia line
April 11, 1834; $100. Age 75. Died January 5, 1833.
Faris, Elijah, private, ... Virginia militia
August 10, 1833; $80. Age 72.
Graham, Amos, private, ... Virginia militia
February 28, 1833; $40. Age 74.
Herbert, Jeremiah, private, ... Maryland militia
February 23, 1833; $23.33. Age 72.

Hardin, Mark, captain, ... Pennsylvania militia
    March 2, 1833; $600. Age 84.
Lambert, James, private, ... South Carolina line
    February 1, 1833; $20. Age 74.
Lawson, Nathan, private, ... Virginia line
    March 30, 1833; $50. Age 79.
McKitrick, sr., John, captain, ... Virginia militia
    February 28, 1833; $95. Age 75.
Nance, Frederick, sergeant, ... Virginia line
    December 2, 1833; $120. Age —.
Overton, Samuel, commissary, ... Virginia State troops
    February 2, 1833; $320. Age 74.
Seay, Jacob, private, ... Virginia militia
    August 10, 1833; $20.88. Age 76.
Scherlin, James, private, ... Pennsylvania militia
    July 10, 1834; $30. Age 77.
Sweeney, Joseph, private, ... Virginia militia
    March 10, 1834; $26.66. Age 75.
Webster, William, private, ... Virginia militia
    October 1, 1833; $25.77. Age 70.
Wright, Jonathan, private, ... North Carolina line
    April 3, 1834; $26.66. Age 71.
Wright, Thomas, private, ... Virginia line
    May 23, 1834; $44.44. Age 83.
Webb, Lewis, captain, ... Virginia line
    April 26, 1834; $480. Age 89.
Young, Andrew, private of cavalry, ... Virginia line
    November 7, 1833; $41.66. Age 74.

PENSIONERS UNDER THE ACT OF MAY 15, 1828.
(Began March 3, 1826.)

Fleece, John, dragoon, ... Lee's legion
    March 11, 1829; $100.
Gilliham, Clammaus, private, seventh regiment, . . Virginia line
    October 6, 1828; $80. Died July 30, 1830.
Thompson, Barnard, dragoon, ... Armand's corps
    August 19, 1828; $100.

REVOLUTIONARY PENSIONERS LIVING IN THE COUNTY IN 1840.
(Collins, Vol. I, p. 8.)

Adams, Peter, age 79.	Combs, John, age 81.
Booker, Samuel, age 82.	Lea, Jacob, age 75.
Burns, Philip, age 84.	White, Jonathan, age 78.

Total for the County, 49.

WAYNE COUNTY.

PENSIONERS UNDER THE ACT OF MARCH 18, 1818.

Cooper, Frederick, private, ... North Carolina line
March 31, 1820; October 20, 1818; $96. Age —.
Thomas, Elisha, private, ... Virginia line
January 28, 1818; October 24, 1818; $96. Age 60.

PENSIONERS UNDER THE ACT OF JUNE 7, 1832.
(Began March 1, 1831.)

Acre, William, private, ... North Carolina line
September 5, 1833; $40. Age 82. Died March 3, 1833.
Adair, John, private, ... North Carolina line
September 5, 1833; $40. Age 79.
Bleakley, Robert, private, ... North Carolina line
September 5, 1833; $52.77. Age 76.
Butram, William, private, ... North Carolina militia
March 4, 1834; $23.33. Age 84.
Brown, James, private, ... North Carolina line
April 14, 1834; $20. Age 79.
Bruton, George, private, ... South Carolina militia
December 21, 1833; $50. Age 72.
Covington, Robert, private, ... Virginia militia
April 10, 1833; $80. Age 72.
Cooper, Frederick, private, ... Pennsylvania militia
September 5, 1833; $80. Age 75.
Carpenter, William, private, ... Virginia militia
October 31, 1833; $26.66. Age 73.
Coffey, Reuben, private, ... North Carolina State troops
October 31, 1833; $40. Age 74.
Coyle, Patrick, private, ... Virginia line
February 7, 1834; $40. Age 71.
Catron, Peter, private, ... Virginia militia
February 12, 1834; $40. Age 80.
Davis, John, private, ... Virginia line
September 2, 1833; $63.33. Age 76.
Decker, George, private, ... Virginia line
September 2, 1833; $56.66. Age 92.
Durham, Mastin, private, ... North Carolina militia
September 2, 1833; $20. Age 79.
Dabney, George, private, ... Virginia militia
October 18, 1833; $40. Age 74.
Daffron, Rody, private of inf. and cav., . . North Carolina militia
November 7, 1833; $22.50. Age 77.

Hunt, Abraham, private, ... Virginia line
    April 14, 1834 ; $26.21. Age 72.
Henegan, Conrad, private, ... North Carolina line
    May 29, 1834 ; $20. Age 80.
Johnson, 2d, William, sergeant, ... Virginia line
    September 2, 1833; $120. Age 77.
Jones, James, private, ... Virginia line
    October 18, 1833; $80. Age 74.
Keath, William, private, ... Virginia line
    October 31, 1833; $23.33. Age 73.
Merritt, Thomas, private, ... North Carolina line
    September 2, 1833; $60. Age 73.
Miller, Frederick, private, ... Virginia militia
    October 31, 1833; $20. Age 82.
Moreland, Dudley, private, ... Virginia militia
    October 31, 1833 ; $60. Age 73.
Majors, John, private, ... North Carolina line
    January 3, 1834 ; $80. Age 77.
McHenry, James, private of inf. and cav., N. Carolina State troops
    January 21, 1834; $51.33. Age 73.
McGee, James C., private, ... Pennsylvania line
    February 25, 1834; $80. Age 72.
Pratt, Stephen, private, ... Virginia militia
    October 18, 1833; $30. Age 70.
Pierce, James, private, ... Virginia militia
    October 31, 1833.
Powers, Jesse, private, ... Virginia line
    November 9, 1833; $30. Age 75.
Rogers, George, private, ... Virginia militia
    September 2, 1833; $30. Age 70.
Stephens, Isaac, private, ... Virginia line
    December 5, 1832; $66.66. Age 74.
Sanders, Zachariah, private, ... Virginia militia
    September 5, 1833; $80. Age 75.
Thomas, Elisha, private, ... Virginia line
    September 2, 1833; $80. Age 75.
Turner, James, private, ... Virginia line
    October 21, 1833; $40. Age 72.
Walters, John, private, ... North Carolina line
    October 31, 1833; $20. Age 72.
Warham, Charles, private, ... Virginia line
    November 7, 1833; $36.94. Age 78.
Woody, James, private, ... North Carolina militia
    July 10, 1834; $23.33. Age 70.

REVOLUTIONARY PENSIONERS LIVING IN THE COUNTY IN 1840.
(Collins, Vol. I, p. 9.)

Cooper, Caleb, age 80.   Doss, William, age 76.
Crabtree, Isaac, age 82.   Piercy, James, age 80.
                Washam, Charles, age 80.

Total for the County, 46.

WHITLEY COUNTY.

PENSIONERS UNDER THE ACT OF MARCH 18, 1818.

Moore, Joseph, private, ... New Jersey line
    January 28, 1819; October 19, 1818; $96. Age 83.
Rogers, James, private, ... North Carolina line
    November 1, 1828; October 8, 1828; $96. Age 74.
Sexton, William, private, ... Virginia line
    October 21, 1826; July 16, 1826; $96. Age 81. Died Dec. 31, 1830.
Twigg, Daniel, private, ... North Carolina line
    May 12, 1829; February 2, 1829; $96. Age —.

PENSIONERS UNDER THE ACT OF JUNE 7, 1832.
(Began March 4, 1831.)

Anderson, John, sergeant, ... North Carolina line
    November 15, 1833; $51.66. Age 76.
Gatliff, Charles, private, ... Virginia militia
    November 15, 1833; $51.66. Age 86.
Hood, John, private, ... North Carolina line
    February 18, 1834; $36.66. Age 72.
Laughlin, Thomas, private, ... North Carolina line
    November 15, 1833; $36.66. Age 71.
Moses, Joshua, private, ... North Carolina militia
    November 15, 1833; $53.33. Age 81.
Mahan, James, private, ... Virginia militia
    November 15, 1833; $80. Age 79.
Porch, Henry, private, ... North Carolina militia
    December 2, 1833; $60. Age 76.
Rose, William, ensign, ... North Carolina line
    December 7, 1833; $160. Age 77.

REVOLUTIONARY PENSIONERS LIVING IN THE COUNTY IN 1840.
(Collins, Vol. I, p. 9.)

Adkins, Thomas, age 82.   Trigg, Daniel, age 86.
Smithheart, Darley, age 81.   Witt, Anes, age 80.

Total for the County, 16.

WOODFORD COUNTY.

PENSIONERS UNDER THE ACT OF MARCH 18, 1818.

Allison, John, sergeant, ... Pennsylvania line
April 22, 1818; April 2, 1818; $96. Age 75. Died June 16, 1823.
Barnet, Daniel, private, ... Maryland line
July 15, 1819; January 7, 1819; $96. Age 75. Died Jan. 23, 1823.
Baker, Nicholas, private, ... Virginia line
June 11, 1819; June 16, 1818.
Booz, John, private, ... Virginia line
December 1, 1820; June 9, 1818; $96. Age 92.
Coleman, Thomas, private, ... Virginia militia
April 19, 1820; June 9, 1818; $96. Age 68.
Dale, William, private, ... Virginia line
March 5, 1819; June 18, 1818; $96. Age 64.
Dossey, John, private, ... New York line
February 7, 1828; February 1, 1828; $96. Age 74.
Goodloe, Henry, private, ... Virginia line
January 11, 1832; December 28, 1831; $96. Age 95.
Malone, John, private, ... Virginia line
May 17, 1820; May 6, 1818; $96. Age 80.
Mosley, Leonard, private, ... Virginia line
July 7, 1819; June 16, 1818; $96. Age 78. Died December 9, 1829.
McCoy, William, private, ... Virginia line
April 19, 1819; June 10, 1818; $96. Age 80.
Mix, Enos, private, ... Connecticut line
July 15, 1819; June 2, 1818; $96. Age 91.
Pullen, William, private, ... Virginia line
August 19, 1819; June 15, 1818; $96. Age 75.
Pollet, John, private, ... Virginia line
May 29, 1819; May 11, 1818; $96. Age 78.
Peyton, George, private, ... Virginia line
Sept. 21, 1819; June 17, 1818; $96. Age 71. Died June 17, 1831.
Terrill, Presley, private, ... Virginia line
February 17, 1819; June 6, 1818; $96. Age 72.
Yancey, Robert, captain, ... Virginia line
June 28, 1819; May 23, 1818; $96. Age 84. Died Nov. 17, 1824.

PENSIONERS UNDER THE ACT OF JUNE 7, 1832.
(Began March 4, 1831.)

Arnold, James, private, ... Virginia line
October 20, 1832; $80. Age 79.
Allen, John, private, ... Virginia line
September 3, 1832; $80. Age 91.

16

Booth, James, orderly sergeant, ... Virginia line
  October 19, 1832; $120. Age 77.
Bull, Edmund, private, . . . North Carolina and Virginia militia
  May 13, 1833; $20. Age 79.
Black, Robert, private, ... Virginia militia
  September 23, 1833; $20. Age 84.
Calmes, Marquis, captain, ... Virginia line
  December 1, 1832; $480. Age 80. Died February 27, 1834.
Carter, John B., private, ... Virginia line
  February 11, 1833; $80. Age 84.
Chelton, George, private, ... Virginia line
  June 3, 1833; $20. Age 86.
Chelton, Stephen, private, ... Virginia line
  June 3, 1833; $80. Age 73.
Davis, 1st, Thomas, private, ... Virginia militia
  July 30, 1832; $80. Age 84.
Eaton, Joseph, private, ... Pennsylvania line
  December 2, 1833; $20. Age 88.
Green, Paul, private, ... Maryland line
  December 12, 1832; $80. Age 81.
Gaines, Robert, private, ... Virginia militia
  August 26, 1833; $28.88. Age 69.
Gregory, John, private, ... Virginia militia
  September 18, 1832; $36.66. Age 76.
Humble, Robert, private, ... Pennsylvania militia
  January 10, 1833; $80. Age 80.
Harris, Nathaniel, private, ... North Carolina line
  May 23, 1834; $20. Age 74.
Jackson, Francis, private, ... Virginia line
  December 10, 1832; $60. Age 77.
Kirkham, Michael, ensign, ... Virginia militia
  $39.66. Age 87.
Minzies, Samuel P., captain, ... Virginia line
  January 19, 1833; $235.83. Age 76.
Mitchell, John, private, ... Virginia line
  February 12, 1833; $80. Age 72.
McKinney, John, lieutenant, ... South Carolina line
  $186.66. Age 76.
Martin, William, private, ... Virginia militia
  June 5, 1833; $80. Age 72.
McGee, Samuel, private, ... Virginia militia
  July 11, 1833; $80. Age 85.
Milton, Elijah, private, ... Virginia militia
  August 26, 1833; $25. Age 78.

McQuady, John, private, ... Virginia line
    October 26, 1833; $40.   Age 74.

Smith, John, private, ... Pennsylvania line
    August 17, 1833; $43.33.   Age 82.

Smithy, William, private, ... Virginia militia
    September 6, 1833; $80.   Age 85.

Smithey, Reuben, private, ... Virginia militia
    October 2, 1833; $30.   Age 75.

Smith, Henry, private, ... Virginia militia
    May 23, 1834; $33.33.   Age 80.

Taylor, Zachariah, private, ... Virginia line
    August 7, 1832; $80.   Age 78.

Twyman, Reuben, private, ... Virginia militia
    October 23, 1832; $26.66.   Age 75.

Tinder, James, private, ... Virginia militia
    March 25, 1833; $53.33.   Age 72.

Wilson, Jeremiah, ... Virginia line
    October 19, 1832; $46.66.   Age 76.

Wingfield, Enoch, private, ... Virginia militia
    February 11, 1833; $40.   Age —.

REVOLUTIONARY SOLDIERS LIVING IN THE COUNTY IN 1840.

(Collins, Vol. I, p. 9.)

Alexander, Peter, age 83.   Hamilton, James, age 77.
Cox, John, age 78.   McQuiddy, John, age 80.
Daily, Dennis, age 79.   New, George W., age 76.
        Ellis, Jane (widow), age 77.

Total for the County, 59.

NUMBER OF REVOLUTIONARY PENSIONERS IN EACH COUNTY, ETC.

COUNTY.	PENSIONERS.	COUNTY NAMED IN HONOR OF
Adair,	48	John Adair, a major in the Revolutionary army.
Allen,	27	Colonel John Allen, killed at the River Raisin, War of 1812.
Anderson,	18	Richard Clough Anderson, whose father was a colonel in the Revolutionary army.
Barren,	70	From its numerous barren plains when first discovered.
Bath,	29	From its numerous medicinal springs.
Boone,	38	Daniel Boone, colonel of Virginia militia in the Revolution.
Bourbon,	66	The royal family of France, who befriended America during the Revolution.
Bracken,	24	William Bracken, a private in the Revolutionary militia.
Breathitt,	3	Governor John Breathitt, son of a Revolutionary soldier.
Breckinridge,	28	John Breckinridge, a soldier in the Revolutionary war.
Bullitt,	28	Alexander Scott Bullitt, whose father was a colonel in the Revolutionary war.
Butler,	17	William Butler, of Pennsylvania, a colonel in the Revolutionary war.
Caldwell,	34	John Caldwell, a private in the Revolution; a major-general of militia in the War of 1812.
Calloway,	22	Richard Calloway, a colonel of Virginia militia in the Revolution.
Campbell,	36	John Campbell, a brigadier-general of Virginia militia in the Revolution.
Carroll,	6	Charles Carroll, of Carrollton, a signer of the Declaration of Independence.
Carter,	1	William G. Carter, a colonel in the War of 1812.
Casey,	18	William Casey, a colonel of Virginia militia in the Revolution.
Christian,	31	William Christian, a captain in Braddock's war, a colonel in the Revolution.
Clark,	59	George Rogers Clark, colonel-commandant of "the Illinois Regiment" in War of the Revolution.
Clay,	15	Green Clay, a soldier boy in the Revolution; a major-general in the War of 1812.
Clinton,	7	DeWitt Clinton, whose father was a general in the Revolutionary army.
Cumberland,	46	The Cumberland river.
Daveiss,	11	Colonel Joseph Hamilton Daveiss, killed at the battle of Tippecanoe, War of 1812.
Estill,	27	James Estill, a captain of militia in the Revolution.
Fayette,	93	The Marquis de La Fayette, a major-general in the Revolutionary army.

COUNTY.	PENSIONERS.	COUNTY NAMED IN HONOR OF
Fleming,	61	John Fleming, an officer in the Revolutionary army.
Floyd,	36	John Floyd, a colonel of Virginia troops during the Revolution.
Franklin,	48	Benjamin Franklin, a statesman and patriot of the Revolution.
Gallatin,	32	Albert Gallatin, a Massachusetts volunteer in 1780.
Garrard,	52	James Garrard, a Virginia militia officer in the Revolution.
Grant,	14	John Grant, a colonel of Virginia militia in the Revolution.
Graves,	17	Captain Benjamin Graves, who was probably a soldier of the Revolution.
Grayson,	18	William Grayson, a Colonel in the Revolutionary army.
Green,	54	Nathanael Greene, a major-general in the Revolutionary army.
Greenup,	13	Christopher Greenup, a lieutenant in the Revolutionary army.
Hancock,	2	John Hancock, first signer of the Declaration of Independence.
Hardin,	34	John Hardin, a lieutenant in the Revolutionary army.
Harlan,	10	Silas Harlan, a captain under Colonel George Rogers Clark in 1779.
Harrison,	56	Benjamin Harrison, a soldier of the Revolution.
Hart,	16	Nathaniel T. G. Hart, a captain in the War of 1812; assassinated at the River Raisin.
Henderson,	10	Richard Henderson, founder of the "Transylvania Colony."
Henry,	92	Patrick Henry, the orator of the Revolution.
Hickman,	16	Paschal Hickman, a captain in the War of 1812; assassinated at the River Raisin.
Hopkins,	32	Samuel Hopkins, a lieutenant-colonel in the Revolution; a major-general in the War of 1812.
Jefferson,	45	Thomas Jefferson, author and signer of the Declaration of Independence.
Jessamine,	42	Jessamine Creek.
Kenton,	7	Simon Kenton, a scout under Colonel G. R. Clark, and a famous Indian fighter.
Knox,	19	Henry Knox, a major-general in the Revolutionary army.
Laurel,	11	Laurel river.
Lawrence,	22	Captain James Lawrence, U. S. navy.
Lewis,	15	Captain Meriwether Lewis, of the "Lewis and Clark Expedition."
Lincoln,	40	Benjamin Lincoln, a major-general in the Revolutionary army.
Livingston,	19	Robert R. Livingston, Secretary of Foreign Affairs of the Continental Congress.
Logan,	42	Benjamin Logan, a general of Virginia militia in the Revolution.

COUNTY.	PENSIONERS.	COUNTY NAMED IN HONOR OF
McCracken,	5	Captain Virgil McCracken, killed at the River Raisin, in the War of 1812.
Madison,	88	James Madison, a congressman from Virginia during the Revolution, and afterward President.
Marion,	16	Francis Marion, a brigadier-general in the Revolutionary war.
Mason,	43	George Mason, of Gunston Hall, a statesman of the Revolution.
Meade,	4	Captain James Meade, killed at the River Raisin, War of 1812.
Mercer,	122	Hugh Mercer, a brigadier-general in the Revolutionary army.
Monroe,	21	James Monroe, a lieutenant in the Revolutionary army; afterward President of United States.
Montgomery,	59	Richard Montgomery, a major-general in the Revolutionary army.
Morgan,	32	Daniel Morgan, a brigadier-general in the Revolutionary army.
Muhlenberg,	22	Peter Muhlenberg, a brigadier-general in the Revolutionary army.
Nelson,	38	Thomas Nelson, signer of Declaration of Independence; brig.-gen. in Revolutionary army.
Nicholas,	37	George Nicholas, a captain in the Virginia State line, Revolutionary war.
Ohio,	18	The Ohio river.
Oldham,	22	William Oldham, captain in Revolutionary army; killed at St. Clair's defeat, 1791.
Owen,	38	Abraham Owen, lieutenant; wounded at St. Clair's defeat; colonel under Wayne.
Pendleton,	31	Edmund Pendleton, a member of the Continental Congress from Virginia.
Perry,	27	Commodore Oliver Hazard Perry, the hero of the Battle of Lake Erie.
Pike,	5	Zebulon Pike, a brigadier-general in the War of 1812.
Pulaski,	43	Count Joseph Pulaski, a brigadier-general in the Revolutionary army.
Rockcastle,	35	Rockcastle river.
Russell,	16	William Russell, a colonel in the Revolutionary army.
Scott,	86	Charles Scott, a brigadier-general in the Revolutionary army.
Shelby,	93	Isaac Shelby, a brigadier-general in the Revolutionary army.
Simpson,	16	John Simpson, a captain in the War of 1812; killed at the River Raisin.
Spencer,	31	Spear Spencer, a captain in the War of 1812; killed at the Battle of Tippecanoe.
Todd,	24	John Todd, an officer under General Clark in the Illinois expedition.
Trigg,	15	Stephen Trigg, a colonel of Virginia militia in the Revolution.
Trimble,	9	Judge Robert Trimble. son of a Revolutionary officer.
Union,	15	Named in honor of the American Union.

COUNTY.	PENSIONERS.	COUNTY NAMED IN HONOR OF
Warren, · · · · ·	38	General Joseph Warren, the hero of Bunker Hill.
Washington, · · ·	49	George Washington.
Wayne, · · · · ·	46	Anthony Wayne, a brigadier-general in the Revolutionary army.
Whitley, · · · · ·	16	William Whitley, a colonel of Virginia militia in the Revolution.
Woodford, · · · ·	59	William Woodford, a brigadier-general in the Revolutionary army.

NUMBER OF PENSIONERS FURNISHED BY THE ORIGINAL THIRTEEN COLONIES.

STATE.	LINE.	MILITIA.	STATED.	NOT STATED.	TOTAL.
Virginia,	950	527	42	. . . .	1,519
North Carolina,	195	142	14	. . . .	351
Pennsylvania,	174	55	4	. . . .	233
Maryland.	96	49	1	. . . .	146
South Carolina,	48	21	8	. . . .	77
New Jersey,	43	16	3	. . . .	62
New York,	20	5	. . . .	. . . .	25
Connecticut,	14	1	. . . .	. . . .	15
Georgia,	8	7	. . . .	. . . .	15
Delaware,	9	3	. . . .	. . . .	12
Massachusetts,	10	. . . .	. . . .	. . . .	10
New Hampshire,	6	1	. . . .	. . . .	7
Rhode Island,	1	. . . .	. . . .	. . . .	1
Not stated,	. . . .	. . . .	. . . .	423	423
Totals,	1,574	827	72	423	2,896

NUMBER OF PENSIONERS OF CERTAIN SEVERAL AGES.

AGE.	NO.	AGE.	NO.	AGE.	NO.	AGE.	NO.
54	2	71	131	85	54	99	3
58	3	72	179	86	35	100	4
59	1	73	179	87	39	101	1
60	12	74	211	88	21	102	4
61	7	75	187	89	30	103	1
62	17	76	169	90	19	104	1
63	7	77	158	91	15	106	3
64	11	78	176	92	19	107	1
65	17	79	171	93	7	108	2
66	11	80	131	94	13	109	1
67	24	81	92	95	7	Not stated }	243
68	33	82	103	96	5		
69	47	83	80	97	2		
70	115	84	94	98	4	Total,.	2,896

Average age of the 2,653 whose ages are stated: 76.22 years

ALPHABETICAL INDEX OF PENSIONERS, WITH REFERENCE TO COUNTIES.

Austin, John, ... Oldham
Awby, Samuel, . . . Hardin
Aycock, Robert, . . . Todd
Backnel, Thomas, . . Madison
Bailey, Elisha, ... Adair
Bailey, Callow, ... Barren
Bailey, James, ... Garrard
Bailey, Richard, . . . Barren
Bagley, John, ... Barren
Baker, Bowling, . . . Clay
Baker, John, ... Cumberland
Baker, Joseph, ... Garrard
Baker, Nicholas, . . . Woodford
Baker, Thomas, . . . Henderson
Baker, William, . . . Cumberland
Baldwin, Edward, . . Henderson
Baldwin, John, ... Mason
Baley, Abraham, . . . Franklin
Baley, Samuel, ... Campbell
Ball, James, ... Fayette
Ballanger, William, . Nicholas
Ballard, Bland W., . . Shelby
Ballew, Charles, . . . Shelby
Ballew, Richard, . . . Harlan
Ballew, Richard, . . . Knox
Bamhill, Samuel, . . Scott
Bane, John, ... Hickman
Bane, Richard, . . . Lewis
Barbee, Daniel, . . . Mercer
Barbee, Elijah. See Barbey.
Barbee, Elias, . . . Green
Barber, John, ... Mercer
Barbey, Elijah, ... Bourbon
Barham, James, . . . Trigg
Barham, John, ... Calloway
Barlow, Joseph, . . . Boone
Barker, George, . . . Morgan
Barker, John, ... Pulaski
Barker, Stephen, . . . Grant
Barker, William, . . . Fayette
Barnard, William L., . Ohio
Barnes, Benjamin, . . Gallatin
Barnes, George, . . . Christian
Barnes, John, ... Harrison
Barnes, Nicodemus, . Clinton
Barnes, Shadrach, . . Gallatin
Barnet, Daniel, . . . Woodford
Barnett, Ambrose, . . Nicholas

Barnett, Andrew, . . Green
Barnett, James, . . . Madison
Barnett, James P., . . Lincoln
Barnett, William, . . Green
Barnhill, Samuel, . . Scott
Barr, John, ... Spencer
Barrett, Francis, . . . Cumberland
Barron, John, ... Pulaski
Barron, William, . . . Pulaski
Barton, John, ... Fayette
Bartlett, John, ... Jefferson
Bartlett, William. See Berkley.
Bartley, Thomas, . . Monroe
Bassam, Obadiah, . . Breckinridge
Basey, William, . . . Mercer
Baskett, Martin, . . Shelby
Bateman, Thomas, . . Jefferson
Bates, James, ... Grant
Bates, Humphrey, . . Rockcastle
Bates, Thomas, . . . Bourbon
Bates, William, . . . Carter
Bates, William, . . . Lawrence
Batterton, Samuel, . . Bourbon
Baugh, Henry, ... Pulaski
Bauldwin, Edward, . Hopkins
Bayliss, William, . . Union
Bayor, Edward, . . . Fleming
Beakman, Michael, . . Pulaski
Beams, Conrad, . . . Marion
Bean, Conrad, ... Washington
Bean, James, ... Harrison
Bean, Leonard, . . . Mason
Bean, Richard, ... Lewis
Beasley, William, . . Butler
Beatty, Daniel, ... Montgomery
Beatty, John, ... Montgomery
Beatty, Joseph, ... Grayson
Beatty, William, . . . Scott
Beavers, John, ... Barren
Beck, Thomas, ... Caldwell
Beech, Asa, ... Boone
Beeton, Adam, ... Henry
Beggs, Moore, ... Harrison
Belew, Solomon, . . . Henry
Belknap, James, . . . Hardin
Bell, Archibald, . . . Bourbon
Bell, Daniel, ... Mason
Bell, John (2), ... Nelson

Brady, John, ...	Garrard	Brown, William, . . .	Lawrence
Brady, William, . . .	Boone	Brown, William, . . .	Shelby
Bramblett, James, . .	Breckinridge	Brown, William, . . .	Warren
Brandon, Peter, . . .	Ohio	Browning, Edward, .	Knox
Branham, William, . .	Bourbon	Brownlee, John, . . .	Barren
Brank, Robert, . . .	Garrard	Bruce, William, . . .	Lincoln
Breast, John, ...	Bourbon	Brumback, Peter, . .	Boone
Breckinridge, Robert,	Jefferson	Brumback, Peter, . .	Shelby
Breedlove, William, .	Simpson	Brummel, Benjamin, .	Cumberland
Breeze, John, ...	Mason	Bruner, Jacob, ...	Boone
Brevard, Benjamin, .	Shelby	Brunson, Stout, . . .	Allen
Brewer, Henry, . . .	Christian	Bruster, James, . . .	Mercer
Brewer, Samuel, . . .	Mercer	Bruton, George, . . .	Wayne
Brewer, William, . . .	Henry	Bryan, Barich, ...	Henderson
Briant, Zachariah, . .	Daveiss	Bryan, Daniel, ...	Jessamine
Bridges, Benjamin, . .	Calloway	Bryan, Daniel, ...	Scott
Bridges, John, ...	Boone	Bryant, Benjamin, . .	Warren
Bridges, John, ...	Mercer	Bryant, George, . . .	Nicholas
Bridwell, Simon, . . .	Spencer	Bryant, John, (3) . . .	Garrard
Brierly, George, . . .	Mason	Bryant, Peter, ...	Shelby
Briggs, Benjamin, . .	Lincoln	Bryant, Thomas, . . .	Henry
Bright, Wyndle, . . .	Green	Buford, Abraham, . .	Scott
Brimmage, John, . .	Graves	Buford, John, ...	Garrard
Briscoe, Henry, . . .	Jefferson	Buford, Simeon, . . .	Barren
Brittain, Jeremiah, . .	Spencer	Bull, Edward, ...	Woodford
Brittain, Samuel, . . .	Mercer	Bunch, Richard, . . .	Washington
Brock, Henry, ...	Jefferson	Burbridge, George, .	Scott
Brook, Jesse, ...	Harlan	Burbridge, Lincefield,	Clark
Brooks, James, . . .	Nelson	Burch, Benjamin, .	Ohio
Brook, John, ...	Allen	Burch, John, ...	Barren
Bromigin, Jarvis, . .	Bath	Burch, Joseph, ...	Scott
Brothers, Elijah, . . .	Cumberland	Burchett, John, . . .	Cumberland
Broughton, Job, . . .	Knox	Burchett, William, . .	Cumberland
Brown, Arabia, . . .	Garrard	Burge, David, ...	Clay
Brown, Charles, . . .	Hopkins	Burgess, Edward, . .	Lawrence
Brown, Charles, . . .	Mercer	Burgess, Joshua, . . .	Mason
Brown, Edward, . . .	Knox	Burk, Samuel, ...	Jessamine
Brown, Frances, . . .	Franklin	Burke, Michael, . . .	Madison
Brown, Henry, ...	Scott	Burke, Robert, . . .	Owen
Brown, James, ...	Wayne	Burke, Samuel, . . .	Shelby
Brown, John, ...	Montgomery	Burns, Andrew, . . .	Perry
Brown, Joseph, . . .	Spencer	Burns, Jeremiah, . . .	Greenup
Brown, Peter, ...	Butler	Burns, James, ...	Boone
Brown, Robert, . . .	Hopkins	Burns, John, ...	Nicholas
Brown, Thomas, . . .	Estill	Burns, Philip, ...	Washington
Brown, Thomas, . . .	Monroe	Burns, Philip, ...	Mercer
Brown, Thomas, . . .	Scott	Burns, William, . . .	Clay
Brown, Thomas C., . .	Floyd	Burnside, Robert, . .	Madison

Chandler, James, . . . Owen
Chandler, John, . . . Clay
Chapman, Amos, . . . Shelby
Chapman, John, . . . Cumberland
Chappell, William, . . Bullitt
Chasteen, James, . . . Rockcastle
Chelton, George, . . Woodford
Chelton, Stephen, . . Woodford
Chetham, William, . . Cumberland
Chick, James, ... Knox
Chisham, James, . . . Scott
Chism, George, . . . Scott
Childers, Goolsberry, Garrard
Childers, Henry, . . . Grant
Childers, Pleasant, . . Floyd
Christian, Andrew, . . Fayette
Christian, John, . . . Fayette
Christian, William, . Fayette
Christie, James, . . . Shelby
Clack, Moses, ... Fleming
Clark, David, ... Hopkins
Clark, Elijah, ... Laurel
Clark, James, ... Casey
Clark, James, ... Mercer
Clark, John, ... Butler
Clark, John, ... Garrard
Clark, John, ... Logan
Clark, Jonathan, . . . Christian
Clark, Joseph, ... Montgomery
Clark, Micajah, . . . Warren
Clark, Moses, ... Fleming
Clark, Obadiah, . . . Shelby
Clark, Patrick, ... Mercer
Clark, Thomas, . . . Fayette
Clark, William, . . . Livingston
Clarkson, David, . . . Boone
Clasby, John, ... Warren
Clayton, Augustine, . Warren
Claywell, Shadrach, . Cumberland
Cleveland, William, . Pendleton
Cleaver, William, . . Grayson
Clement, Roger, . . . Montgomery
Clemons, Bernard, . . Franklin
Cleveland, John, . . . Harrison
Clinkenbeard, Isaac, . Bourbon
Clinton, James, . . . Livingston
Clinton, James, . . . Caldwell
Cochran, Thomas, . . Adair

Cockerell, James, . . Marion
Cockerel, Peter, . . . Bourbon
Cockrum, Wm., . . . Hickman
Coffey, Osbourne, . . Casey
Coffey, Reuben, . . . Wayne
Coffman, Jacob, . . . Casey
Coghill, James, ... Carroll
Coghill, James, . . . Gallatin
Cohoon, Joel, ... Trigg
Cole, Benjamin, . . . Mason
Cole, John, ... Barren
Coleman, Robert, . . Mercer
Coleman, Thomas, . . Barren
Coleman, Thomas, . . Woodford
Collett, Isaac, ... Henry
Collier, Coleman A., . Nicholas
Collier, John, ... Lincoln
Collins, John, . . . Fleming
Collins, Joshua, . . . Bath
Collins, Stephen, . . Campbell
Collins, Stephen, . . Kenton
Colvin, Henry, ... Pendleton
Combes, William, . . Fleming
Combs, John, ... Perry
Combs, John, ... Washington
Comingore, Henry, . Mercer
Comingore, John, . . Mercer
Compton, Edmund, . Marion
Conine, Andrew, . . Henry
Conn, James, ... Russell
Conn, Samuel, ... Jefferson
Conn, Timothy, . . . Mercer
Conn, William, . . Henry
Connelly, Henry, . . Floyd
Conner, John, ... Christian
Conner, Isaac, ... Pendleton
Conner, Lawrence, . . Cumberland
Conner, William, . . . Montgomery
Conover, Lewis, . . . Adair
Conway, Hugh, . . . Owen
Conway, John, ... Nicholas
Conyers, Benjamin, . Shelby
Cook, John, ... Butler
Cook, John, ... Madison
Cook, William, ... Graves
Cooke, Robert, . . . Calloway
Cooke, William, . . . Morgan
Cookendorfer, Mich'l, Pendleton

David, Michael, . . . Mason
Davidson, Joshua, . . Fleming
Davis, Anthony, . . . Spencer
Davis, Forrest, ... Hardin
Davis, Henry, ... Christian
Davis, James, ... Bourbon
Davis, John, ... Clinton
Davis, John, ... Hopkins
Davis, John, ... Wayne
Davis, Jesse, ... Fleming
Davis, Joseph, . . . Fleming
Davis, Joseph, ... Henry
Davis, Joseph, ... Lawrence
Davis, Nancy, ... Shelby
Davis, Nathaniel, . . Caldwell
Davis, Samuel, . . . Campbell
Davis, Samuel, ... Henry
Davis, Samuel C., . . Gallatin
Davis, Snead, ... Livingston
Davis, Septimus, . . . Clark
Davis, Thomas, . . . Woodford
Davis, William, . . . Fleming
Davis, William, . . . Hopkins
Dawson, William, . . Bourbon
Day, John, ... Morgan
Dean, Benjamin, . . . Mercer
Dean, John, ... Gallatin
Dean, Michael, . . . Bracken
Deaver, William, . . Mason
Decker, George, . . . Pulaski
Decker, George, . . . Wayne
Decker, John, . . . Grayson
Decker, Samuel, . . . Mercer
Decker, William, . . . Grayson
DeCourcey, William, . Campbell
Defever, John, ... Hart
De Hart, Samuel, . . Mason
De Haven, Edward, . Breckinridge
De Haven, Edward, . Grayson
Demaree, John, . . . Mercer
Dement, Jarret, . . . Gallatin
Demoss, Peter, . . . Pendleton
Demott, Peter, ... Mercer
Denham, Hardin, . . Monroe
Denny, Elijah, ... Rockcastle
Denton, David, . . . Barren
De Peyster, John, . . Hickman
Depp, William, . . . Barren

Deshazure, Henry, . . Mercer
Deskins, Daniel, . . . Bath
De Spain, Peter, . . . Green
Devine, William, . . . Mason
Dewitt, Peter, ... Clark
Dicken, Ephraim, ...
Dicken, John, ... Green
Dickens, Joseph, . . . Campbell
Dickerson, Solomon, . Monroe
Dickey, Ebenezer, . . Simpson
Dickey, Robert, . . . Mercer
Diddleston, Thomas, . Garrard
Dilman, Andrew, . . . Bracken
Dimkinson, Thomas, . Christian
Dinwiddie, John, . . Lincoln
Dishman, William, . . Barren,
Divin, James, ... Lincoln
Dixon, Wynne, . . . Henderson
Dodson, William, . . Nelson
Dogan, Lovel H., . . Pulaski
Dogan, Jeremiah J., . Henry
Doherty, John. See Dougherty.
Dooley, Jacob, ... Madison
Dooley, James, . . . Scott
Dorch, William, . . . Lawrence
Doss, William, ... Wayne
Dossett, Thomas, . . Hopkins
Dossey, John, ... Woodford
Doudon, Clementius, . Bourbon
Dougherty, John, . . Shelby
Dougherty, William, . Lincoln
Douthitt, Silas, . . . Franklin
Dowden, James, . . . Madison
Downey, John, ... Henry
Downey, Samuel, . . Hopkins
Downey, Thomas, . . Henry
Downing, Francis, . . Scott
Downing, Samuel, . . Barren
Downs, Robert, . . . Montgomery
Drebuler, John, . . . Bourbon
Drennon, Hugh, . . . Fleming
Driggs, David, ... Logan
Driskell, David, . . . Gallatin
Driver, Francis, . . . Scott
Ducker, John, ... Campbell
Ducker, John, ... Kenton
Duff, John, ... Barren
Duke, Henry, ... Madison

17

Fitzgerald, Benjamin, Mason
Fitzgerald, Daniel, . . Franklin
Fitzpatrick, James, . . Nicholas
Fitzsimmons, Thos., . Shelby
Flack, James, ... Todd
Flanders, Jacob, . . . Hardin
Fleece, John, ... Lincoln
Fleece, John, ... Washington
Fletcher, James, . . Fayette
Fletcher, John, . . . Clark
Flick, James, ... Madison
Floyd, George, . . . Garrard
Floyd, Henry, ... Union
Floyd, John, ... Garrard
Fons, John, ... Fleming
Forbes, John, . . . Laurel
Force, Jesse, ... Oldham
Force, Joseph, ... Shelby
Force, Peter, ... Henry
Ford, Elisha, ... Shelby
Ford, Jesse, ... Livingston
Ford, Joseph, . . . : Pike
Ford, William, ... Caldwell
Foree, Joseph, ... Shelby
Forgey, Hugh, ... Bourbon
Forgueran, Peter, . . Bourbon
Forrester, John, . . . Barren
Forsee William, . . . Franklin
Fosbrook, John, . . . Bath
Foster, John, ... Barren
Foster, Henry, ... Nicholas
Foster, Nathaniel, . . Montgomery
Foster, William, . . . Clark
Fowler, John, ... Fayette
Fox, Daniel, ... Graves
Foxworthy, John, . . Harrison
Franklin, Absalom, . Christian
Franklin, James M., . Shelby
Franklin, John, . . . Warren
Franklin, Joseph, . . Bracken
Franklin, Reuben, . . Clark
Franklin, Stephen, . Anderson
Fraseur, John, ... Fleming
Freeman, Aaron, . . . Caldwell
Freeman, John, . . Laurel
Freeman, Michael, . . Caldwell
Freer, Samuel, ... Caldwell
French, James, . . . Laurel

French, William, . . Shelby
Fritter, Moses, . . . Mason
Frizell, Nathan, . . . Calloway
Frogget, William, . . Barren
Frost, Micajah, . . . Lincoln
Frost, Micajah, . . . Rockcastle
Fry, Joshua, ... Garrard
Fugate, Randall, . . . Scott
Fulcher, Richard, . . Barren
Fulkerson, John, . . Grayson
Fullilove, Anthony, . Madison
Furnish, James, . . . Gallatin
Furnish, James, . . . Harrison
Furnish, Thomas, . . Harrison
Gabbert, George, . . Mercer
Gabbert, Michael, . . Mercer
Gadd, Thomas, . . . Rockcastle
Gaines, Thomas, . . . Green
Gaines, Robert, . . . Woodford
Gale, Anthony, . . . Lincoln
Gale, Robert, ... Shelby
Galloway, Charles, . . Calloway
Galloway, James, . . Mercer
Galloway, John, . . . Madison
Gamblin, Joshua, . . Graves
Gamblin, Joshua, . . McCracken
Garland, John, ... Clay
Garland, John, ... Knox
Garven, Isaac, ... Lincoln
Garvey, Job, ... Gallatin
Gano, Daniel . . . . Scott
Garnett, John, ... Owen
Garrett, John, ... Scott
Garrett, Robert, . . . Montgomery
Garris, Sikes, ... Muhlenberg
Garrison, Samuel, . . Warren
Garth, John, ... Scott
Gatewood, John, . . . Allen
Gatewood, John, . . . Scott
Gatliff, Charles, . . . Woodford
Gay, sr., James, . . . Clark
Gentry, Richard, . . . Madison
Gentry, Richard, . . . Rockcastle
George, John, ... Mercer
George, Jordan, . . . Russell
George, Thomas, . . Oldham
Geoghan, John, . . . Nicholas
Gevedann, John, . . . Henry

Griffin, Sherrod, . . . Green
Griffin, William, . . . Jefferson
Grigsby, Benjamin, . Montgomery
Grigsby, Benjamin, . Shelby
Grill, John, ... Owen
Grimes, Leonard, . . Henry
Grindstaff, Jacob, . . Jessamine
Grindstaff, Michael, . Jessamine
Grinter, John, ... Logan
Gritton, John, ... Mercer
Groom, Major, ... Caldwell
Grosvenor, Richard, . Nicholas
Grover, Jonathan M., . Lewis
Gryder, Martin, . . . Cumberland
Gryder, Valentine, . . Cumberland
Guess, Joseph, ... Caldwell
Guffey, Alexander, . . Logan
Guill, John, ... Scott
Gunison, Samuel, . . Madison
Guthery, William, . . Henry
Guthrie, Nathaniel, . Madison
Guttridge, Nathan, . Madison
Hackney, Samuel, . . Garrard
Hackney, Samuel, . . Mercer
Hackworth, Thomas, Greenup
Hagan, James, ... Nelson
Haggard, Henry, . Rockcastle
Haggard, William, . . Garrard
Hagins, William, . . Perry
Haines, Evan, ... Madison
Hains, Christopher, . Allen
Haley, Morris, ... Scott
Haley, Pleasant, . . . Monroe
Haley, Randall, . . . Fayette
Halfpenny, John, . . Clark
Hall, Anthony, . . . Floyd
Hall, Anthony, . . . Perry
Hall, Edward, ... Clark
Hall, James, ... Daveiss
Hall, James, ... Harlan
Hall, John, ... Russell
Hall, Joseph, ... Lincoln
Hall, Robert, ... Simpson
Hall, Thomas, ... Montgomery
Halley, Benjamin, . . Clark
Ham, Drury, ... Lincoln
Ham, John, ... Logan
Hamblin, Pierce Dant, Knox

Hamilton, Abner, . . Barren
Hamilton, B., ... Morgan
Hamilton, Benjamin, . Morgan
Hamilton, James, . . Fayette
Hamilton, James, . . Pulaski
Hamilton, James, . . Woodford
Hamilton, John, . . . Adair
Hamilton, John, . . . Bracken
Hamilton, John, . . . Caldwell
Hamilton, Thomas, . Morgan
Hamilton, William, . Boone
Hamler, Henry, . . . Mercer
Hamlett, John, ... Calloway
Hamlin, John, ... Montgomery
Hamm, John, ... Rockcastle
Hammerly, James, . . Pendleton
Hammerty, John, . . Pendleton
Hammock, William, . Union
Hammon, Obadiah . . Knox
Hammon, Philip, . . Montgomery
Hammond, John, . . . Fleming
Hammond, Peter, . . Perry
Hammonds, Peter, . . Knox
Hancock, Isaiah, . . . Muhlenberg
Hand, John, ... Pendleton
Haney, William, . . . Floyd
Hawkins, John, . . . Hopkins
Hanna, John, ... Nicholas
Hansford, Charles, . . Daveiss
Hansford, Charles, . . Nelson
Hansford, William, . . Pulaski
Harber, Jeremiah, . . Hart
Hard, Zadock, ... Meade
Hardin, Benjamin. . . Henry
Hardin, Mrs., ... Marion
Hardin, Mark, ... Washington
Hardin, Thomas, . . . Gallatin
Hardin, Thomas, . . . Trigg
Harding, Thomas, . . Green
Harding, Vachel, . . . Jefferson
Hardwick, George, . . Lawrence
Hargin, Michael, . . . Hardin
Hargate, Peter, . . . Mason
Hargis, John, ... Nicholas
Harlan, George, . . . Mercer
Harlew, George, . . . Rockcastle
Harlow, George, . . . Rockcastle
Harlow, John, ... Christian

Hillen, George, . . . Warren	Howell, Jonathan, . . Fayette
Hindley, John, ... Oldham	Howerton, William, . Morgan
Hines, Hardy, ... Muhlenberg	Howke, Laurence, . . Logan
Hines, James, ... Bath	Hubbard, Eppa, . . . Bullitt
Hiser, John, ... Barren	Hubbell, Richard, . . Boone
Hitchcock, Joshua, . . Floyd	Hubbell, William, . . Scott
Hite, Abraham, . . . Jefferson	Hubbs, Jacob, ... Bullitt
Hodges, Jesse, ... Madison	Hubbs, John, ... Knox
Hogue, Andrew, . . . Casey	Huff, Peter, ... Mercer
Hollady, Zacharias, . Adair	Huffman, Ambrose, . Barren
Holland, James M., . . Shelby	Huly, John, ... Caldwell
Holley, Samuel, . . . Shelby	Huey, Lewis, ... Hickman
Holliday, Benjamin, . Owen	Hugh, Moses, ... Spencer
Holliday, Stephen, . . Clark	Hughs, William, . . . Lincoln
Hollis, John, ... Franklin	Hughes, Absalom, . . Barren
Hollowell, Miles, . . . Trigg	Hughes, John, ... Henderson
Holman, Richard, . . Mercer	Huguely, Charles, . . Henry
Hood, John, ... Whitley	Hukill, Abiah, ... Mason
Hoover, Lawrence, . . Owen	Hukins, Daniel, . . . Mason
Hopkins, David, . . . Fleming	Hulet, James, ... Lewis
Hopkins, Garner, . . Floyd	Huling, Jonathan, . . Campbell
Hopkins, Mary, . . . Morgan	Humble, Robert, . . . Woodford
Hopkins, Robert, . . Nicholas	Humfres, John, . . . Jefferson
Hopkins, William, . . Adair	Humphrees, Samuel, . Fleming
Hopkins, William, . . Muhlenberg	Humphries, Joseph, . Bourbon
Horn, Christopher, . . Knox	Humphrey, John, . . Bullitt
Horn, Matthias, . . . Estill	Humphrey, John, . . Hart
Hornbeck, Samuel, . . Bullitt	Humphrey, Merritt, . Oldham
Horrell, James, . . Pulaski	Humphreys, Absalom, Trigg
Horton, James P., . . Knox	Hunt, Abraham, . . . Wayne
Horseley, James, . . . Jefferson	Hunter, Jacob, ... Owen
Hoskins, James, . . . Oldham	Hunt, John, ... Muhlenberg
Hoskins, Randall, . . Washington	Hunt, Jonathan, . . . Barren
Hoskins, Thenas, . . Hardin	Hunt, Richard, . . . Lincoln
Hoskinson, Charles, . Breckinridge	Hunt, Wilson, ... Fayette
Houchins, Edward, . Mercer	Hunter, Ann . . . . . Jessamine
Houk, Nicholas, . . . Rockcastle	Hunter, John, ... Fayette
House, Audrew, . . . Bourbon	Hunter, John, ... Madison
Houseworth, Henry, . Henry	Hurst, Henry, ... Perry
Howard, Benjamin, . . Madison	Hurst, Henry, ... Scott
Howard, James, . . . Montgomery	Hutchins, Edward, . . Mercer
Howard, James, . . . Perry	Hutton, James, . . . Mercer
Howard, John, ... Mason	Hurt, William, ... Adair
Howard, Thomas, . . Perry	Hurtt, John, ... Cumberland
Howe, David, ... Fleming	Huston, William, . . Jefferson
Howe, John, ... Hardin	Hutchinson, Joseph, . Breckinridge
Howe, John W., . . . Greenup	Ingram, Jeremiah, . . Adair
Howell, John, ... Ohio	Ingram, Jeremiah, . . Green

Justice, Simeon, . . . Perry
Karr, James, ... Logan
Kay, James, ... Boone
Kearns, William, . . Bath
Keath, William, . . . Wayne
Keech, John J. S., . . Nelson
Keen, John, ... Campbell
Keen, John, ... Kenton
Keeton, John, ... Franklin
Keeton, Isaac, ... Morgan
Kelly, Beall, ... Warren
Kelly, James, ... Daveiss
Kelly, John, ... Barren
Kelly, John, ... Perry
Kelly, John, ... Simpson
Kelly, Samuel, ... Morgan
Kelly, Thomas, . . . Bourbon
Kelly, Thomas, . . . Jefferson
Kelly, William, . . . Mercer
Kelso, Thomas, . . . Shelby
Kendall, Aaron, . . . Bracken
Kendall, Peter, . . . Fleming
Kendrick, Benson, . . Bourbon
Kendricks, William, . Shelby
Kenner, Rodham, . . Logan
Kennedy, Charles, . . Trigg
Kennedy, David, . . . Garrard
Kennedy, Joseph, . . Boone
Kennedy, Joseph, . . Madison
Kennedy, Thomas, . . Garrard
Kenny, Edward D., . Owen
Kenny, Edward D., . Scott
Kenny, John, ... Scott
Kercheval, John, . . . Mason
Kerr, David, ... Scott
Kerrick, Benjamin H., Spencer
Kersey, John, ... Nicholas
Key, Price, ... Clark
Key, Sarah, ... Barren
Kidwell, John, ... Madison
Kidwell, Jonathan, . . Henry
Kidwell, Matthew, . Monroe
Kilander, Philip, . . . Harrison
Kimmer, Nicholas, . . Bracken
Kincheloe, Thomas, . Breckinridge
Kindred, William (2), . Madison
Kindrick, Benjamin, . Bourbon
King, George, ... Cumberland

King, Jeremiah, . . . Jessamine
King, John, ... Bracken
King, William, ... Bracken
Kinnard, Joseph, . . . Madison
Kiphart, Henry, . . . Henry
Kirby, Jesse, ... Warren
Kirk, Robert, ... Livingston
Kirk, Thomas, ... Mason
Kirkham, Michael, . . Woodford
Kirkland, John, . . . Mercer
Kirley, John, ... Scott
Kirley, Leonard T., . . Warren
Knight, Betsy, ... Jessamine
Knight, John, ... Shelby
Knight, Night, ... Christian
Knight, William, . . . Henry
Knox, John, ... Shelby
Kugel, John, ... Owen
Kulby, John, ... Morgan
Kuykendall, Matthew, Butler
Kutan, Isaac, ... Morgan
Kyle, Thomas, ... Mercer
Lackey, Andrew, . . . Estill
Lackland, John, . . . Scott
Land, John, ... Madison
Lane, Isham, ... Madison
Lafferty, John, ... Mercer
Laffoon, James, . . . Fayette
Lainhart, Isaac, . . . Madison
Lamb, George, ... Nelson
Lamb, Thomas, . . . Madison
Lambert, James, . . . Washington
Lambert, Matthias, . Madison
Lander, Charles, . . . Bourbon
Landrum, Thomas, . . Scott
Lang, William, ... Harrison
Langsdon, Charles, . . Bullitt
Lanter, Jacob, ... Harrison
Lanter, Thomas, . . . Madison
Larrance, Rodham, . Barren
Lastey, John, ... Lawrence
Latimer, William, . . Pendleton
Laughlin, Thomas, . . Whitley
Laurence, Thomas, . . Butler
Laurence, William, . . Owen
Laurence, William, . . Rockcastle
Lane, Henry, ... Russell
Law, John, ... Oldham

McCoy, Alexander, . . Fleming
McCoy, Daniel, . . . Gallatin
McCoy, William, . . . Woodford
McCrasky, James, . . Scott
McCulley, James, . . Montgomery
McCulloch, James, . . Montgomery
McCullough, William, Fleming
McCullum, James, . . Hardin
McDaniel, George, . . Perry
McDonald, William, . Franklin
McDougall, Alex'r, . . Hardin
McDowell, Alexander, Gallatin
McDowell, Daniel, . . Bourbon
McDowell, James, . . Fayette
McDowell, John, . . . Fayette
McDowell, William, . Gallatin
McElhany, James, . . Bath
McElroy, John, . . . Allen
McGannon, Darby, . . Gallatin
McGee, James C., . . Wayne
McGee, John, ... Jessamine
McGee, Ralph, ... Madison
McGee, Samuel, . . . Woodford
McGinness, Andrew, . Barren
McGlassen, Matthew, Adair
McGlassen, Nancy, . Kenton
McGlasson, John, . . Campbell
McGohan, Mark, . . . Mercer
McGoodwin, Daniel, . Logan
McGuire, Daniel, . . Barren
McGuire, James, . . . Anderson'
McGuire, John, . . . Morgan
McGuire, Joseph, . . . Henry
McGraw, Christopher, Fayette
McGrew, Thomas, . . Calloway
McHargue, William, . Knox
McHatton, John, . . . Scott
McHenry, James, . . . Wayne
McIntire, William, . . Gallatin
McIntosh, Thomas, . Trimble
McIsaacks, James, . . Fayette
McKee, Guion, ... Fleming
McKee, John, ... Fleming
McKee, Samuel, . . . Montgomery
McKinney, Dennis, . . Lincoln
McKinney, John, . . . Campbell
McKinney, John, . . Woodford
McKinney, Thomas, . Jefferson

McKinney, William, . Adair
McKinzee, Isaac, . . . Morgan
McKitrick, John, . . . Warren
McLardy, Alexander, . Logan
McMahon, John, . . . Muhlenberg
McMannis, Charles, . Bullitt
McMasters, Michael, . Spencer
McNab, John, ... Caldwell
McPherson, Alex'r, . . Boone
McPherson, Mark, . . Lincoln
McQuady, John, . . . Woodford
McQueen, Joshua, . . Franklin
McQueen, Joshua, . . Madison
McQuiddy, John, . . . Woodford
McVay, Daniel, . . . Fayette
McVey, Hugh, ... Caldwell
McWhorter, John, . . Casey
McWilliams, James, . Hardin
Mabry, John, ... Trigg
Madden, Joseph, . . . Fleming
Maddox, John, ... Ohio   *NOT LISTED*
Maddox, Sherwood, . Owen
Maddox, William, . Shelby   *WILSON*
Madison, Ambrose, . Todd
Maffett, Jacob, ... Harrison
Maffitt, William, . . . Spencer
Magill, John, ... Franklin
Mahan, James, ... Whitley
Mahan, Henry, ... Todd
Maines, George, . . . Bracken
Major, Alexander, . . Hopkins
Majors, John, ... Wayne
Malone, John, ... Woodford
Maloney, Robert, . . Jefferson
Mann, Benjamin, . . . Pendleton
Mann, Francis, ... Harrison
Manzy, Peter, ... Fleming
March, Samuel, . . . Scott
Marcum, Josiah, . . . Lawrence
Maren, Benjamin, . . Cumberland
Marshall, Humphrey, . Franklin
Marshall, John, . . . Lawrence
Marshall, Robert, . . Campbell
Marston, James, . . . Campbell
Martenson, John, . . . Nelson
Martin, Azariah, . . . Clay
Martin, Benjamin, . . Barren
Martin, Gideon, . . . Warren

Moore, Abraham . . . Shelby
Moore, Charles, . . . Adair
Moore, David, ... Jefferson
Moore, Hugh, ... Warren
Moore, James, ... Fleming
Moore, James, ... Harrison
Moore, James, ... Mercer
Moore, John, ... Floyd
Moore, Joseph, ... Whitley
Moore, Michael, . . . Bath
Moore, Nicholas, . . . Montgomery
Moore, Thomas, . . . Bracken
Moore, Thomas, . . . Mercer
Moore, William, . . . Rockcastle
Moore, Wilson, . . . Allen
Morehead, Charles, . . Logan
Morehead, John, . . . Monroe
Moreland, Dudley, . . Wayne
Morgan, John, ... Oldham
Morgan, Morgan, . . Cumberland
Morgan, Thomas, . . Oldham
Morgan, Thomas, . . Trimble
Morgan, William, . . Shelby
Morin, Edward, . . . Campbell
Morrell, Benjamin, . . Fayette
Morris, Daniel, ... Hart
Morris, Jacob, ... Bracken
Morris, Jesse, ... Green
Morris, Nathaniel, . . Bracken
Morris, Thomas, . . . Madison
Morris, Thomas, . . . Mason
Morris, Thomas, . . . Nicholas
Morrison, Ezra, . . . Lincoln
Morrison, James, . . . Union
Morrison, Hugh, . . . Allen
Morrow, Thomas, . . Casey
Morrow, Thomas, . . Harrison
Morse, Alexander, . . Shelby
Morton, Samuel, . . . Madison
Mosby, Joseph, . . . Fayette
Mosby, William, . . . Adair
Moseby, Thomas, . . Montgomery
Moses, Joshua, ... Whitley
Mosley, Leonard, . . Woodford
Mosley, Robert, . . . Ohio
Moss, John, ... Henderson
Moss, John, ... Montgomery
Mothershead, Nathn'l, Scott

Mountjoy, Alvin, . . . Pendleton
Mountjoy, John, . . . Pendleton
Moxley, George, . . . Nelson
Mulberry, James, . . . Bath
Mullikin, John, . . . Shelby
Mullins, Charles, . . . Calloway
Mullins, Gabriel, . . . Pendleton
Mullins, John, ... Floyd
Mullins, Joshua, . . . Knox
Mullins, Joshua, . . . Perry
Mullins, Matthew, . . Madison
Murphy, Gabriel, . . . Nelson
Murphy, James, . . . Nelson
Murphy, John, ... Jefferson
Murphy, Leander, . . Spencer
Murrah, Joshua, . . . Logan
Murray, Barnabas, . . Pulaski
Murray, James, . . . Fayette
Murray, Thomas, . . . Floyd
Murrell, Samuel, . . Barren
Murvin, Patrick, . . . Hardin
Muse, George, ... Fleming
Nabois, Nathan, . . . Warren
Nailor, Isaac, ... Fayette
Nance, Frederick, . . Washington
Neal, Benjamin, . . . Logan
Neal, Benjamin, . . . Muhlenberg
Neal, Charles, ... Scott
Neal, Micajah, ... Shelby
Neil, James, ... Union
Neill, Lewis, ... Henry
Nelson, Moses, ... Bath
Nelson, John, ... Fayette
Nelson, John, ... Jefferson
Netherland, Benjamin, Jessamine
Netherton, John, . . . Oldham
Neves, Daniel, ... Nicholas
Nevill, James, ... Barren
New, George W., . . . Woodford
New, Jacob, ... Grant
Newby, John, ... Pulaski
Newell, Samuel, . . . Pulaski
Newman, Edward, . . Hancock
Newton, Benjamin, . . Mercer
Newton, John, ... Hardin
Newton, Robert, . . . Hopkins
Nicks, John, ... Laurel
Nixon, Absalom, . . . Christian

Petit, Thomas, ... Shelby
Petree, Peter, ... Todd
Petty, Rodham, . . . Anderson
Pew, Reuben, ... Rockcastle
Peyton, George, . . . Woodford
Phelps, John, ... Grayson
Phelps, Josiah, ... Madison
Philips, George, . . . Mercer
Phillips, Jacob, ... Mercer
Phillips, John, ... Christian
Phillips, John, ... Clay
Phillips, Zachariah, . Estill
Phipps, John, ... Hopkins
Phipps, Joshua, . . . Green
Pickett, Henry, . . . Hickman
Pickford, Daniel, . . . Allen
Pierce, Frances, . . . Clay
Pierce, Francis, . . . Cumberland
Pierce, James, ... Wayne
Pierceall, Richard, . . Green
Piercey, James, . . . Wayne
Pierson, John, ... Union
Pike, Robert, ... Jefferson
Piles, William, ... Mercer
Pilkinton, Larkin, . . Bullitt
Pilkinton, Larkin, . . Jefferson
Pindell, Richard, . . Fayette
Pipes, Mary, ... Mercer
Pitkins, William G., . Livingston
Pitt, Joseph, ... Muhlenberg
Pittinger, Abraham, . Spencer
Pittman, Ambrose, . . Laurel
Pitts, Mexico, ... Floyd
Poe, Benjamin, . . . Allen
Poe, Virgil, ... Franklin
Pollard, Absalom, . . Garrard
Pollard, Braxton, . . Pendleton
Pollard, Edmund, . . Harrison
Pollard, William, . . Anderson
Poller, John, ... Mercer
Pollet, John, ... Woodford
Polly, John, ... Russell
Polly, Edmund, . . . Perry
Polly, Edward, ... Perry
Pool, John, ... Clark
Porch, Henry, ... Whitley
Porter, Ephraim, . . Todd
Porter, James, ... Floyd

Porter, John, ... Butler
Porter, William, . . . Butler
Porter, William, . . . Caldwell
Potter, John, ... Mercer
Pounds, Hezekiah, . . Jefferson
Powe, William, . . . Garrard
Powell, Ambrose, . . Estill
Powell, Nathaniel, . . Logan
Powell, Richard, . . . Garrard
Powell, Sarah, . . . Henry
Powers, Jeremiah, . . Scott
Powers, Jesse, ... Wayne
Pratt, Jacob, ... Boone
Pratt, James, ... Lawrence
Pratt, Stephen, . . . Wayne
Preston, Moses, . . . Floyd
Preston, Nathan, . . . Floyd
Prewitt, Byrd, ... Fayette
Prewitt, John, ... Morgan
Prewitt, Joshua, . . . Henry
Prewitt, Joshua, . . . Trimble
Prewitt, Solomon, . . Cumberland
Prible, James, ... Pendleton
Price, Isaac, ... Scott
Price, William, . . . Scott
Price, William H., . . Green
Priest, Peter, ... Barren
Prior, Simon, ... Grayson
Pritchard, James, . . Bourbon
Pritchett, James, . . . Bourbon
Proctor, George, . . . Fayette
Proctor, George, . . . Rockcastle
Proctor, Joseph, . . . Estill
Proctor, William, . . Fleming
Pruett, John, ... Rockcastle
Pullen, William, . . . Woodford
Pullin, George, . . . Bourbon
Pullins, Loftus, . . . Madison
Pumphrey, Peter, . . Rockcastle
Purcell, Richard, . . Green
Purvis, William, . . . Bath
Puryear, Jesse, ... Green
Pytts, Jonathan, . . . Floyd
Quarles, Elizabeth, . Todd
Radcliff, Minus, . . . Owen
Radford, James, . . . Cumberland
Ragland, John, . . . Warren
Ragsdale, Godfrey, . Shelby

Rogers, George, . . . Wayne
Rogers, James, . . . Whitley
Rogers, Thomas, . . Bourbon
Rogers, William, . . Adair
Roll, Michael, ... Morgan
Rooksbury, Jacob, . . Jefferson
Roper, David, ... Pulaski
Roper, James, ... Simpson
Rose, Benjamin B., . Mercer
Rose, Jesse, ... Harrison
Rose, William, ... Whitley
Ross, Alexander, . . . Boone
Ross, Daniel, ... Jessamine
Ross, John, ... Adair
Ross, John, ... Fleming
Ross, John, ... Graves
Ross, John, ... Madison
Ross, Nathaniel, . . . Jefferson
Rosser, Richard, . . . Mercer
Roundtree, Nathaniel, Hart
Rouse, Jacob, ... Boone
Rouse, Lewis, ... Lewis
Rouse, Samuel, . . . Boone
Rowden, George, . . Graves
Rowe, James, ... Shelby
Rowe, John, ... Grayson
Rowe, John, ... Hart
Rowe, William, . . . Cumberland
Rowland, Samuel, . . Bullitt
Royaltree, John, . . . Casey
Royse, Solomon, . . . Adair
Rucker, Elliott, . . . Shelby
Ruddeel, James, . . . Boone
Rule, Thomas, ... Mercer
Russell, Absalom, . . Casey
Russell, Robert S., . . Fayette
Rust, John, ... Mason
Rutherford, Archibald, Logan
Sacrey, James, ... Shelby
Salmon, John, ... Mason
Salter, Michael, . . . Garrard
Salyas, Dunn, ... Lincoln
Sampson, Isaac, . . . Shelby
Sampson, William, . . Lincoln
Sanders, John, ... Owen
Sanders, Philemon, . Barren
Sanders, Reuben, . . Shelby
Sanders, Zachariah, . Wayne

Sandifer, James, . . . Mercer
Sartin, Clayburn, . . Greenup
Satterwhite, John S., . Franklin
Saunders, David, . . Logan
Saunders, Joseph, . . Bullitt
Sayers, Robert, . . . Pulaski
Scherlin, James, . . . Washington
Scholfield, Jesse, . . . Butler
Schooler, William, . . Fayette
Scott, Drury, ... Clark
Scott, Francis, ... Barren
Scott, James, ... Caldwell
Scott, Jesse, ... Rockcastle
Scott, John, ... Cumberland
Scott, John, ... Hardin
Scott, John, ... Harrison
Scott, Reuben, ... Gallatin
Scott Robert, ... Carroll
Scott, Thomas, . . . Henry
Scott, William, . . . Bourbon
Scroggin, Thomas C., Franklin
Scruggs, William, . . Scott
Seaburn, Jacob, . . . Clay
Searcy, John, ... Owen
Searcy, Richard, . . . Anderson
Seaton, George, . . . Breckinridge
Seaton, Thomas, . . . Pulaski
Seay, Jacob, ... Washington
Sebree, Richard, . . . Franklin
Self, John, ... Cumberland
Sellers, Isham, . . . Henderson
Sellers, Samuel, . . . Harrison
Sergeant, William, . . Bracken
Servants, William, . . Mercer
Severn, David, ... Gallatin
Seward, Daniel, . . . Grant
Sewell, Joseph, . . . Cumberland
Sexton, John, ... Lawrence
Sexton, William, . . . Whitley
Shackleford, Henry, . Harlan
Shanks, John, ... Madison
Shanks, John, ... Meade
Shannon, Andrew, . . Fayette
Sharp, Isham, ... Russell
Sharp, John, ... Scott
Sharp, sr., Samuel, . . Breckinridge
Sharp, William, . . . Fayette
Sharp, William, . . . Jessamine

Sorrells, John, ...	Ohio		Stilth, Joseph, ...	Meade
Spalding, Aaron, . . .	Washington		Stinson, John, ...	Clark
Spalding, George, . .	Marion		Stipp, John, ...	Bourbon
Spalding, George, . .	Washington		Stipp, Moses, ...	Pike
Sparks, Henry, . . .	Owen		Stitt, Samuel H., . . .	Mason
Sparrow, Henry, . . .	Marion		Stivers, Reuben, . . .	Fayette
Sparrow, Henry, . . .	Mercer		Stober, Edward, . . .	Nicholas
Speak, George, . . .	Mercer		Stocker, William, . .	Fleming
Speaks, Hezekiah, . .	Bourbon		Stoker, Edward, . . .	Bourbon
Spencer, Hezekiah, .	Montgomery		Stoker, William, . . .	Fleming
Spencer, Joseph, . . .	Grant		Stokes, John, ...	Graves
Spencer, William, . .	Bullitt		Stone, Bryant, ...	Spencer
Spillman, George, . .	Henry		Stone, Cudbeth, . . .	Floyd
Spillman, James, . . .	Barren		Stone, Rowland, . . .	Calloway
Spillman, James, . . .	Clark		Story, John, ...	Franklin
Spoffner, Henry, . . .	Green		Stout, Elijah, ...	Fayette
Spring, Levin, ...	Meade		Stout, Elijah, ...	Spencer
Stafford, John, ...	Graves		Stout, Reuben, . . .	Shelby
Stamper, Jacob, . . .	Owen		Stovall, George, . . .	Allen
Stansbury, Solomon, .	Laurel		Strahan, Samuel, . .	Fleming
Staples, Isaac, ...	Adair		Strange, John, ...	Spencer
Stapleton, Thomas, .	Clay		Stratton, Seth, ...	Shelby
State, James, ...	Hardin		Street, Anthony, . . .	Garrard
Steen, Edward, . . .	Montgomery		Stringer, John, . . .	Bullitt
Steerman, William W.,	Green		Stroud, Isaac, ...	Christian
Steers, Hugh, ...	Boone		Strubling, Samuel, . .	Boone
Stephens, John, . . .	Franklin		Strufflebean, John, . .	Estill
Stephens, John, . . .	Montgomery		Styvers, William, . .	Estill
Stephens, Joseph L., .	Bourbon		Sublett, Abraham, . .	Lincoln
Stephenson, James, .	Boone		Suggett, John, ...	Scott
Stephenson, James, .	Logan		Sullenger, James, . .	Christian
Steuart, James, . . .	Christian		Sullinger, James, . .	Livingston
Stevens, Gilbert, . . .	Morgan		Sullivan, Cornelius, .	Fayette
Stevens, Isaac, . . .	Wayne		Sullivan, Peter, . . .	Floyd
Stevens, Jacob, . . .	Madison		Summers, John, . . .	Fleming
Stevens, Jacob, . . .	Rockcastle		Sutherland, Traverse,	Henry
Stevens, James, . . .	Rockcastle		Sutherland, Walter F.,	Henry
Stevens, James, . . .	Warren		Sutherland, William, .	Casey
Stevens, John, ...	Fayette		Sutton, Benjamin, . .	Campbell
Stevenson, John, . . .	Clark		Sutton, Benjamin, . .	Garrard
Stevenson, Levi, . . .	Morgan		Sutton, Richard F., .	Marion
Stevenson, William, .	Jefferson		Swanson, Levi, . . .	Morgan
Stewart, Charles, . .	Scott		Sweeney, Moses, . . .	Warren
Stewart, David, . . .	Livingston		Sweeney, Joseph, . .	Washington
Stewart, Ezekiel, . .	Montgomery		Sweeny, William, . .	Rockcastle
Stewart, Robert, . . .	Owen		Swindle, John, ...	Boone
Stewart, William, . .	Fayette		Swift, Thomas, . . .	Henry
Stidham, Samuel, . .	Perry		Swingle, George, . .	Franklin

Trigg, Daniel, ... Wayne
Trimble, John, ... Harrison
Trimble, William, . . Pulaski
Triplett, George, . . . Spencer
Triplett, Hedgman, . Franklin
Triplett, Thomas, . . Bath
Trower, Solomon, . . Mercer
True, James, ... Fayette
True, John, ... Oldham
Tubbs, Cyrus, ... Gallatin
Tucker, John, ... Bracken
Tucker, John, ... Scott
Tucker, William, . . Adair
Tudor, John, ... Madison
Tuggle, William, . . Clark
Turner, George, . . . Campbell
Turner, James, . . . Wayne
Turner, Roger, . . . Breathitt
Turner, Roger, . . . Perry
Turner, Solomon, . . Hardin
Turner, William, . . . Todd
Turpin, Martin, . . . Pulaski
Tutwiler, John, . . . Madison
Twigg, Daniel, . . . Whitley
Twyman, James, . . . Scott
Twyman, Reuben, . . Woodford
Tyler, Charles, ... Franklin
Tyler, William, . . . Jefferson
Underdoun, Stephen, Russell
Urton, James, ... Jefferson
Utterbach, Hammon, ...
Vallandigham, Geo., . Fayette
Vallandingham, Lewis, Oldham
Vanarsdall, Cornelius, Mercer
Vanarsdall, Cornel. C., Mercer
Vanarsdall, Lawrence, Mercer
Vance, Joseph, ... Scott
Vance, Thomas, . . . Boone
Vanhorn, Samuel, . . Trimble
Vanhorne, Samuel, . Henry
Vanmeter, Isaac, . . . Grayson
Vanmeter, Jacob, . . Hardin
Van Swearingen, ——, Shelby
Vaughan, Nathan, . . Fayette
Veach, Elijah, ... Caldwell
Veach, Elijah, ... Monroe
Veatch, Jeremiah, . . Jessamine
Venard, William, . . . Harrison

Verbryck, Rebecca, . Mercer
Vertress, Isaac, . . . Hardin
Vest, George, ... Boone
Vincent, Thomas, . . Hickman
Vinzant, John, ... Scott
Vittilon, Samuel, . . Nelson
Voris, John, ... Mercer
Wade, John, ... Owen
Wade, Obadiah, . . . Barren
Wade, Richard, . . . Cumberland
Wade, Richard, . . . Clinton
Wages, Benjamin, . . Morgan
Waggoner, Thomas, . Christian
Walden, James, . . . Spencer
Walden, John, ... Garrard
Waldren, John, . . . Henry
Walker, James, . . . Jessamine
Walker, James, . . . Livingston
Walker, Philip, . . . Marion
Walkup, Samuel, . . Madison
Wallace, John, ... Henry
Wallace, William B., . Anderson
Waller, Joshua, . . . Henry
Walls, Reuben, . . . Nicholas
Walsh, William, . . . Morgan
Walters, John, ... Wayne
Ward, Elizabeth, . . . Estill
Ward, James, ... Lawrence
Ward, John, ... Mason
Ward, Lawrence, . . Estill
Warden, Elisha, . . . Allen
Warford, Benjamin, . Anderson
Warham, Charles, . . Wayne
Warmack, William, . Adair
Warmouth, Thad. H., Garrard
Warnock, Abner, . . Butler
Warren, Hugh, . . . Green
Warren, William, . . Christian
Washam, Charles, . . Wayne
Washburn, Benjamin, Shelby
Waterfield, Peter, . . Caldwell
Waters, John, ... Estill
Watkins, Benedict, . . Floyd
Watkins, John, . . . Harrison
Watkins, Thomas, . . Shelby
Watson, David, . . . Green
Watson, Evan T., . . Warren
Watson, John, ... Barren

Watson, John,	Anderson	Whitman, Richard,	Hart
Watson, Joseph,	Madison	Whittaker, Ann,	Harrison
Watson, Joseph,	Spencer	Whittaker, Mark,	Butler
Watson, William,	Madison	Whittaker, William,	Cumberland
Watts, Peter,	Shelby	Whittington, John,	Bourbon
Wayland, Joshua,	Shelby	Wickliffe, Charles,	Fayette
Weatherhall, Jacob,	Breckinridge	Wigginton, Henry,	Bourbon
Weaver, John,	Allen	Wilcoxen, Daniel,	Shelby
Weaver, Philip,	Fleming	Wiley, Henry,	Shelby
Webb, Augustine,	Bullitt	Wilhite, John,	Owen
Webb, Isaac,	Fayette	Wilhite, Tobias,	Mercer
Webb, John,	Garrard	Wilkenson, Benjamin,	Jefferson
Webb, Lewis,	Mercer	Wilkerson, Francis,	Breckinridge
Webb, Lewis,	Washington	Wilkins, Thomas,	Hardin
Webster, William,	Washington	Wilkinson, Joseph,	Montgomery
Weeks, David,	Hopkins	Williams, Abraham,	Mason
Weeks, James,	Spencer	Williams, Benjamin,	Bourbon
Weinand, Philip,	Jefferson	Williams, Benjamin,	Pendleton
Weir, Joseph,	Adair	Williams, Elijah,	Garrard
Welch, James,	Monroe	Williams, Gerard,	Fleming
Wells, James,	Breckinridge	Williams, Isaac,	Grayson
Wells, John,	Gallatin	Williams, Jacob,	Hickman
Wells, Littlebury,	Henry	Williams, James,	Cumberland
Wells, Richard,	Floyd	Williams, James,	Simpson
Wells, Samuel,	Scott	Williams, John,	Henry
Wells, William,	Livingston	Williams, John,	Simpson
Welsh, James,	Jefferson	Williams, Judith,	Logan
Wentworth, Levi,	Shelby	Williams, Lawrence,	Fleming
West, Leonard,	Calloway	Williams, Philip,	Floyd
West, Thomas,	Scott	Williams, Philip,	Morgan
Whaley, William,	Harrison	Williams, Thomas,	Caldwell
Wharton, William,	Pendleton	Williams, Thomas,	Cumberland
Whedon, Ichabod,	Lewis	Williams, Thomas,	Lewis
Wheeler, John,	Livingston	Williams, William,	Mason
Wheley, Benjamin,	Bourbon	Williamson, James,	Allen
White, Ambrose,	Franklin	Willis, Britton,	Muhlenberg
White, Aquilla,	Montgomery	Wilmott, Robert,	Bourbon
White, David,	Jefferson	Willoughby, Alex.,	Jessamine
White, Galen,	Madison	Wills, Henry,	Montgomery
White, James,	Campbell	Wilson, Andrew,	Fleming
White, John,	Mason	Wilson, David,	Nelson
White, Jonathan,	Washington	Wilson, Henry,	Bourbon
White, Nathan,	Fayette	Wilson, Henry,	Montgomery
White, Thomas,	Adair	Wilson, James,	Clark
White, Thomas,	Monroe	Wilson, James,	Nicholas
Whitecotton, James,	Marion	Wilson, Jeremiah,	Woodford
Whitecotton, James,	Mercer	Wilson, Jeremiah,	Hopkins
Whitehead, John. See Wited.		Wilson, John,	Pulaski

Wilson, Mary, ... Mercer
Wilson, Robert, . . . Jefferson
Wilson, Samuel, . . . Logan
Winchester, Richard, Hardin
Winfrey, Philip, . . . Adair
Wingate, John, . . . Fayette
Wingfield, Enoch, . . Woodford
Winkler, Henry, . . . Estill
Winlock, Josiah, . . . Shelby
Winsett, Raphael, . . Nelson
Winstead, Maudley, . Hopkins
Wirble, Henry, . . . Oldham
Wise, Samuel, ... Jessamine
Wited, John, ... Logan
Witt, Agnes, ... Wayne
Witt, Elisha, ... Estill
Wolf, Lewis, ... Harrison
Wood, Jonathan, . . . Nelson
Wood, Joseph, ... Garrard
Wood, Samuel, . . . Clay
Woodall, Charles, . . Rockcastle
Woodall, Jesse, . . . Rockcastle
Woodard, George, . . Green
Woods, Archibald, . . Madison
Woods, Caldwell, . . Lincoln
Woods, Samuel, . . . Mercer
Woods, William, . . . Harrison
Woodson, Samuel, . . Barren
Woody, James, ... Clinton
Woody, James, ... Wayne
Woodyard, Richard, . Union
Wooldridge, Josiah, . Todd
Wooldridge, Thomas, Henry
Woolfolk, Robert, . . Shelby
Wooton, Silas P., . . Lawrence
Womack, Massanello, Spencer
Worsham, Charles, . . Clinton
Worthington, William, Muhlenberg

Wright, Elijah, . . . Bullitt
Wright, George, . . . Hopkins
Wright, George, . . . Oldham
Wright, George, . . . Trimble
Wright, James, . . . Scott
Wright, Jarrett, . . . Allen
Wright, John, ... Hart
Wright, Jonathan, . . Washington
Wright, Thomas, . . Green
Wright, Thomas, . . Washington
Wright, William, . . Henry
Wyath, Henry, ... Pendleton
Yager, Samuel, . . . Shelby
Yancey, Robert, . . . Woodford
Yancey, Philemon, . . Franklin
Yates, Robert, ... Washington
Yeager, Elisha, . . . Jefferson
Yelton, James, ... Pendleton
York, John, ... Fayette
York, Joshua, ... Mason
Young, Alexander, . . Floyd
Young, Andrew, . . . Washington
Young, John, ... Fayette
Young, Joseph, . . . Spencer
Young, Michael, . . . Pulaski
Young, Nathan, . . . Scott
Young, Ralph, ... Warren
Young, Thomas, . . . Mason
Young, William, . . . Adair
Young, William, · · · Muhlenberg
Younger, Kanard, . . Henry
Younger, Kennard, . Trimble
Younglove, Samuel, . Christian
Yount, John, ... Fayette
Zerry, Josiah, ... Grayson
Zinn, John, ... Grant
Zornes, Andrew, . . . Greenup